American Gourmet

American

Gourmet

Classic Recipes,
Deluxe Delights,
Flamboyant Favorites,
and Swank "Company" Food
from the '50s and '60s

JANE and MICHAEL STERN

HarperCollinsPublishers

FIRST EDITION

Designed by JOEL AVIROM

Library of Congress Cataloging-in-Publication Data

Stern, Jane.
    American gourmet: classic recipes, deluxe delights, flamboyant favorites, and swank "company" food from the '50s & '60s / Jane and Michael Stern.
        p.   cm.
    Includes bibliographical references and index.
    ISBN 0-06-016710-6
    1. Cookery, American.   I. Stern, Michael, 1946–   . II. Title.
TX715.S8386   1991
641.5973—dc20   90-56399

---

91 92 93 94 95 CG/RRD 10 9 8 7 6 5 4 3 2 1

CONTENTS

ACKNOWLEDGMENTS

Too may cooks may spoil a broth, but our experience writing *American Gourmet* has been greatly enriched by the contributions of others. Susan Friedland, our inspiring editor, rolled up her sleeves and joined us in the kitchen on the quest for perfect baked Alaska. Joseph Montebello and Joel Avirom translated the gourmet life into a feast for the eyes. At the head of the table at HarperCollins, William Shinker made us feel right at home.

As always, Brooke Dojny and Melanie Barnard worked their magic as test cooks to transform even the most muddled vintage recipes into ones that are clear and foolproof.

For help in locating and providing some of the important illustrations in *American Gourmet* we thank Barbara Kuck of the Johnson & Wales Culinary Library, Rozanne Gold and Michael Whiteman, and Michael DeLuca of *Restaurant Hospitality*. David J. Colella of the Omni Ambassador East and Connie Costello of Sheila King Public Relations supplied exceptional images of Chicago's Pump Room. Jessica Miller unearthed fine pictures of Joseph Baum and the early days of Restaurant Associates. Julia Child was kind enough to send photographs taken by Paul Child from her television show "The French Chef"; and Alice Waters contributed her portrait taken by Robert Messick at Chez Panisse.

We also want to thank Narcisse Chamberlain for some enlightening correspondence about America's rediscovery of French food; and thanks, too, to our longtime eating companion, Bob Gottlieb, for sharing an especially evocative recipe for cassoulet.

America's appetite soared as the baby boom was born. A nation once known for square meals and the bluenose abstinence of Prohibition fell in love with deluxe food, vintage wine, and the joy of cooking. *American Gourmet* is about that quarter century between the first nationally televised cooking show in 1946, fittingly titled "I Love To Eat!," and the opening of Alice Waters's restaurant, Chez Panisse, in 1971—an ambitious era when fine dining was in style. At no other time in America's gastronomic history were recipes so brimful of idealism; never have so many people been enchanted by the excitement, mystique, and sheer sensual delight of eating.

We wrote this book to chronicle the passion of America's midcentury gourmets. Theirs was a time unspoiled by today's nutritional sanctimony and the unseemly one-upmanship of the yuppie years. For people learning the pursuit of pleasure after a depression and a world war, discovering such delectables as Swiss fondue, flaming shashlik, and baked Alaska was an exhilarating adventure. For us, it was inspiring to travel back to that time and feel the thrill that fancy food had for unjaded palates. Happily, we found that many of those long-since forgotten fondues are truly delicious; and a spear of sizzled-crusty lamb chunks is a dazzling dish with power to pique even blasé appetites; and there are few desserts as wondrous to eat as a monumental flaming baked Alaska.

Some of the foods gourmets once relished are ridiculously rich by today's austere dietary standards—goose liver pâté, dozen-yolk mousses, and fat-marbled meats in oceans of butter and cream sauce. Eating rich was once equated with eating well. James Beard said, "A gourmet who counts calories is like a whore who looks at her watch." But not all gourmet fare was nutritionally wanton; and it wasn't richness alone that defined the gourmet way of eating. Three decades ago, learning about fine food was a noble quest with an agenda beyond personal satisfaction. Those who determined to elevate their taste honestly (and correctly) believed that they were a force that would help uplift American foodways and the quality of American life in general. Despite the depreciation of the term *gourmet* and the consignment of many overexposed gourmet dishes to the oblivion of culinary history, it can be a real joy to cook and savor some of the authentically fine food from this era of great aspirations. American gourmets ate very well indeed; their pioneering palates affected the way nearly all Americans think about gastronomy. And we believe the best recipes from that era (as well as its hunger to explore the culinary unknown) are well worth reclaiming.

About the Recipes

Unlike today, when parsimonious portions are fashionable, in the heyday of the American gourmet no self-respecting host or restaurant chef would dare serve a meal that looked skimpy with too much bare plate showing around the food. For true gourmets, to eat well was to eat plenty; and when we give recipe yields, we have generally stayed true to that ideal. So if a recipe in this book indicates it feeds four people, that means it feeds four generously.

Some of the fundamental gourmet dishes depend on raw or barely cooked eggs. Because of current fears about salmonella, wherever sensible we offer suggestions for making them another way. There are some classic recipes, however, such as freshly made aïoli and true chocolate mousse, that would change too much if rewritten to eliminate the risk. Such recipes are presented in their original formulation, but with a note of warning for those worried about contaminated eggs. In these instances, as is the case for all recipes in *American Gourmet*, we have standardized measurements and directions and adjusted them as necessary to make certain that they work properly in a modern kitchen and produce food that is good, as well as true to the taste of yesterday's gourmets.

LIST OF RECIPES

on The Flaming Sword

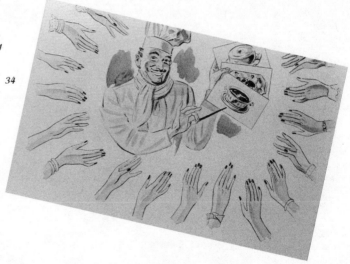

American Gourmet

AMERICAN GOURMET:
Beyond Square Meals

*G*ourmet was once a noun that meant a rich libertine with tastes above the means and manners of the hoi polloi. Originally from the Old French *gromet*, meaning servant, it had come to mean vintner's assistant, then had risen to become a universally recognized adjective for elegant food as well as the *bec fins* who ate it. America had gourmets since Thomas Jefferson; and a century ago gluttonous robber barons established standards of Lucullan gastronomy not since equaled; but it was not until the end of World War II that the gourmet point of view became popular.

As great numbers of citizens gleefully found themselves moving up the social ladder into the middle class comfort zone, they felt discontented with plebeian pleasures and square meals; they craved to refine their taste in all things, which included cultivating their palates. Good food was an essential component of The Good Life they wanted. It was championed on television by charismatic chefs who said anyone could eat like a king; *coq au vin* replaced dowdy casseroles on the women's pages of upwardly striving daily newspapers; before long, travelers could enjoy such delicacies as coquilles St.-Jacques and crème brulée in the dining room of nearly any Holiday Inn and eat duck à l'orange on an airplane flight from Omaha to Oklahoma City; and Americans who might once have been content to feed on chicken 'n' biscuits and tapioca pudding learned to appreciate epicurean delights from quiche Lorraine to chocolate mousse.

Those who felt part of the gastronomic rebirth were proud to call themselves gourmets because it meant that

Good food was an essential component of The Good Life they wanted.

*. . . so they set sail
on an expedition to
establish culinary
standards more
sophisticated than those
symbolized by Ike and
Mamie Eisenhower . . .*

they were people who sought the best life had to offer. Imbued with the heady enthusiasm of an insurrection whose time had come, they were fighters against America's notorious Puritanism, which had stamped out so much gustatory pleasure with Prohibition and frowned on all sensual delights; they attacked this country's traditionally xenophobic attitude toward other cultures—they wanted to be citizens of the world and world-class eaters; and they sought to tear down the old barriers of class and snobbery that once kept haute cuisine a prerogative reserved for the upper classes. These new epicures were not necessarily high-born or wealthy; they were college professors, footloose graduate students, free-thinking champions of fine art, professionals who could afford a trip to Paris and handsome travel books for their coffee tables, and anyone dissatisfied with America's maddeningly unsophisticated (and ever more ubiquitous) pop culture.

For many of them, being a gourmet was not just a hobby. It was a lifestyle that rippled out from the dinner table and added zest and spice and also a kind of broad-minded philosophy to everything they did. Gourmets formulated a new set of cultural priorities correlated to the exultations of gastronomy. They discovered pleasure not only in exquisite things to eat and majestic wines to wash them down, but also in art films with subtitles, sleek skyscrapers designed by Mies, abstract modern paintings and primitive African masks, and cultural splendors newly discovered in interesting localities from Rio and Paris (bikinis, bouffants, and baguettes) to Bombay and Singapore (dhurries and curries). They were reaching out for excellence, and they felt like nothing less than cultural pathfinders who had found a wondrous doorway into the modern world's Elysian Fields.

In its inaugural issue in January 1941, emblazoned with a painting of a succulent roasted boar's head on the cover, *Gourmet* magazine expounded, "The word *gourmet* signifies far more than just food perfection. It is a synonym for the honest seeker of the *summum bonum* of living"; and it went on to promise that "*Gourmet* will speak that esperanto of the palate that makes the whole world kin—good food, good drink, fine living—the universal language of the gourmet." Five years later at the end of the war, when suddenly it seemed there was a whole wide world of tantalizing food to bring to light, *Gourmet*, published from the penthouse suite of New York's Plaza hotel, surveyed America's future and proclaimed, "Delicious, Delectable, Delovely!" The Populuxe era was about to unfurl: a time of stunningly modern, brilliantly advertised opportunities to make life fun. By the fifties, plane travel was getting cheaper and faster; credit was looser; time was freer; there were so many new things to buy, foreign lands to discover, and food to relish. The horizon was infinite.

American gourmets were dissatisfied with the status quo (drab plowman's stews, penurious old fowl casseroles, and trite ladies' magazine recipes for layer cakes); so they set sail on an expedition to establish culinary standards more sophisticated than those symbolized by Ike and Mamie Eisenhower, the corn-fed Kansans in the White House in the fifties, or, even worse, the LBJ whole-side-of-cow-eating Texans of the sixties. They stocked their kitchens with such fascinating foreign ware as couscous pots, copper soufflé pans, romertoffs, and inspiring framed prints of street scenes in Aix-en-Provence. They gave cocktail parties and served hors d'oeuvre ("French for appetizers," advised Lawton Mackall's 1948 guidebook, *Knife and Fork in New York*) such as saumon fumé with capers, prosciutto, and pâté maison, drinking cocktails with ice fetched from a well-proportioned Dansk bucket. By candlelight, using napkins held in handsome teak napkin rings, they ate their dinner *en croute, au vin, au gratin, à l'orange, au poivre,* or *cordon bleu*, accompanied by imported wines and climaxed by a majestic soufflé, the glow of café brûlot and a dénoument of ripe-smelling mature cheese. Gourmets abjured hamburgers, Coke, white bread, TV dinners, and anything with ketchup on it—all emblems of Amer-

The first *Gourmet*, January 1941:

" *. . . to whet their appetites and excite their senses so that they will strive for broader horizons in their dinning and wining adventures.* "

ica's sorry lack of savoir faire—in favor of foods with character, history, and breeding such as beef Wellington, cassoulet, moussaka, and Swiss fondue.

Not content to lie in a Barcalounger watching *Andy of Mayberry* (sponsored by Cool Whip), American gourmets roamed the globe intellectually as well as literally. To know and to eat the cuisines of the family of man was the broad-minded thing to do. Neither elitist snobs like the stereotypical finicky gastronomes who preceded them, nor irritatingly materialistic like so many avaricious foodies of the 1970s and 1980s, midcentury American gourmets were earnest believers in the power of knowledge (in this case, of foods of the world) to make them better human beings.

They were true connoisseurs who saw cooking as a fine art and cooks as noble artists. "The composer arranges sounds, or notes, in harmonious, fecund relationship to make what, when recreated, we call music," wrote Merle Armitage in *"Fit For A King,"* an early (1937) compendium of essays by famous chefs and celebrities about sophisticated food. "The chef, or cook, proportions, assembles, and prepares various products of the animal, vegetable, and mineral kingdoms, creating food for the epicure. The aesthetic pleasure induced by food can be so closely related to that produced by certain music and other arts, as to defy separation or separate identification." Allying fine food with fine art (and thus distancing it from sheer gluttony and unseemly hedonism) was a favorite strategy of early apologists for the gourmet life.

Food, however, was different from the other arts. You could only *look* at Picasso's *Guernica* or listen to Stravinsky's "Rite of Spring"; you could *possess* a *soufflé au grand marnier* like La Tour d'Argent's right in your own kitchen; with a bit of effort, you could make it yourself, you could serve it to your friends, you could EAT it! Furthermore, gourmet cookery provided its cosmopolitan adherents with handy trophies of their travels. Exotic dishes on the dinner table at home were valued souvenirs of places they had been (or wanted to go). Like a living room slide show of the market in Morocco, a wall poster of a bullfight in Madrid, or a stereo tape of bossa nova music from Rio de Janeiro, a meal of paella à la Valenciana or ossobuco alla Milanese or tempura shrimp and hibachi steak evoked the far-flung delights of the planet. "When we come back home from any trip to anywhere we try to bring something of that place with us, including menus from the restaurants and recipes," wrote Mary and Vincent Price, guiding lights of the gourmet revolution, whose *Treasury of Great Recipes* (1965) compares their collection of recipes from grand restaurants to their equally beloved collection of pictures and objets d'art collected in foreign lands.

Prior to the gourmet revolution, if you were to ask John and Jane Q. Public to describe a gourmet, they might have told you with some suspicion about an offbeat voluptuary who ate sheep's eyes and chocolate-covered grasshoppers, then smoked a cigarette in a bejeweled holder or puffed on a hookah pipe. Before World War II, gourmets—particularly those of the male gender—seemed especially effete because their fussy kind of hedonism simply didn't jibe with most Americans' ideals of two-fisted, democratic square meals. A gourmet was considered by many to be a self-indulgent dilettante; at best, he might be an amusing old fop like Adolphe Menjou with his hankie in his sleeve or a spoiled aesthete like Charles Laughton making a sour face about some plate of food he didn't like; at worst, he was just about the most annoying thing a person could be in America during the depression or the war—a snob. A letter printed in the July 1946 *Gourmet* from Robert M. Morris of S. Ardmore, Pennsylvania, nicely sums up the hostility that gourmets' pleasure-loving life was able to engender:

> We are firm believers in simple home-cooked meals, without sauce, without incredible mixtures as you suggest in your epicurean journal. . . . How any human being with an average digestive tract can force down some of the things with which you try to enlighten the gastronomic world is quite beyond us. Not only did we refuse to try them or waste precious foods in their preparation, we tore your magazine into wee bits and deposited them in the incinerator. Fie on the lot of you!

Gourmet's response was: "Please pass the oil and we'll make a salad dressing."

To know and to eat the cuisines of the family of man was the broad-minded thing to do.

Average Joe Americans suspected gourmets not only because they seemed like elitists. They were also reviled by many as infirm old fussbudgets. "When the waitress puts the dinner on the table the old men look at the dinner. The young men look at the waitress." So proclaimed Gelett Burgess's *Look Eleven Years Younger*, written in 1937 during an earlier self-help book bonanza, in which the author advises readers how to enjoy life by behaving youthfully. "The old men sniff and fondle their wine and sip it lingeringly. The young men gulp it down. When ladies foregather the elderly matrons are particular about their sugar and cream, and the choosing of cakes is apt to be important. The young girls watch the styles and see who's there." The author asserts that connoisseurs who prate of brands and vintages of wine, study menus in restaurants, swap recipes, and show other signs of having a "culinary complex" do so because life's *real* pleasures have passed them by. He concludes, "An exaggerated delight and satisfaction in eating is one of the salient features of advancing age."

This dapper bon vivant appeared in an early *Gourmet* to illustrate an article about exotic foods of the world.

From the gourmet's point of view, such an attitude typified so many Americans' dismal inability to live life to the hilt. The gourmet considered the pleasures of the table, like art and even like sex, to be part of a full and happy modern existence; and he was quick to point out that most Americans were no more comfortable discussing cubism or kissing techniques than sauce béchamel. Alas, Americans viewed gastronomy, like all pleasures of the senses, with apprehension. In an essay about epicureanism written in the early sixties, card-carrying gourmet Joseph Wechsberg observed, "To descendants of the Puritans it is all but inconceivable that a man should spend hours talking about the great meal he plans to have, enjoying the meal, and then talking about how wonderful it was."

Before World War II, there had been glimmers of a mellowing of this country's much-lamented abstemiousness. When Prohibition ended in 1933, a small cadre of epicures vowed to recover the era of sophisticated gastronomy it had suppressed. A breathtaking, pleasure-filled modern life was consecrated at the New York World's Fair of 1939; and in the years before that, there was a budding renaissance of ambitious home cooking and an advent of a new class of serious gastronomes. The first commercially published edition of *Joy of Cooking* came out in 1936 after five years of expanding self-published mail order sales to housewives; M.F.K. Fisher debuted in 1937 with the dazzlingly literate *Serve It Forth*; and a year before *Gourmet*'s appearance in 1941, James Beard produced his first cookbook, *Hors d'Oeuvre and Canapés*, devoted entirely to finger food for swank cocktail parties.

James Beard's big impact on American cookery came after the war and on television (see Chapter 3), but in the late thirties he had already begun to formulate attitudes and ideas that became the basis of the gourmet revolution. His first well-known recipes were an impudent break with tradition. Instead of the customary nibbles of pale paste on itty bitty crackers or rounds of white bread (which he denigrated as insubstantial "doots"), and "the ghastly potato-chip-dip invention" (which he recalled had only just begun to spread across the country), his catering company, named Hors d'Oeuvre, Inc., and operated in concert with Bill Rhode and Rhode's sister Irma Rhode, invented hearty, appetizing finger foods out of identifiable ingredients with robust flavors. "We shopped in foreign sections of the city for unusual items," Beard recalled. "We discovered the trick of using various smoked sausages and meats as cornucopias and developed a dozen ways to offer stuffed eggs." Nearly everything Hors d'Oeuvre, Inc. served was strong, novel, and exciting. There was

"Your friends may laugh as they sit down at your table to partake of a meal you have prepared, but believe me, they'll applaud when the meal is over."

—Morrison Wood
in his introduction to
With a Jug of Wine, 1949

chopped raw beef (in the form of "tartar balls"); there were garlicky salami slices fashioned into cornucopias packed with grated parmigiana and anchovies; there were cheese tartlets (soon to become known as quiche); and there were fist-size squares of hearty pissaladière.

Beard's recipes were radical because they were ballsy. They broke rules with glee. Introducing his chapter about canapés, he wrote, "The canapé world presents all sorts of problems and rules which have been laid down by one person and another. I think I shall disregard the majority of them and proceed under my own power and see if I can't reach a logical and fairly simple conclusion." He then went on to suggest such provocative items as *brioche en surprise*, spicy curried chicken, and raw beef paste. ("That raw meat idea again. Somehow I think I must have a complex about it! However, I am sure there is nothing more delicious if the meat is properly seasoned and very tender.") What a break this was from the tradition of pedagogues like Fanny Farmer of the Boston Cooking School with all her *shoulds* and *musts* about level measurement! And from all the bespectacled schoolmarms who had addressed American home cooks in conventional cookbooks with seven-day menus and scientific strategies for getting each of the four basic food groups into every meal!

Beard's relish for raw beef, as well as for anchovies, strong cheeses, garlic, spiced tongue, onion-smothered liver, and ultra-rich sweetbreads, shows the high-spirited side of his personality that made him so appealing to people who had little interest in fussy connoisseurship or in dainty ladies' teatime recipes. "For so many years, fun was lacking in our kitchens," he recalled in 1983. "The home economists approached their task with such solemnity . . . just like the nutritionists of today. I say, to hell with all their rules." Enjoyment was James Beard's battle cry; and it became one of the fundamental principles of America's gourmet revolution. Many early gourmets were iconoclasts who relished joining him in saying "to hell with rules." They took pride in treating food with panache that would not have been sanctioned by earlier, more tradition-bound connoisseurs of the gastronomic arts. They ate whole cloves of garlic, roasted or marinated in olive oil; they sat cross-legged on pillows in the living room to feast on sukiyaki; they used empty Mateus bottles to hold candles on the table and tore at loaves of crusty French bread with their hands; they were a generation learning to eat, drink, and be merry.

Beard was a fitting leader for a movement with a strong streak of culinary insolence. He was a bigger-than-life bon vivant for whom cooking was always a provocative event—great fun for any adventurer with a healthy appetite. More than three hundred pounds at the peak of his celebrity and influence, he was hearty and hammy; he carried himself with western bravura (he hailed from Oregon); and he loved to deliver gastronomic pronouncements with insouciance. He was an epicure who was distinctly American—hungry, loud, happy, and impatient. Although obstinate by nature and nonconformist as a matter of principle, he was no philistine. From his earliest fame in the late thirties as the caterer who revolutionized the cocktail party, James Beard was a man with a mission: to encourage Americans to cook better and eat better.

During the war, despite rationing and shortages and a government-encouraged campaign to make people believe that self-indulgence was unpatriotic, civilian gourmets did indeed find a way to eat, drink, and be merry—mostly in restaurants. The military-stoked economy was a shot in the arm for the restaurant business: Their clientele had less time to cook but more money to spend; cities were crowded with newcomers ranging from blue-collar factory workers (who patronized cafeterias and luncheonettes) to war tycoons and home-front personnel (who joined what remained of café society in nightclubs where they could relieve wartime tensions); also, many restaurant kitchens were enriched by refugee chefs from France, Italy, Spain, and Middle Europe. Top-of-the-line restaurants patronized by serious gourmets always seemed to find ways around rationing and shortages. And besides, as Bill Rhode wrote in February 1945, tough times separated the truly great restaurateurs—those with "knowledge, experience, and integrity"—from the pretenders; and thus, in a sense, the war brought out the *crème de la crème* for connoisseurs of fine dining to enjoy.

For most people who were not devoted epicures, the war made gourmet living seem like wasteful indulgence at best, or possibly even unpatriotic: Fancy cookery used too much fat, which could be put to better use as a component of synthetic rubber for gas masks and truck tires; and it took too much time, which could be better spent building tanks and airplanes. The popularization of gourmet ideals was therefore forcibly deferred, although you would scarcely know there was a war being waged by looking at the increasingly sumptuous pages of *Gourmet* between 1941 and 1945. Occasionally, the magazine intimated that the high life it celebrated was what the boys in uniform were fighting for (wasn't "the pursuit of happiness" one of our democracy's cornerstones?); but by and large its writers smacked their lips and relished good food as though every meal was a carefree celebration. In December 1945, when the fighting was concluded, Lucius Beebe initiated a new column, called "Along the Boulevards," by admitting that the war hadn't had much effect at all on serious epicures. Beebe was an old-fashioned, prewar gourmet, one of the last of a line of Café Society sybarites for whom fine food was a patrician privilege rather than a middle class opportunity. He wrote that his deluxe life of "taxicabs, T-bone steaks, whitewall tires, and desirable travel accommodations never entirely disappeared. . . . The torch which set the cherries jubilee in flames was never wholly extinguished." To Beebe, such irrepressible joie de vivre was cause for pride in the pleasure-loving character of America, which he praised as "accustomed by long use to the best of everything." He wondered if "perhaps, indeed, there has been no serious dislocation of living at all, just a momentary turning down of the lights." Now, he rejoiced, everything was hunky-dory again: "Even the editorial Cassandras of Harold Ross's *New Yorker* are hard put to read direful and ghastish omens into 'The Talk of the Town' "; and with the war officially over, he noted, no one needed to feign austerity consciousness anymore.

In the years after the war, many more Americans learned to relax and enjoy life the way gourmets such as Beebe had been doing all along. It happened slowly and selectively, and there were—still are—plenty of spiritual descendants of the Puritans among us; but in the late forties, many signals appeared that greater numbers of Americans were hungry for a good time. When the war ended, tabled luxuries were advertised, acquired, and relished with gusto. Within a decade, it was possible to believe that The Good Life was arriving in a tide of material wonders. To growing numbers of Americans, a canary yellow and black tu-tone hardtop in the driveway and a salmon pink linoleum kitchen with an oh-so-moderne aqua blue refrigerator and matching deep freeze were a dream that could actually come true. And for those who took particular pleasure in gastronomy, once unheard-of extravagances abounded: frozen rock lobster tails by the dozen from halfway around the world to stock that deep freeze! Lancers rosé from Portugal in its interestingly shaped, hand-molded earthenware crock! New ways of cooking and serving meals (the fondue pot, the hibachi)! And fascinating desserts that could be flambéed to make dinner glow!

Here was a nation ready to indulge itself: Men's ties got wider and louder and women's hats blossomed in styles with flair not seen since the twenties; cars got longer, lower and sportier, sprouted fins, and appeared in gay new colors. And suddenly, it was OK to eat red meat, bacon fat, and sweet cakes with plenty of frosting. After years of ration points and government-enforced glorification of plain food with little sex appeal, Americans were eager to sit down to a meal that was fun, even frivolous. Hedonism was in style. "It's a psychological fact: PLEASURE HELPS YOUR DISPOSITION," boasted advertisements for Camel cigarettes. In 1946 *Gourmet* introduced its first *Guide to Good Eating* (a national restaurant Baedeker) with a sigh of relief—"now that we are done with the more serious business of the past four years"; and it promised anyone who subscribed to the magazine "good food with ALL the fixings," including "the newest fashions in silver, table linen, glassware, china . . . new and unusual foods," and "nothing about bombs, budgets—or diets!"

It wasn't only moneyed urbane citizens who felt they were entitled to an extra-large helping of postwar prosperity. The riches of The Good Life were available to nearly everybody! When the *Silver Jubilee Super Mar-*

"The lights have gone up and the fiddles and woodwinds may be heard again behind the velvet hangings and through the tall French windows of a hundred premises of pleasure."

—Lucius Beebe,
December 1945

ket Cook Book was published in 1953 to celebrate the twenty-fifth anniversary of the supermarket industry, it contrasted the old way Mrs. Housewife shopped—in small, inefficient, poorly stocked grocery stores—to the glories of the modern "SUPERmarket," where "thousands of products help make the American family the best fed and most supplied in the world."

The impulse to enjoy was abetted by newfound sophistication that many GIs brought back from overseas. It is all too easy to overstate their familiarity with exotic cuisines while in Europe or the South Pacific—most ate powdered eggs and mess hall mystery meat (not to mention Spam and K-rations); but even those who weren't lucky enough to *taste* cassoulet in France or pizza margherita in southern Italy or a luau in Hawaii returned to the cities and small towns of America having at least *seen* some of the rest of the world; and for a good number of veterans, as well as home-front guys and gals who had drastically changed their lives in service of the war effort, that experience made them feel different from previous generations who had been content at the family dinner table eating plain meat and potatoes. Many of these people who were second-generation Americans had parents who had forsworn ethnic ways, including foreign recipes and uncommon spices, so that they could blend into the melting pot and see themselves as regular, average citizens. (A lot of prewar cookbooks celebrate blandness as more patriotic than exotic seasonings.) The budding postwar yearning for sophistication, not only among soldiers who had been overseas but also among younger college students and older professors and the newly minted upper middle class, made that old goal of conforming seem provincial. And greater numbers of Americans were coming to see provincialism as something to be ashamed of.

For those men and women who wanted to include deluxe cookery as part of their postwar good life, tides of materiel were soon made available by manufacturers of everything from dry instant onion soup mix to color-coordinated boomerang-patterned linoleum for kitchen counters and floors. Meals once considered the domain of the professional chef were suddenly a lead-pipe cinch for industrious gourmets, who availed themselves of all the new frozen and prepared foods and stocked their modern Formica-fronted cabinets with miraculous kitchenware. "This is the Golden Heyday of the Marvelous Mechanical Appliance!" gushed John and Marie Roberson in their *Complete Small Appliance Cookbook* (1953), which featured separate chapters on such marvels as the infrared broiler, the mixer, the blender, the deep-fat fryer, the electric grill, the electric egg cooker, the automatic bean pot, and the "scientific electric tea maker." Over six million refrigerators were produced in 1950 (compared with two-and-a-half million in 1940), and within a few years they were self-defrosting and had automatic ice-makers. "Relax and Rejoice!" begins the *Mr. & Mrs. Roto-Broil Cookbook* of 1953, touting the infrared electric cooker as "the greatest cooking advance in a century" because it produced whole meals that were tasty, colorful, and fit for the sophisticate. In 1953, Club Aluminum developed "Velvaglaze" to put a cheerful (and practical) porcelain finish on aluminum cookware. Not only was cooking becoming easier and prettier; it was fun! Even a chore as simple as making toast took on nearly magical qualities in 1949 when Sunbeam introduced the first self-lowering toaster, which also ejected the toast when done. (Six years later, the task of toasting bread reached epiphany when General Electric created the Toast-R-Oven.)

Inventions such as the Toast-R-Oven and the electric rotisserie made cooking easier for nearly everyone. And in the beginning, even for many who considered themselves aspiring gourmets, ease was a vital ingredient in the recipes. While on the one hand *Gourmet* magazine was publishing complex and laborious formulas for *Canard à la presse Tour d'Argent* and *Lapins Rôtis en Accolade*, its pages also told readers how to make turkey hash in a chafing dish and tuna salad from a can; and vast numbers of late-forties and early-fifties cookbooks took readers by the hand and assured them,

Raytheon's amazing Radarange cooked hot dogs and heated buns simultaneously. The electronic oven, forebear of the modern microwave, was supposed to appeal to women because it ended drudgery, and to men because it was a gadget. (1947)

as did Jean Hamilton Campbell and Gloria Kameran in *Simple Cooking for the Epicure* (1949), that "given a little special knowledge and imagination it is still possible to produce interesting cosmopolitan dishes with less time and money than are required for dull and traditional ones." Ever since fancy food had been equated with the elaborate folderol of French haute cuisine as prepared in this country in pre-Prohibition days (always by professional chefs or servants), gourmet cookery had suffered from a daunting stigma as nearly impossible for ordinary housewives or hobbyist male cooks to create. The postwar gourmet revolution conscripted many of its recruits because cookbooks and cooking teachers were able to assure people that it really didn't need to be so difficult, that with a little extra effort and an epicurean attitude, any cook could elevate a meal from tried-and-true to transcendent.

The driving force of the gourmet revolution was not the search for authenticity (that would come later) or status (that, too, would come), but the desire to make food special. Three squares a day no longer interested the gourmet, who wanted every meal to have interesting angles. Conventional wisdom saw the old days as a time when cooking was not only difficult but drab. *Simple Cooking for the Epicure* began as a stirring manifesto: "There has been a cooking revolution in the past few years"; then went on to explain, "Gone are the days of yesteryear, and the daily grind of soups, stews, and suet puddings that bogged down the family board and bored the family." *Simple Cooking for the Epicure* incited readers to "Use your imagination! Cook the way Gauguin painted—the way you want to." Among the artistic dishes the book suggests are Caesar salad ("it will make *your* reputation if you prepare it correctly"), rice pilaf ("when mother isn't present we admit that [it] has her mushy product backed off the map"), and crêpes suzette ("really just thin pancakes with a simple sauce"). In 1949, to present family or company such dishes, instead of a casserole and a layer cake, was to declare oneself at the front lines of the revolution—you were a gourmet, for whom fine foods and, by implication, all the best things in life were delights you intended to savor.

Recipes

Liptauer Cheese

Beard's Famous Onion Rings,
   Actually Sandwiches

Anti-Doot Salami Parmigiana
   Cornucopias

A Man's Tartar Balls

Original Caesar Salad

Gourmet Pâté of Chicken Liver

Vincent Price Paella à la Valenciana

Breast of Pheasant Under Glass

Quick Brown Sauce

Ossobuco alla Milanese

Shashlik Impaled on a Skewer

International Rice Pilaf

Sybaritic Potatoes Suzette

Sophisticated Garlic Bread

Beginners' Crêpes Suzette

Classic Flaming Baked Alaska

Cheese for Dessert

Coeur à la Crème

Liptauer Cheese

SERVES 6 TO 8 (1 CUP)

"Cheese is a gourmet's food," proclaimed *The Gourmet Cookbook* in 1950. One of the surest pathways to culinary sophistication was to disavow such placid American cheeses as Velveeta bricks ("smooth as velvet") and Pimento Cream Spread jars in favor of sophisticated, and usually strong-smelling, cheese. With nothing but a crusty loaf of bread and a jug of *vin ordinaire*, a hunk of bleu or provolone was the soul of culinary honesty; along with a crisp green salad bowl, Dutch Edam or buttery Camembert made a transcendent informal lunch; and on a cheese board after dinner, with ripe figs and a glass of fine old port, nothing was more cosmopolitan than a robust Pont l'Eveque or Camembert *à point*. Many American gourmets began their journey toward savoir faire in the late 1940s with the discovery of a Hungarian-accented cheese spread known as Liptauer, traditionally made from goat's milk pot cheese and served as hors d'oeuvre. The recipe that follows is an old family favorite around our house, probably originally based on one *Gourmet* printed in 1947.

6 ounces cream cheese, softened
4 tablespoons butter, softened
1 shallot, minced
1 teaspoon capers, drained
½ teaspoon caraway seeds
½ teaspoon Hungarian paprika
1 teaspoon prepared Dijon mustard
¼ teaspoon anchovy paste
1 teaspoon grated Parmesan or Romano cheese
1 to 2 tablespoons flat beer

Mash cream cheese together with butter. Chop together the shallot, capers, and caraway seeds, then blend them into the cheese. Season with paprika, mustard, anchovy paste, Parmesan or Romano cheese, and enough beer to create a spreadable consistency. Pack the cheese into an earthenware pot, cover and allow to ripen in the refrigerator overnight. Serve with cocktail rye or pumpernickel bread.

"The favorite of all our offerings," James Beard wrote in his memoirs, *Delights and Prejudices*, "was something we named 'onion rings.' I have never known any hors d'oeuvre to catch the fancy as this one did. And if I serve onion rings nowadays, they are eaten by the hundreds. . . . I guarantee they will disappear faster than anything else you can serve!" Beard sometimes varied this formula, using dark pumpernickel bread instead of a brioche loaf; he preferred the name "onion ring" to "onion sandwich," he once said, because *sandwich* sounds so ordinary, and these are anything but.

Beard's Famous Onion Rings, Actually Sandwiches

SERVES 6 TO 8

  1 fresh brioche loaf or challah bread
  1 large bunch of parsley
  6 to 8 small, sweet white onions
  ½ cup mayonnaise
  Salt

Chill the bread several hours in the refrigerator to facilitate slicing it.

Chop the parsley very fine. Slice the onions extremely thin. Cut the bread into ¼-inch slices, then use a 1¼- to 1½-inch cookie cutter to cut the bread into rounds. Arrange the rounds on a board or table. Spread them lightly with mayonnaise. Place a single onion round on half of the bread rounds; lightly salt them. Top with the remaining rounds of brioche. Press gently.

Place the remaining mayonnaise on a flat plate and the parsley on a separate plate. Roll the circumference of each round first in mayonnaise, then in parsley. The parsley should make a fairly heavy wreath around the rim.

Cover sandwiches and chill for about an hour.

Anti-Doot Salami Parmigiana Cornucopias

SERVES 4 TO 6

*B*ecause he was fed up with the cliché of "doots"—his name for cream cheese spreads on crackers or crustless white bread—James Beard was fond of serving hors d'oeuvre that needed no bread or crackers at all. These cornucopias were among the inventions of which he was proudest. They can be filled with nearly any kind of herbed, spreadable cheese. His favorite was a zesty combination accented by Parmesan and anchovies. He suggests in lieu of anchovies that one might use "Gentleman's Relish"—a fish-spiked, odoriferous condiment gone the way of top hats and spats, but still available in some fancy food shops.

15 to 18 large, thin slices of fine-grained salami
½ cup (4 ounces) cream cheese
2 tablespoons freshly grated Parmesan cheese
1 tablespoon chopped chives
1 teaspoon chopped anchovies

Fold each slice of salami around your finger and pinch the edges together, threading a toothpick through the salami to form a cornucopia shape. Place each cornucopia between the rungs of a cake rack to hold it in position and chill 30 minutes to 1 hour so that the salami stiffens.

Combine cream cheese, Parmesan, chives, and anchovies. Use a pastry tube to fill the cornucopias. They may be kept in the rack and refrigerated, draped with plastic wrap, for several hours before serving.

NOTE: Beard recommends sticking each slice of salami into a cornucopia shape using raw egg white. Out of deference to salmonella germs, we suggest using toothpicks.

*B*eef used to be considered among the most healthful foodstuffs, and dieters often forswore potatoes and bread in favor of nothing but red meat. Raw beef, with all its blood and protein, was also thought to be the most macho food, so strong it could cure a hangover and even counteract drunkenness. James Beard, who loved raw beef anyway, suggested serving about half a dozen tartar balls to any party guest who needed to be sobered up. What is crucial to this recipe is *good* beef: freshly butchered, very lean, and ground just minutes before the tartar balls are made. Do the grinding and mixing in a food processor, and tartar balls are easy as pie.

A Man's Tartar Balls

SERVES 6 TO 8

> 1 pound very lean sirloin
> ½ cup chopped onions
> 1 teaspoon salt
> 1 teaspoon freshly ground pepper
> 1 small garlic clove, minced
> 2 teaspoons chopped anchovies
> 1 cup chopped parsley
> ½ cup finely chopped toasted walnuts

Grind beef fine, then mix it with onions, salt, pepper, garlic, and anchovies. Form the mixture into tiny balls, about ½ inch in diameter. Toss the parsley with the walnuts. Roll the tartar balls in the parsley-nut mixture, pressing to make it cling. Refrigerate before serving.

Original Caesar Salad

SERVES 2 AS A
MAIN COURSE,
4 AS AN APPETIZER

*A*lthough it was allegedly invented for a bunch of Hollywood movie stars on a binge in Tijuana one wild weekend in the 1920s, Caesar Cardini's bread-and-romaine salad, with all its tableside commotion by waiters in restaurants, became one of the foremost emblems of high-class dining out. At home, for Americans who wanted salad that was something grander than the usual things from the garden, it was a wondrous big course (or small meal) to serve, especially with home-made croutons and hand-grated Parmesan cheese. To this day—despite arriviste salads made with lettuce leaves of all tints and tastes—a freshly made Caesar salad is the king of greens. *Freshly made* is the key: Make your own croutons, grind the cheese, and squeeze the lemon just before mixing, and use the best olive oil. Any shortcuts in this formula diminish Caesar salad's greatness. No one knows exactly how anchovies made their way into it (Señor Cardini's original version, a close facsimile of which follows, had none); and some reports of its original form say that he served the leaves of romaine lettuce *whole*, and the salad was eaten without utensils, by hand. That might have been fine for vulgarians from the movie colony, but true gourmets tore their lettuce into fork-size pieces before tossing it.

Among many gourmets, and especially in swank restaurants, salad making (of Caesar and other types, too) was itself a fine art, carried on with much pageantry in great, seasoned hardwood bowls reserved only for the use of the saladier. The bowls were never, ever washed with water; they were merely wiped clean with a lightly oiled cloth, the logic being that over time the bowl would imbibe the flavor of the garlic with which it was rubbed and, in turn, impart that flavor to subsequent salads. Eventually, many bowls made of wood that wasn't hard enough turned rancid from the salad oils; and for most cooks (ourselves among them), a salad bowl merely wiped with an oiled cloth is not really clean. Nonetheless, wooden behemoths are still marketed as tableside pieces of furniture on turntables for dramatic spinning-and-tossing rituals, accoutered with giant wooden tongs reminiscent of Bora Bora pitchforks.

20 large, fresh romaine lettuce leaves
2 garlic cloves
½ cup olive oil
1½ cups stale French bread cubes (½ inch)
1 egg
¼ teaspoon salt
Juice of ½ lemon
½ teaspoon Worcestershire sauce
¼ cup coarsely grated Parmesan cheese
Freshly ground pepper

Wash the lettuce and tear it into bite-size pieces. Spin dry or roll the leaves in towels to dry. Wrap them in paper towels and refrigerate.

Make croutons: Preheat oven to 300 degrees. Heat ¼ cup of the olive oil in an ovenproof frying pan. Crush 1 garlic clove and add it to the oil, then add bread cubes. Toss, coating bread with oil. (Add salt, if desired.) When the bread begins to brown, transfer the pan to the oven and heat the bread, tossing occasionally, until the cubes are crisp and nicely browned, about 15 minutes.

Cut the remaining garlic clove and rub the cut edges against the inside surface of the salad bowl.

Ease the egg into boiling water. Cook exactly 1 minute, remove from water, and crack it into the salad bowl. Mix it with a fork. Add the remaining ¼ cup olive oil, salt, lemon juice, and Worcestershire sauce. Mix well. Add lettuce, tossing well to coat with dressing. Add grated cheese and toss again. Arrange the salad on plates—two plates if the salad is a main course, four if it is an appetizer. Add pepper to taste. Top with croutons.

NOTE: A raw or coddled egg is traditional in Caesar salad. In compliance with today's raised salmonella consciousness, the egg may be omitted from this recipe. In that case, to encourage the dressing to cling to the leaves of lettuce, we recommend adding a tablespoon of commercial mayonnaise to the bowl and mixing it with the olive oil.

Gourmet Pâté of Chicken Liver

SERVES 4 TO 6 (1 CUP)

*C*anned pâté seemed like a miracle in 1945, when June Platt wrote *Serve it and Sing* (published by Alfred A. Knopf), about the joys of Sell's Liver Pâté in its convenient tin. Mrs. Platt called ready-made pâté "magic in our kitchens" and she waxed rhapsodic in the introduction to her book of serving ideas and recipes: "Give it to me well chilled and straight from the can, spread it on a good piece of bread, and I'll make my own music, singing from pure and unadulterated joy." By the 1950s, canned pâté had become an emblem of utmost elegance in homes and restaurants, served *en gelée* (with a decoratively sliced cornichon), still shaped like the rounded-corner triangular can in which it came. Some epicures remained stubborn purists, and having savored real French pâté *not* from a can, wanted theirs freshly made. The home cook, however, was stymied: Strasbourg geese, from which genuine pâté de foie gras is made, are not available in America. Instead, the *Gourmet* cookbook of 1950 recommended ordinary chicken livers and plenty of fat, ground in a food chopper. A modern food processor works even better. And although *Gourmet* suggested softened butter as a substitute for chicken (or goose) fat, we do not recommend it. It's chicken fat that gives this pâté its savor.

½ pound chicken livers
½ cup rendered chicken fat (or softened butter)
1 teaspoon salt
Pinch of cayenne
¼ teaspoon grated nutmeg
1 teaspoon dry mustard
⅛ teaspoon ground cloves
2 tablespoons finely minced onion
1 tablespoon sherry or port
Truffle shavings as garnish

Sauté the livers in 2 tablespoons of chicken fat or butter, mashing and stirring them until cooked through. Put them into a food processor and process to a paste, adding the remaining ingredients except the truffle shavings. Pack mixture into a crock. Chill. Garnish with truffle before serving.

By the mid-sixties, when the cooking of the Mediterranean was as fashionable as that of Paris and the north, paella (like bouillabaisse, but classier) had become a requisite badge on the gourmet cook's escutcheon. Iberian cuisine had a swarthy mystique all its own, complemented by sherry aperitifs, posters of bullfights and sexy matadors, records of flamenco guitarists, dinnertable talk about Ernest Hemingway, and bottles of Lancers or Mateus wine or pitchers of sangria. Recipes for paella range from the simplest chicken-and-rice casseroles to elaborate full-dress versions such as this one, which Mary and Vincent Price attribute to the Palace Hotel in Madrid. The Prices reported that the Palace itself offered two versions of the dish: paella "good friend," which was basically arroz con pollo, and was considered the informal version of the dish for casual company, and paella "à la Valenciana" for epicures. Valencia was known as the home of the best paella—a prodigious, expensive meal with many ingredients but no complicated cooking techniques.

¼ cup olive oil
1 frying chicken (3 to 3½ pounds), cut up
¼ pound veal, diced
¼ pound lean pork, diced
2 garlic cloves, minced
1 medium onion, finely chopped
1½ teaspoons salt
¼ teaspoon freshly ground pepper
2 ripe medium tomatoes, peeled and chopped
2 cups uncooked rice
½ teaspoon saffron
4 cups boiling water
Cooked meat from a 1½-pound lobster
½ pound picked-over crabmeat
1 red pepper, chopped
1 package (10 ounces) frozen peas
1 package (10 ounces) frozen artichoke hearts
6 cherrystone clams, well scrubbed
6 mussels, well scrubbed
12 asparagus stalks, top 2 to 3 inches only
Pimiento strips as garnish

Vincent Price Paella à la Valenciana

SERVES 6 TO 8

continued

Heat the oil in heavy deep skillet. Add the chicken, veal, and pork and cook over medium-high heat until the chicken pieces are browned on all sides. Add half the garlic and onion; cook over medium-low heat until the onion is limp but not browned, 3 to 5 minutes. Add salt, pepper, and tomatoes. Cover and cook over medium heat 10 minutes. Add the rice, saffron, and boiling water. Stir well. Cover and simmer slowly for 20 minutes.

Add remaining garlic. Using a large spoon or spatula, turn the rice and mix well. Add lobster, crabmeat, pepper, peas, and artichoke hearts. Cover and cook 5 to 10 minutes longer.

Put clams and mussels in a heavy pot with ½ cup water. Cover and bring to a high boil. Cook 2 minutes, or just until shells open.

Cook the asparagus tips until tender.

Arrange the rice mixture in a large shallow casserole. Place the open mussels and clams in their shells on top. Garnish with asparagus tips and strips of pimiento.

"*T*ell me what you eat and I will tell you what you are," wrote Jean Anthelme Brillat-Savarin, the nineteenth-century bon vivant whose *The Physiology of Taste* established him as the supreme oracle of haute cuisine. Curiously, he preferred the taste of chicken to that of pheasant, but among most gourmets, pheasant became the ultimate symbol of epicureanism, mostly because it was game and therefore more scarce than any domestic fowl. In light of Brillat-Savarin's famous axiom, game is especially interesting foodstuff: relished both by connoisseurs and by toothless hillbillies who shoot it themselves, but scorned by most of us with taste somewhere in between the high and low extremes. To this day, such fare as venison, pheasant, rabbit, and quail remain the province of epicures in search of novelty and yokels who kill to eat, having made virtually no inroad into middle-class eating habits.

Presented under a glass dome that served the dual purpose of keeping it warm and on display, breast of pheasant was enshrined as the height of luxe well before the midcentury gourmet revolution; and for most newcomers to the gourmet way of eating, although it represented an outdated, fussier kind of connoisseurship, it nonetheless stood as the epitome of gastronomic hedonism, along with caviar, truffles, and champagne. In *A Treasury of Great Recipes* of 1965, Vincent Price raved about the pheasant under glass he ate at Antoine's in New Orleans as positively gorgeous. Antoine's presentation offered only breasts under glass, however, so Price noted, "I don't know what Mr. Alciatore [Antoine's proprietor] did with the rest of our pheasants, but at home we have the most elegant snacks the next day!"

Breast of Pheasant Under Glass

SERVES 4

2 pheasants, cleaned and dressed (reserve livers)
½ lemon
Salt and pepper
6 tablespoons butter
2½ cups brown sauce (recipe follows)
¼ cup Madeira
2 tablespoons minced truffles
4 slices white bread

continued

Preheat oven to 350 degrees.

Rub cavities and skin of pheasants with cut side of lemon, then season them inside and out with salt and pepper.

Melt 4 tablespoons of the butter in a heavy ovenproof pan. Brown the birds in the butter on all sides. Place the pan in the oven. Roast 45 to 50 minutes, until done, basting the birds with pan juices every 10 minutes. Remove and keep them warm.

Simmer the brown sauce until it is reduced by one quarter. Add Madeira and truffles. Season to taste with salt and pepper.

Cut the bread into rounds and toast them.

Sauté the 2 pheasant livers in the remaining 2 tablespoons butter. Mash them well and spread them on the toast rounds.

Carve pheasants so you have 4 breast pieces. (Reserve remaining meat for snacks the next day.) Place a roasted breast of pheasant on each prepared round of toast. Cover with sauce and place a glass bell over the dish. Serve at once, with much fanfare.

At Antoine's, the breast of pheasant that made Vincent Price swoon was served with brown sauce enriched by Madeira wine and two tablespoons of minced truffles. Because they were (and are) so expensive, and because they have a wild, woodsy taste, truffles were frequently the favored flavor accent for pheasant and other game birds on show-offs' tables. We couldn't afford any, so instead we made this quick and easy sauce for our pheasant's breast.

> 6 tablespoons vegetable oil
> 6 tablespoons flour
> 1 small carrot, chopped
> 1 small celery rib, chopped
> 1 small onion, chopped
> 6 cups beef broth (homemade or low-salt canned)
> 2 tablespoons tomato paste
> 1 cup red wine
> 1 bouquet garni

In a heavy saucepan, heat the oil and stir in the flour until smooth. Cook, stirring constantly, over medium-high heat for about 5 minutes, or until the roux is medium brown and has a nutty aroma. Keep the heat low enough to prevent burning.

Stir in the vegetables and cook, stirring, for 3 minutes over medium heat. Add 2 cups of the broth and the tomato paste and simmer, stirring until smooth. Add wine, bouquet garni, and the remaining 4 cups of broth. Simmer over medium-low heat, partially covered, 1½ hours, stirring occasionally until sauce coats the back of a spoon and is just lightly thickened. Strain.

Sauce may be stored in the refrigerator for up to 3 days or frozen for later use.

Ossobuco alla Milanese

SERVES 6

*N*ot all dishes favored by midcentury gourmets were expensive ones. In fact, some of the favorite new discoveries among connoisseurs of international cuisine were robust peasant meals—ragouts, fisherman's stews, and entrées made from thrifty parts of animals that middle-brow Americans traditionally disdained (kidneys, brains, sweetbreads). Ossobuco, made with shinbones of veal, is just such a dish, popularized before so many people developed consideration for the welfare of the young calves that provide the shins. It was frequently introduced in cookbooks as a real man-pleaser, presumably because men derive special pleasure from gnawing on bones.

6 lengths (3 inches) of veal shanks, with marrow
  (about 3 pounds)
¾ cup flour
¾ teaspoon salt
½ teaspoon freshly ground pepper
3 tablespoons butter
3 tablespoons olive oil
½ cup finely chopped carrots
½ cup finely chopped onion
½ large ripe tomato, peeled, seeded, and finely chopped
½ cup finely chopped mushrooms
½ teaspoon crumbled dried sage
½ teaspoon crumbled dried rosemary
2 tablespoons tomato purée
2 cups white wine
Grated peel of 1 lemon
3 tablespoons chopped parsley
1 anchovy, mashed
1 garlic clove, finely chopped

Roll the shanks in flour seasoned with salt and pepper. Heat butter and oil in a large skillet over high heat. Sauté the shanks on all sides until well browned, taking care to turn them on their sides so the marrow stays in.

Add carrots, onion, tomato, mushrooms, sage, rosemary, and tomato purée. Reduce heat, cover, and braise 10 minutes.

Add wine. Cover and simmer gently 2 hours, or until meat is tender and nearly falling off the bone. For the last 20 minutes or so, remove the lid to reduce sauce.

Before removing the shanks from the heat, combine lemon peel, parsley, anchovy, and chopped garlic. Stir this mixture into the sauce. Remove from heat and serve, accompanied with rice.

Shashlik Impaled on a Skewer

SERVES 6

*L*amb has never been favored on average American dinner tables as much as beef, but for gourmets its Mediterranean tang made it one of the most fancied entrées. It was uncommon yet not dauntingly exotic (like snails or fish eggs), therefore something that could be appreciated by advanced epicures and novices alike. Furthermore, its robust flavor encouraged piquant and sometimes elaborate strategies of seasoning and preparation that might have obliterated the blander taste of beef. Certainly, no meat developed a more succulent crust than lamb that was quickly broiled with intense heat and served enrobed in flames. Shashlik, the Russian word for lamb, was customarily cubed and marinated, then cooked and served on a skewer; it was a standard company dish in many gourmet kitchens by the mid-fifties. Our recipe is based on one from Chicago's Pump Room, where it arrived at the table skewered on a sword and hissing in a spire of flames. This recipe eliminates the flaming razzle-dazzle, which is not at all necessary to create the crusty succulence that made this dish such a delectable showpiece.

MARINADE

- 2 cups Burgundy wine
- ½ cup minced onion
- 2 bay leaves
- 1 tablespoon Worcestershire sauce
- 1 garlic clove, crushed
- 1 teaspoon salt
- ¼ teaspoon freshly ground pepper
- 2 pounds lamb from leg, cut into 1½-inch cubes

FOR SKEWERS

- 1½ cups unseasoned bread crumbs
- 2 large firm tomatoes, cut into bite-size wedges
- 24 large fresh mushroom caps
- 2 green peppers, cut into bite-size pieces
- 2 red onions, cut into small wedges
- ¼ cup olive oil

SHASHLIK SAUCE

> 2 cups chili sauce
> 1 cup ketchup
> 2 tablespoons piccalilli
> 1 tablespoon honey
> 1 tablespoon prepared horseradish
> 2 tablespoons chopped prepared chutney

Combine the marinade ingredients in a crock or bowl with the lamb cubes. Cover the bowl, refrigerate, and marinate 48 hours, stirring occasionally.

Remove the meat from the marinade and roll it in the bread crumbs. Thread it on skewers alternating with tomatoes, mushroom caps, pepper, and onions. Brush the meat and vegetables with olive oil. Broil about 6 inches under high heat (or on an outdoor barbecue grill) about 20 minutes, turning frequently, until the lamb is crusty outside, pink inside.

As the lamb cooks, combine the ingredients for the shashlik sauce in a saucepan. Mix well and bring them to the lowest possible simmer. Cook, stirring almost constantly, about 10 minutes.

To serve, use a fork to push the lamb and vegetables off the skewers onto a warm platter. Serve hot shashlik sauce on the side, and accompany the meat with saffron rice or rice pilaf.

International Rice Pilaf

SERVES 6

*I*n the quest for a starch that was different and more interesting than potatoes, American gourmets discovered rice—not just white rice, but rice with saffron, rice with pine nuts and mushrooms ("Caucasian rice"), rice seasoned with cumin seed and chili powder and brightened with tomatoes and peppers ("Mexican rice"), rice with chicken, ham, and curry (*nasi goreng*, the Indonesian specialty), rice à la Grecque (with garlic and sausage), Chinese fried rice, Rice-a-Roni in a box, and rice pilaf, which could be seasoned in any number of ways to suit the main course it accompanied. This recipe was *Simple Cooking for the Epicure*'s suggestion to accompany dolma (minted ground lamb); it goes equally well with flamed shashlik.

    8 tablespoons (1 stick) butter
    1 cup chopped onion
    1 garlic clove, chopped
    2 cups long-grain rice
    1/4 teaspoon ground cinnamon
    1/4 teaspoon ground allspice
    1/4 teaspoon ground cloves
    Salt
    1 cup tomato juice
    1 cup chicken broth
    1/4 cup golden raisins
    2 tablespoons blanched almonds

Melt butter in a deep heavy saucepan. Add onion and garlic. Sauté over medium heat until onion is soft but not yet browned. Add rice and cook, stirring occasionally, 6 minutes. Stir in cinnamon, allspice, cloves, and salt.

Combine tomato juice, broth, raisins, and almonds. Add to the saucepan along with enough water to cover the rice by 1 1/2 inches. Bring to a boil, cover pan tightly, and simmer slowly until all liquid has been absorbed and the rice is tender.

The dowdiest starch, a baked potato, was made voluptuous in at least two ways. The more expensive way—
simple and elegant—was to bake it, butter it, then dollop
it with sour cream and as much high-quality caviar as
you could afford: a true luxury, and generally considered a small meal (i.e. late supper or brunch) rather than
a supporting member of a large cast of dinner courses.
(Diamond Jim Brady was supposed to have enjoyed
mashing a pound of caviar into every spud he ate.) The
more traditional and affordable way to glorify a baked
potato was to bake it, scoop it out, enrich the pulp with
cheese, cream, etc., then restuff it and bake it again.
This created not only maximum richness, unobtainable
in plain potato pulp, but also a silky, worked-over texture that had a more epicurean feeling than the chunky
composition of unadulterated potato. Twice-baked potatoes have a long history in American cookery, and
although always deluxe, could seem somewhat home-
spun; hence, when *Gourmet* magazine wrote about them
in the fifties, they were given a more elegant title:
POTATOES SUZETTE.

Sybaritic Potatoes Suzette

SERVES 6 TO 12,
DEPENDING ON HOW MUCH
THE EATERS LIKE POTATOES

6 large Idaho potatoes, well scrubbed
6 tablespoons butter, softened
½ cup sour cream
1 egg yolk, well beaten
Salt and pepper
¼ cup chopped chives
12 tablespoons grated cheese of choice (Cheddar,
Swiss, Parmesan)

Preheat oven to 400 degrees. Place potatoes an inch or
two apart on a middle oven rack and bake 1 hour, or
until soft inside.

Remove the potatoes from the oven with a heatproof
mitt. When they are cool enough to handle, cut each in
half horizontally. Scoop out the pulp and place it in the
bowl of an electric mixer. At high speed, beat in the butter, sour cream, and egg yolk. Add salt and pepper to
taste. Mix in chives. Restuff the potato skins. Press a
tablespoon of grated cheese on top of each potato half.
Bake 15 to 20 minutes, or until browned on top.

Sophisticated
Garlic Bread

SERVES 4 TO 6

*G*arlic was one of the great windfalls of the gourmet revolution. For many years considered the mark of unassimilated (hence unsophisticated) immigrants, garlic-love became the mark of a daring, high-spirited, audacious (and therefore enlightened) palate in the 1950s. It found its way into nearly every kind of interesting foreign stew or ragout; some culinary bohemians actually served it raw in a marinade on plates of crudités with Kalamata olives and chunks of feta cheese; and nearly all gastronomically adventurous Americans learned to enjoy it as a component of garlic bread. Bland dinner rolls and ordinary sliced bread were so square by comparison! Of course, garlic bread was essential to accompany Italian food; but its excellence as a companion for bouillabaisse or any stew that needed mopping up made garlic bread a gourmet standard that has never gone out of style.

The most familiar way to make garlic bread is to take a knife and cut an Italian loaf into slices that don't go all the way through to the bottom of the loaf, spread the slices with garlic butter, sprinkle on some oregano, then wrap the loaf in foil and bake it at 350 degrees for 20 to 25 minutes so the garlic-butter flavor steams into the bread, unwrapping it for the last 5 to 10 minutes so it gets crisp. The fun of this method is that the whole hot loaf is brought to the table where diners tear off their own hunks of bread with gusto. The method that follows, which in effect makes jumbo croutons (well suited for the bottom of a bowl of French onion soup [page 73]) doesn't provide the sleeves-up fun of tearing at the loaf, but it does yield elegant tiles of toast that are an interesting hors d'oeuvre—like open-face garlic-and-cheese sandwiches. The recipe calls for garlic that is minced; but if you have a garlic press (no well-equipped midcentury gourmet kitchen was without one), it will make spreading the garlic butter easier.

1 long baguette
**1 to 3 garlic cloves (to taste), minced (or mashed in
  garlic press)**
4 tablespoons butter, softened
¼ cup olive oil
2 tablespoons grated Romano cheese
½ teaspoon dried oregano
Salt and pepper

Preheat oven to 350 degrees.

Slice the baguette horizontally, then into 4-inch lengths.

Mix the garlic into the softened butter and butter the inside of each piece of bread. Use a pastry brush to brush olive oil over the buttered part *and* along the outside crust of the bread. Sprinkle the buttered parts of bread with cheese, oregano, and (if desired) salt and pepper.

Bake 10 to 15 minutes, until bread begins to brown. Place the pieces 4 to 6 inches under the broiler and cook 2 to 3 minutes more, until sizzling brown on top. Watch carefully so as not to burn the bread.

Beginners' Crêpes Suzette

SERVES 4

*C*rêpes suzette were a fancy-restaurant dish usually served with maximum tableside fanfare. One story about their origin, which we came across in a privately commissioned history of the Rainbow Room restaurant, attributes their invention to Henri Charpentier, chef/owner of La Maison Française of Rockefeller Center, where they "epitomized the total caring great restaurants lavished upon their guests. . . . Crêpes suzette symbolized what occasionally bordered on frenzied drama. A team of waiters hovered around the table, whispering, peeling, sprinkling, lighting matches, clinking bottles, juggling dishes, and bumping into each other with the urgency of brain surgeons." To prepare such a specialty at home, complete with flaming finale, was the mark of utmost culinary confidence. The following recipe, from *Simple Cooking for the Epicure,* involves only one sauce rather than the traditional two, but "it gets the same result, thus saving time and dishes."

CRÊPES

3 eggs
¾ cup milk
¾ cup flour
1 teaspoon salt
2 teaspoons sugar
1 tablespoon butter, melted

SAUCE

5 tablespoons butter
4 tablespoons confectioners' sugar
2 teaspoons grated orange peel
¼ cup Cointreau or curaçao
½ cup orange juice

To prepare crêpes, whisk eggs slightly, add milk, then sift in the flour, salt, and sugar. Whisk well until smooth. Let stand at least 10 minutes, or up to an hour.

Heat a 6-inch nonstick frying pan until a drop of water sizzles on it, then brush it with melted butter. Using 1½ to 2 tablespoons, cover bottom of pan with a thin layer of batter, tipping the pan to spread the batter in an even circle. Brown crêpes lightly on both sides (30 to 45 seconds on first side, 15 to 20 seconds on second side), and set them in a warm place, separated by wax paper, until all are done. (These can be made ahead and stored a couple of days in the refrigerator or frozen, separated by sheets of wax paper.)

For the sauce, cream the butter and sugar with the orange peel. Add 1 tablespoon of the liqueur and 3 tablespoons of orange juice. Use half this mixture to spread lightly inside each pancake. Roll up each pancake and place in a heatproof serving dish. Keep them warm in a low oven. To the remaining half of the mixture, add the rest of the orange juice and half the remaining liqueur. Heat to boiling point. Pour over the pancakes. Heat remaining liqueur, pour over top of pancakes, and ignite. Serve immediately.

Classic Flaming Baked Alaska

SERVES 6

*I*nvented by an American scientist named Benjamin Thompson not long after ice cream was popularized in the late 1700s, this seemingly anomalous combination of baked-crisp meringue, soft cake, and frozen-stiff ice cream was enjoyed by gourmets as far back as Thomas Jefferson. It was given its name later by Charles Ranhofer, chef of Delmonico's in New York, to commemorate the American purchase of Alaska in 1867. Always a tour de force for its dazzling textural range, baked Alaska is frequently served garlanded with piped-on meringue birds, trellises, and flowers, and bedecked with eggshell halves filled with burning high-proof rum. The festoonery isn't necessary, but you don't want to omit the flaming liquor. It adds a toasted-marshmallow flavor kick to the meringue, and turns a merely delicious dish into a breathtaking spectacle that is surprisingly easy to prepare.

> 1 half-gallon brick of ice cream, whatever flavor you like, soft enough to cut but not drippy
> 1 poundcake (12 to 16 ounces), about 7 x 4 x 2 inches
> 4 egg whites, at room temperature
> Pinch of salt
> ½ cup confectioners' sugar
> 2 tablespoons high-proof rum or flammable liqueur of choice

Cut the ice cream to the exact dimensions of the cake. (There will be some ice cream left over.) Cut the cake in half horizontally and place the ice cream brick in the center, making a giant ice cream sandwich. Put the sandwich on an ovenproof platter and cover lightly. Place in the freezer long enough to refreeze the ice cream, until ready to serve.

Just before serving, preheat oven to 450 degrees. Beat egg whites and salt until frothy and gradually beat in the sugar until the whites are thick and glossy. Remove the frozen brick of ice cream and cake from the freezer and cover it with the egg whites, swirling them festively. Bake 4 to 6 minutes, or until meringue is lightly browned. Watch carefully so as not to burn the meringue.

Heat the liqueur. As soon as the baked Alaska is pulled out of the oven, set the liqueur on fire and pour it all over the meringue. Blow out the flames when the meringue begins to singe.

Cheese for Dessert!

*I*t is a bit of a mystery why so many aspiring American hosts—gourmet and otherwise—came to think of mass quantities of cheese *before* dinner as an appropriate hors d'oeuvre; but cheese for dessert was strictly for the sophisticated set. Savoring ripe Brie after dinner, with only a Spartan cracker and a piece of fruit to satisfy the sweet tooth, was a great way to certify the sophistication of one's palate, particularly if one could choose the cheese intelligently from a significant "cheese board" on which several ripe varieties from different countries were displayed. We have a New York friend who tells a story about his "pretentious days" in the 1960s when he was visiting Cleveland and ate in a hotel dining room, where he requested a cheese board for dessert. Although it was a relatively ambitious restaurant and served duck à l'orange and offered sweet sherbet between courses to cleanse the palate, the kitchen was unprepared for this much refined taste; but they did not want to admit their naiveté. So after much scurrying about by the staff, the waiter paraded forth from the kitchen with a plate on which the chef had arranged a few ungainly logs of Swiss and American cheese, apparently purloined from a chef's salad, alongside a Delicious apple.

The following after-dinner combinations, suggested by Betty Wason's *A Salute to Cheese* (1966), are more appropriate. Ms. Wason recommends that an hour should elapse before the end of dinner and the serving of cheese (preferably in the living room, with Cognac and coffee). "Any one of [these] would make a superb dessert to follow the most elegant gourmet dinner."

Stilton with ripe figs or plums
Gorgonzola with ripe peaches
Crème Chantilly with strawberries
Chabichou with bananas
Provolone with red grapes or pears
Danish Blue with red Delicious apples
Pont l'Evêque with tart white Thompson grapes
Taleggio with Queen Anne (white) cherries
Feta or creamy goat cheese with red Emperor grapes

Americans had long known about two kinds of cheesecake for after meals, but both of them were emblematic of immigrant cuisines that were considered informal: Italian cheesecake made with ricotta, and Jewish cheesecake made with cream cheese. For those who wanted to serve a more aristocratic cheese dessert, there was coeur à la crème—a simple formula for elegance and Valentine's Day tours de force. Traditional coeur à la crème is made from cheese curds beaten and drained in muslin-lined basket molds. This easier recipe, adapted from Betty Wason's *A Salute to Cheese* (1966), requires only a Jell-O mold and large perfect strawberries.

Coeur à la Crème

SERVES 6 TO 8

> 1½ cups (12 ounces) ricotta cheese
> 1 cup (8 ounces) cream cheese
> ½ cup heavy cream
> 2 tablespoons butter, softened
> ¼ cup sifted confectioners' sugar
> 1 quart strawberries, preferably with stems still on, washed

Beat together the cheeses, cream, butter, and sugar until they are very smooth. Rub a 3-cup (preferably heart-shaped) Jell-O mold with butter and pack the cheese into it with the back of a spoon. Place a plate on the top and weight it with a heavy object. Chill in the refrigerator overnight.

Dip the mold quickly in warm water to unmold, and turn the coeur out onto a large round platter. Smooth its surface with a knife. If not serving immediately, return it to the refrigerator to keep it chilled. Surround the coeur à la crème with strawberries.

— 2 —
PASSPORT TO SOPHISTICATION:
Discovering Foreign Food

Craig Claiborne pinpointed the beginning of America's gourmet revolution as June 17, 1947, the day of the first scheduled Pan Am round-the-world flight. International travel soon became a real possibility not only for the rich and idle, but also for students and professors, artists and writers, vagabonds who stayed in hostels, young families hungry for adventure, and all kinds of broad-minded citizens eager to know something beyond the culture of the United States. Jet travel, inaugurated by the first 707 flights in 1959 and soon followed by low-cost package tours of twenty countries in twenty days, made globe-trotting even easier; and by the 1960s, worldly sophistication was an alluring and attainable goal for millions. Americans explored the planet, armed with newly issued credit cards and with dollars generated by an explosion of government spending. Many were just curious; some were part of the sixties' wide-ranging cultural insurrection that rejected anything conservative and doctrinally American in favor of what was different and exotic.

To travel was to taste; and the story of this country's culinary awakening after World War II is mostly about the discovery of foreign food. For Americans who learned to be skeptical about their own vulgar pop culture, especially its fast-food-and-ketchup cuisine, the other, more ancient and more mature civilizations were a revelation of culinary goodness. By the 1960s, when Time-Life published twenty-six volumes of a lavish series called *Foods of the World* filled with photos, food lore, and recipes from all over the globe, sophisticates

"When you find yourself irresistibly drawn towards travel poster of moon-drenched Doric columns or yodelers in gray leather britches, of heather-covered moors or whirling street dancers, take care! You're skating on the thin ice of wanderlust."

—Fodor's Woman's Guide to Europe, 1953

had made it their business to taste and perhaps even know how to cook such exotica as tempura shrimp, turkey mole, and fillet of sole bonne femme.

Of all the cuisines of the world, French food was the gourmet's Holy Grail. It was a paradigm of excellence at every level, from tradition-crusted haute cuisine down to hearty ragouts and happy-go-lucky bouillabaisse. Even the most ordinary French foods such as peasant bread and omelets were cause for jubilation among American gourmets. No other western civilization devoted so much attention to the delights of the kitchen and the table as did France; and nowhere else did people find such prodigious pleasure in the art of eating. Yes, the ART of eating! To Americans exasperated with their own country's heritage of prosaic cookery and dour self-denial in all matters of the senses, it seemed that the French had figured out one of life's most exquisite secrets. They knew how to thoroughly enjoy themselves by eating good food and drinking wine.

"Even a cursory visit to France will enrich a visitor more than a journey to any other country," Eugene Fodor wrote in his first postwar guidebook, *France in 1951*. "There is perhaps no other place on earth that can contribute so much to the spiritual development of the individual." For many of those who fell in love with it in the early fifties, French cuisine was not just a matter of good things to eat; it was an edible manifestation of spiritual wisdom. Fodor was one of several convincing adulators who beguiled travelers with descriptions of a race of connoisseurs who applied patience, knowledge, and art to food, and ate not just because they were hungry, but to have an aesthetic experience comparable to a great symphony or a day at the Louvre. After all, Fodor reminded readers, it was a Frenchman, Brillat-Savarin, who declared, "Animals feed, only man can eat." This was what being a gourmet was all about.

The word itself—*gourmet*—was French; and as modifiers in the language of the gastronome, *French* and *gourmet* were virtually synonymous. Aside from its intrinsic excellence, the principal charm of French cuisine was that it was so different from cooking in America, where the accelerating mania for jiffy recipes and conveniently packaged products seemed to be wiping all vestiges of epicureanism off the map, and where even before the popularization of can-opener cookery, native gastronomy seemed either vulgar (hot dogs, etc.), primitive (baked beans and chowder), or embarrassingly jejune (blue-ribbon pies). As America modernized its kitchens and cooking habits with gusto in the 1950s, the quaint and time-honored ways of the French seemed ever more romantic in the eyes of American aesthetes. To some degree, their swelling love affair with French culture was engineered by the French government itself, whose first order of business after the war was to entice tourists and tourist money (dollars especially) to help revive the economy. Along with fashion, *gastronomie* was seen as the way to do it; and so food writers were wined and dined; and a thriving little industry grew up in America celebrating the joys of visiting France and tasting French cuisine.

Gone was the stigma of *haute cuisine* thriftlessness that had been attached to French food in America since pre-Prohibition days, when it was considered the overly rich indulgence of gluttons and patrician snobs. The new, postwar view of French food emphasized *cuisine bourgeoise*—hearty victuals eaten by farmers and townsfolk, friendly meals served in candlelit bistros with gracious hosts, and extraordinary (but inexpensive) feasts prepared in picturesque hostelries by amusing temperamental chefs whose cats curled up by fireplaces in convivial dining rooms. Here was a cuisine *of the people* that any American could enjoy without feeling that democracy was being compromised. "For the foreign tourist in France, it is a wonderful surprise to stop at the small country inn or the 'restaurant de quartier' and be served a regal meal made with relatively inexpensive ingredients," noted Fernande Garvin in *The Art of French Cooking*. "No truffles, no foie gras, but simple foods cooked with what seems to be an intuitive knowledge of the way each ingredient will react when combined with the others."

The image of French food as charming instead of stuffy had been pioneered by the first of *Gourmet*'s serialized articles (turned into a novel with recipes in 1943), called "Clémentine in the Kitchen," by Samuel Chamberlain, an etcher, photographer, and pioneering gourmet, who wrote using the gastronomical pen name Phineas Beck. Clémentine, who debuted in the second issue of the magazine, was a fictional Burgundian cook whose adventures in the Chamberlains' kitchen in Marblehead, Massachusetts, made the idea of French cuisine irresistibly adorable. Her jolly tale is illustrated by Chamberlain's drypoints and drawings, peppered with useful and amusing French phrases (*pièce de résistance; batterie de cuisine; "Ah! Ça, alors! C'est formidable!"*), and larded with recipes for honest French family fare. "Clémentine in the kitchen!" Chamberlain rhapsodized. "The bright-eyed little cook brought new significance to that part of the house, which had waited so long for a presiding genius." Described as "the faithful red-cheeked cuisinière who has presided majestically over [our] kitchen for close to a decade," Clémentine imparts the gastronomic wisdom of the French to the Beck family (as well as teaching their son, little Phinney, the language); and she remains wholly untarnished, even when the Chamberlains reluctantly expose her and their son to the vulgarities of an American supermarket. "What was Bab-O, little Phinney wanted to know? And Karo, Thrivo, Crisco, Bosco, Brillo, Marvo, Rinso, Flako?" Clémentine, dazed by the supermarket, wonders, "Would *madame* tell her why there was so much grape juice for sale, but no red wine?" The French cook is especially perplexed when she confronts the shelf of mixes, where "an immaculate, rather cold young woman with flawless make-up" is regaling customers: "Just add water and mix, ladies. No fuss, no bother, no wasted time." Bewildered but unmoved by the spiel, and by the Andrews Sisters singing the Hut-Sut song on the sound system, and by cans full of French-fried onions and Strawberry Fluff, and even by dog food (which she first assumes is canned dog), clever Clémentine emerges from the market "with precisely the same articles she would have brought home from Rue St. Hilaire." Her admiring biographer, "Monsieur Beck," breathes a sigh of relief when they get home and Clémentine begins singing "Sous les Ponts de Paris" as she whips up a batch of crêpes parysis. "I knew that the Becks were still going to enjoy French food at home," he rejoices.

Clémentine was a popular book for years, but Chamberlain's literary *chef d'oeuvre* came after the war in another series of articles in *Gourmet* called "An Epicurean Tour of the French Provinces." Compiled as a book titled *Bouquet de France* published in 1952 and kept in print for a quarter century, this was the definitive *apologia* for the gourmet life as embodied by France. *Bouquet* was a sumptuous guide to French villages, farms, inns, marketplaces, scenery, and restaurants, including "A Small Treasury of French Regional Recipes," as well as evocative drawings and gorgeous black-and-white photographs by the author. It is impossible to overstate the lyric impact this book had on readers (indeed, continues to have, with the added patina of nostalgia). Here was a brave country that may have been impoverished by the war but was still rich with beautiful cathedrals and chateaux, white seaside cliffs and pastoral vineyards, charming little village streets, and stone-and-timber hostelries from the Middle Ages. And such food! Every restaurant described has its own "fabled way of preparing crayfish," "divine pâté de foie gras en croûte," "gossamer flaky pastry with mild Roquefort stuffing," or "canard aux olives, which was delectable when accompanied by that limpid sunshine, Châteauneuf-du-Pape." Not only the food, but the chefs and waiters and hosts and dining rooms and railway rides in between are all described with such seductive rapture that it is impossible not to fall in love with Chamberlain's France. That was precisely the *raison d'être* for the book. His daughter, Narcisse Chamberlain, esteemed editor of many cookbooks herself, told us, "My father, who loved France for many other reasons, felt that French food was the carrot that would bring Americans back."

Bouquet de France distilled the ideals of growing numbers of postwar epicures who were proud to call themselves gourmets. They saw themselves as an intelligentsia who valued not just good food, but good living, which meant something other than what American businesses were pitching to the multitudes in the early fifties. Good living, for gourmets, was something beyond having some spare money, a television, a new car, and gadgets galore. Good living was travel, connoisseurship, and broadening experiences. It meant striving to be worldly and sophisticated rather than gauche and vulgar. Good living meant rejecting the self-satisfied, leisure-worshiping middle-class dream world celebrated in advertisements for products guaranteed to make life in the kitchen (and beyond) plush. True gourmets spurned the glut of corporate-inspired, jiffy can-opener recipes and TV dinners that promised to minimize time spent cooking. They wanted to savor their wine and food, and even the process of preparing it. They wanted to be different.

Vive la différence! The nauseated reaction described in *Clémentine in the Kitchen* to the supermarket and all the big food corporations' packaged products with Madison Avenue names is a good expression of why French cuisine was so appealing to gourmets. It was personal and idiosyncratic. It appealed to nonconformists for the same reasons some of them began driving Peugeots or Volkswagens rather than big, gross American cars. Along the same lines, a man who fancied himself a connoisseur of fine food and wine might choose to wear an easygoing sporty cap instead of a conservative fedora, and a nubby Rooster tie rather than a slick silk one; a woman might shun the tidy permanent wave or sculpted bouffant to let her hair grow long and artistic, perhaps pulled back tight (to accentuate the large, intelligent forehead) and accented by big, jangly earrings made by the hands of an artisan rather than a factory's machine. To be a gourmet was to set yourself apart from neatly packaged, mass-produced, mainstream culture—an increasingly urgent need for many thinking people in the 1950s when *conformity* was becoming an evil word. Gourmets had no intention of keeping up with the Joneses. They would much rather keep up with *les jambons delicieux* for which recipes were regularly given in *Gourmet* magazine.

Part of the fun of being a gourmet was *not* conforming. Instead of feeding on 1001-things-to-do-with-ground-beef like average American households, gourmets were busy discovering new and different and sometimes thrillingly exotic foods from all over the world, but especially, in the fifties, from France: truffles and chestnuts, tripes à la mode de Caen, couscous marocain, calf's brains with black butter, frogs' legs provençal, and—the one dish that separated the truly devoted epicure from the dilettante—snails. "The thought of eating snails conjures up all kinds of weird mental pictures," *Paris News Post* writer Leon Kafka gulped in 1951, politely expressing the revulsion felt by many non-gourmets over the grotesque things that these effete people put in their mouths. But Kafka assured readers, "This state of mind doesn't last for long upon seeing how snails are prepared in Burgundy. We then realize how corrupt our mental picture of this delicacy was."

For years in America, one commonly held image of the gourmet was of a person who relished food that was not merely exotic, but downright repulsive: oddball root vegetables and flower petals, octopus and offal, tongues and eyes and hearts of strange beasts, beetles, bugs, fish eggs, and horrendously odoriferous cheeses (not to mention the fairly recent gourmet predilection for raw fish in the Japanese style, prepared as sushi). Especially in the early years of the gourmet revolution, when most red-blooded Americans were still proud to eat beefsteak in large quantities and as frequently as possible, the relish of foods outside that meat-and-potatoes mainstream provided gourmets not only with a refined culinary identity, but a delicious way to *épater le bourgeois*, for whom such flavors as kidneys, squid ink, seaweed, and fried brains were a shocking affront to the bland regime most of them knew as normal. Even James Beard, the great popularizer, had a mischievous streak in this direction, frequently expressing his love of outrageous amounts of garlic, mashed potatoes enriched with goose fat and cracklings, dandelion greens, eels ("fascinating and romantic fish"), marinated chicken hearts, and just about any meat or seafood that could be eaten raw.

More than eating weird food, one thing that set gourmets apart from common people and made becoming one especially enjoyable was drinking and appreciating wine. Except for some intransigent ethnic immigrants, this was not a country of wine drinkers, and had not been even before Prohibition. It became litany among oenophiles to inveigh against average Americans as impatient guzzlers who knocked back shots of whiskey and swilled beer, and liked nearly everything we drank to be boiling hot (coffee), ice cold (cocktails), or sugary sweet (soda pop). As late as 1957, 62 percent of all wine consumed by Americans was fortified "dessert wine"— unsophisticated, heavily alcoholic, and sweet, and customarily sold in pints and half-pints and often drunk directly from the bottle wrapped in a brown paper bag.

Learning to enjoy fine wine was an imperative aspect of the gourmet experience, and it became proverbial wisdom among gourmets that *no meal is complete without it.* Of all the hallmarks of an epicurean life, connoisseurship of wine became—and to a considerable degree remains—the bellwether. You can be a bad cook and barely know the difference between *veau Prince Orloff* and *veau Oscar* and eat mashed potatoes with a spoon; but if you put on a good show with your Bordeaux or Burgundy, you will convince nearly everyone you are a knowledgeable gourmet.

As it was presented to American cooks by Francophilic food writers, wine was nothing less than liquid bliss. "Wine makes a symphony of a good meal," Fernande Garvin wrote in *The Art of French Cooking.* "Between drinking water and drinking wine with the meal, there is the same difference as between hearing a melody played with one hand on the piano and listening to it played by a full orchestra. The greater the wine, the more harmoniously the tune sings and the deeper your enjoyment." As for its powers as a stupefacient, Madame Garvin reassures the teetotaling American cook at whom her book is aimed, "Wine contains a very small percentage of alcohol. The low alcoholic content is just enough to create a feeling of well-being and to stimulate conviviality." In addition to its inherent flavor and its vaunted powers to make food even better, wine appreciation gave the aspiring gourmet a veritable armory of ways to make dining a special event even if the soufflé fell or the capon was prosaic: the ritual uncorking, decanting, swirling, sniffing, and sipping, not to mention such oenophilic activities as saving labels for a scrapbook and tending a wine collection in a wine cellar.

Gourmets learned that you didn't just plop a jug of wine on the table to last the meal; you served *a different wine with every course!* "It is possible to have, perhaps, ten kinds of wine with your meal," exulted Leon Kafka in his paean to "The Fine Art of Food and Wine." He wrote, "To the French gourmet, one cannot enjoy the pleasure of the table unless the wine is presented in the proper order. It is important that there should be no incompatibility between the dish and the wine. Therefore dry wines should be served with spicy dishes while the

> "To find the perfect wine partner for your menu, you must think of more than color. There can always be, of course, an element of romance. How often does the lilting name of a lovely wine add to the glamorous moment when a beautifully decorated dish is presented?"
>
> —Roy Andries de Groot

sweet wines and liqueurs should be saved for dessert . . . but remember, always light before heavy." The conceit that a different wine should accompany each course of a gourmet meal created chaos for many a newly minted gourmet (who were frequently stymied when it came to salad and dessert); but most knew to fall back on the fundamental wine rule, as sung by Desi Arnaz as he dances around his house trailer in gleeful anticipation of his first married meal (ragout) in Vincente Minnelli's movie, *The Long, Long Trailer* (1954): "Oh, the red wine with the meat, the white wine with the fish . . ."

To the adventurous gourmet, wine was not only for drinking out of a glass. The pleasure of gastronomy could be magnified many times over if wine was included as an ingredient in the foods one cooked. California's Wine Advisory Board did its best to encourage this idea as early as the mid-forties, in full-page advertisements in cooking magazines that described "the appetite-whetting miracle that comes when food and wine keep company at your dinner," and advising hosts to serve the same kind of wine used to prepare a dish along with the dish—"for taste harmony." Among its suggestions were baked beans Claret, tamale pie Burgundy, wine onion soup, and fish steaks in white wine ("A test dish, for it reveals how much better the eating gets when food is cooked with wine.")

"It is, of course, entirely possible to cook without using wine," Morrison Wood wrote in the introduction to his cookbook, *With a Jug of Wine*, which was first published in 1949 and stayed in print for twenty years. "It is also possible to wear suits and dresses made out of gunny sacks," he continued, "but who wants to?" He explains that Europeans have used wine in their cooking for centuries, which is why they can take ordinary foods and make them edible poetry. Then he provides a hefty book full of recipes for foods thus ennobled, including sherry-flavored liverwurst paste and peanut butter canapés enriched with dry red wine all the way to pineapple boats sauced with champagne syrup for dessert. In between, of course, are more traditional wine- (and other spirit-) enriched recipes for the likes of boeuf bourguignonne, hasenpfeffer, lobster thermidor, and of course, cherries jubilee.

*B*efore midcentury gourmets embraced France and the cult of fine wine, many flirted with the allure of Polynesia and silly drinks decorated with paper parasols. The American rediscovery of French food in the fifties and sixties was preceded by a flurry of interest in the kind of campy, imitation native cuisine that goes by the name "Polynesian," but in fact is only dimly related to what people in the South Pacific eat. It may be hard to believe during our current age of minimalist good taste that Polynesian cuisine, which is now virtually synonymous with outlandish, gummy kitsch, could have seemed sophisticated; but in the late 1940s and early 1950s, exotic frequently equaled soigné. "Those who are discriminating and wish something unusual and fine should not miss this place," wrote Duncan Hines about the original Oakland (California) Trader Vic's in the early 1950s editions of his *Adventures in Good Eating*. "Chinese cuisine, but NOT the chop suey variety," he raved. Similarly, *Gourmet's Guide to Good Eating*, composed mostly of comments by peripatetic readers of the fairly snooty magazine, praised the Trader's San Francisco establishment as "Unparalleled in the preparation of Polynesian and Oriental dishes [with] the most divine atmosphere imaginable . . . the best!" About Don the Beachcomber's Polynesian-themed restaurant in Los Angeles, *Gourmet*'s enthusiastic guides gushed: "Cooking so good it's beyond description," praising "the best almond duck I ever tasted" and "mysterious tropical drinks."

Oriental cuisine had been a familiar presence in America since the last quarter of the nineteenth century, when it had been installed in city neighborhoods and throughout the Southwest by Chinese immigrants. But mostly it was chop suey and egg foo yung—cheap ethnic grub apparently made from scraps of meat instead of royal roasts—and it was denigrated by American epicures as unrefined. "Fifty years ago 'foreign foods' were viewed with suspicion and horror," noted *Simple Cooking for the Epicure* in 1955. In the late 1930s, however, about the time there were glimmerings of a renewed interest in ambitious home cooking (*Joy of Cooking*, etc.), the image of Chinese food began to get embellished. *The Chinese Cook Book* by Mr. M. Sing Au, "Compiled and edited for the American Cook" in 1936, introduced such strange fare as "The Nine-Course Dinner" (from bird's nest soup to sharks' fins and fried pigeons) with these words of wisdom from litterateur Yuan Mei: "There is a difference between dining and eating. Dining is an art. When you eat to get the most out of your meal, to please the palate, just as well as to satiate the appetite, that, my friend, is dining." The cover of the book depicts a wise old Chinese man with his forefinger raised in the air, observing, "Variety is the spice of life."

Despite such efforts to elevate Chinese food from its chop-suey-joint reputation, it had to be repackaged and relabeled as Polynesian before it entered the canon of the American gourmet. The year *The Chinese Cook Book* was published, Victor Bergeron, a saloon keeper from Oakland, California, took a trip to the Gulf Coast and the Caribbean to try to get some new ideas for drinks to serve at his watering hole, which was then called Hinky Dink's. He learned to make daiquiris at La Floradita in Havana, planter's punches at the Bon Ton Bar in New Orleans, as well as Tongo punches and Frankensteins from God-knows-where. And when he returned to Oakland, he started cooking ham-and-eggs "Hawaiian" (with pineapple and banana chunks) to spice up the menu at Hinky Dink's. In 1937, still in search of new ideas, Bergeron went to Hollywood to visit Don the Beachcomber's, where the zombie and the missionary's downfall had first been mixed. He was transfixed by the tropical decor in the dining room, and by the menu of dishes from Hawaii. When he returned to Oakland, he changed the name of Hinky Dink's to Trader Vic's, covered the walls with fabric and bamboo, and started serving what he called Polynesian food, which (as he conceived it) was like Chinese food but not so crude (no fish with their heads on), spiced with some seasoning from France (via Tahiti), and infused with the strong, manly flavor of an open fire. "I call my style of cooking 'imaginative,' Trader Vic wrote in his autobiography, *Frankly Speaking*. "Not the same old junk that the fellow down the street makes. That's no fun."

The secret of Polynesian food, as conceived by Trader Vic, was that it was different, but not *too* exotic. Genuine oriental cookery scared the bejeezus out of most Americans, as evidenced by *American Cookery*'s jingoistic description of how the Japanese soldier ate during the war: "Every Jap is outfitted with a tiny portable stove and a can of Nipponese 'Sterno.' In a small pouch he carries raw rice. He makes a stew of the dirty kernels and if he's lucky, embellishes it with fish heads and tails. These are canned or salted down and, according to GIs, taste like preserved garbage." Despite such repulsive foodways, by the end of World War II many Americans had developed a genuine interest in the South Seas, and many more were looking for imaginative food as a relief from wartime austerity. Trader Vic's brand of eater-friendly Polynesian cuisine—augmented in restaurants by fish nets, tiki god statues, torch-and-candle lighting effects, and in some cases floor shows with fire-eating Samoan sword dancers—was a welcome thrill.

Amazingly, much of the original Trader Vic's repertoire was fairly sophisticated and, if not authentic, at least truly imaginative. Although it has tumbled far down the culinary status ladder, and all its customary synthetic South Seas ambience seems preposterous by modern standards of fine dining, Polynesian cookery as conceived by Trader Vic has many tasty dishes to recommend, some of which are still served at the flagship restaurant in San Francisco. For some who cut their gourmet teeth on pressed duck with sweet-and-sour plum sauce, this brand of ersatz exotica still has a gourmet cachet. Even into the early seventies, Gael Greene, *New York* magazine's trend-conscious restaurant reviewer, wrote about the New York branch of Trader Vic's that it "has a persistent chic that defies the hanging spears and Philippine blowfish and the lumpen tiki gods that flank the entrance on Central Park South." Ms. Greene, of course, found the stuff on her plate insipid: "monumentally unmemorable . . . hideously thickened . . . fatty, demoralized . . . dismally bland." Nonetheless her review quoted *Cosmopolitan* editor Helen Gurley Brown, apparently swept away by the sexy ambience, who said, "The food is heavenly."

For many people concerned with cultivating their palates, Polynesian food was far too silly; furthermore it was—horrors!—inauthentic, not to mention too sugary and Americanized and—to be blunt—primitive. Anyway, it quickly lost its uniqueness. By the late fifties nearly every middle-class American suburban home with a patio had become the site of unsophisticated luaus; and to the average (non-gourmet) housewife, "Polynesian cooking" had become little more than a synonym for dumping chunks of pineapple, banana, and maraschino cherries on otherwise humdrum food. Real gourmets wanted more out of life than that. They wanted to know all the ins and outs of sophistication. They had learned about the exquisite delights of French gastronomy from Clémentine and *Bouquet de France*; and those who could afford it traveled to the Continent (or at least to a serious French restaurant in the U.S.) and tasted heaven-on-earth for themselves. The campy flash of Polynesian pyrotechnics was far beneath the modernistic sensibilities of true epicures.

Clémentine, *Bouquet de France*, and *Gourmet* magazine notwithstanding, cooking genuine French food was not so easily done. Especially for those who had tasted the real thing overseas or in a good French restaurant, few cookbooks provided the necessary guidance for recapturing its magic. Most French recipes available in English were incomplete or difficult, demanded obscure ingredients, or came shrouded in writerly hocus pocus about the *je ne sais quoi* of the techniques and the cook's magic touch. Then in 1961 Julia Child, Louisette Bertholle, and Simone Beck put out a book that suddenly and dramatically provided ambitious gourmets with a bible. *Mastering the Art of French Cooking* was no gay romp through the provinces, nor did it promise jiffy gourmet dishes with little fuss or bother. The first sentence exactly explains its appeal: "This is a book for the servantless American cook who can be unconcerned on occasion with budgets, waistlines, time schedules, children's meals, the parent-chauffeur-den-mother syndrome, or anything else which might interfere with the enjoyment of producing something wonderful to eat."

Here at last was a touchstone that separated gourmets from dilettante pretenders with can openers.

Consider that title: This was not *"Simple Cooking for the Epicure,"* not even the mere *"Art of French Cooking"* (1958). This was *"Mastering the Art of French Cooking"*; and it delivered what it promised in recipes of heretofore unknown length and precision that led aspiring gourmets step-by-step from ignorance to hands-on knowledge—not merely of French food, but of French cooking techniques. Before the first recipe is given, *Mastering the Art* provides its reader with thirty-six pages of instruction concerning the proper "batterie de cuisine," definitions from *baste* and *boil* to *sauté* and *toss*, descriptions of ingredients as basic as butter and flour, measuring charts, temperature conversion tables, a treatise on how to use a knife, and a short course in wine including cooking with it, which one to serve with which food, how to store it, how to uncork it, and how to pour it from bottle to glass. What is missing from this unabashedly instructional tome is the ambience with which so many earlier French cookbooks had been embellished. "We have purposely omitted cobwebbed bottles, the *patron* in his white cap bustling among his sauces, anecdotes about charming little restaurants with gleaming napery, and so forth," the authors write in their introduction. "Such romantic interludes, it seems to us, put French cooking into a never-never land instead of the Here, where happily it is available to everybody." Earlier cookbooks had inspired American gourmets' interest in French food; none did so much to encourage so many to actually take up skillet and balloon whisk and cleaver as did this one.

The whopping success of *Mastering the Art of French Cooking* (reinforced by Mrs. Child's appearance on television beginning in 1962 as "The French Chef"; see Chapter 3) happened about the same time many people were converted to the gourmet point of view by the writing of Craig Claiborne, the restaurant reviewer of *The New York Times*. Whereas restaurant writing had traditionally been a matter of passion and prejudice, Claiborne, starting at the *Times* in 1957, established an objective voice and spoke of gastronomy less as an ineffable art than as a significant commodity to be care-

Here at last was a touchstone that separated gourmets from dilettante pretenders with can openers.

fully studied by serious consumers of culture. He was quiet, unassuming, scrupulous about his weight (158 in the morning; 162 at night), and apparently uninterested in restaurateurs and the business of restaurants. Never swayed by pomp or circumstance, nor by his emotions, his reviews applied fastidious, middle-class values to the unruly business of eating out. His criterion, he told readers, was simple and practical: "How does the food and service compare to the cost of dining?" Unlike swooning gourmands who usually wrote enthusiastically about their favorite restaurants and made their appetites a feature of the writing, Claiborne practiced restaurant reviewing as earnestly as if he were evaluating such serious cultural phenomena as plays or novels.

Born in Mississippi, and avowing that some of his favorite foods included hamburgers and chili, Claiborne's great feat nonetheless was to open the door to complicated and foreign foods for his followers. With him as their guide, diligent *Times* readers learned to appreciate and critique everything from shrimps rémoulade at Absinthe House to roast duck at Zetti Hungarian Restaurant. In Claiborne's book, the loftiest continental restaurant started with the same clean slate as a Lower East Side delicatessen; but those that got four stars were almost invariably such bastions of haute cuisine à la française as La Caravelle, La Côte Basque, Lafayette, and La Grenouille; and it was his dispassionate analysis of complex French fare that made his reputation. "Not until the author [Claiborne] published *The New York Times Cook Book* in 1961 did I make the cooking connection between the dream-like food we ate in France and the dreck we ate at home," Betty Fussell wrote in *Masters of American Cookery*.

Reading Craig Claiborne, gourmets sharpened their favorite simile, that fine food (in particular, foreign food) was like art. In the case of Claiborne's restaurant reviews, it was art that the reader was considering for purchase; and Claiborne assigned it a market value, using the star system. Although foreign food was almost always considered better, it didn't have to be grand to rate his approval; excellence was where you found it, and it was Claiborne's blessing of regional Chinese food that encouraged many New Yorkers to discover the allure of "uptown" Szechuan restaurants and Chinese food beyond Polynesian and Cantonese clichés. "For a man with a conscientious palate," he wrote, "a small Chinese restaurant in mean surroundings, provided it serves excellent food, is just as important as, and perhaps more so than, a gloriously upholstered salon with a mediocre kitchen." That was Claiborne speaking: the man with the conscientious palate, whom readers learned to trust not only for his unemotional reviews (which he himself called "as detached as human nature would allow") but also for the recipes he gathered in the equally prudential but ever-popular standard, *The New York Times Cook Book*.

At the same time Julia Child and Craig Claiborne demystified gastronomy, the art of fine dining continued to have persuasive champions who loved it for its magic and miracles. Nowhere was this classicist attitude better expressed than between the covers (and in the covers themselves, which were padded in thick bronze leatherette) of Vincent and Mary Price's *A Treasury of Great Recipes*, published in 1965. Before writing this ten-pound compendium of recipes from the great restaurants of the world, the Prices were already famous as connoisseurs of fine painting; in 1959 Vincent had written "a visual autobiography" called *I Like What I Know* about his lifelong love affair with beauty. Less an autobiography than an engaging tour guide to the aesthetic splendors of the world, *I Like What I Know* was followed by a marvelous record album called *Gallery*, in which masterpieces by Picasso, Van Gogh, Matisse, et al., were "interpreted" via orchestral arrangements, thus providing the listener, in Price's words, "the pleasant experience of 'hearing' some of your favorite paintings." When it came to cooking, for which Price developed a taste during his world travels as both an actor and an art collector, his approach was a similar fusion of connoisseurship and sorcery. The introduction to his and Mary's cookbook explained, "Behind the scenes we've met the alchemists in tall white hats who have initiated us into their mysteries." As to why these gastronomic wizards were willing to share their secrets, the Prices speculate, "Somehow it has gotten around that we are collectors of everything, all the arts, folk art, decorative art, fine art, and the art of enjoying food—and preparing it.''

Price was a very American character—born in St. Louis to a comfortable family and raised in a childhood home he called a "semi-pretentious Pseudo-Windsor Castle"—and in fact a large number of the recipes he collected came from grand old American restaurants; but there was something so *continental* about the guy in his silk smoking jacket and that neatly tonsured mustache, and with his refined sensibilities about art, poetry, and music. Price was a globe-trotter and world-class collector; and when it came to cooking, the world was his oyster. The Prices' book is a sumptuous gallery of gastronomic treasures plucked from all the earth's great cuisines, its recipes supplemented by stunning glossy color photographs (beautiful food, international dining rooms, picturesque chefs in their toques, genteel maître d's, flaming desserts, and Price himself sniffing some especially delectable dishes), reproductions of grand menus, and dozens of blank pages for listing Your Favorite Recipes,

Vincent Price sips at sauce for crêpes suzette.

Your Favorite Wines, and Your Favorite Guests. (About the latter, the Prices suggest, "When you have had guests to dinner, memorialize the event by asking each of them to write a line or so on the following pages. In years to come, these pages will be a treasured record of your hospitality and friendships.") For the Prices, gourmet cooking was something to savor with the hallowed respect customarily tended to a collection of fine art. With its leatherette covers encased in acetate, two silk ribbon place markers, pages made of sturdy, antiqued paper, and astronomical price of $20 (at the same time Dione Lucas's equally compendious *Gourmet Cooking School Cookbook* was going for $8.50), the book itself was a literary manifestation of gourmet cookery as utmost connoisseurship.

By the 1960s, some of America's favorite culture heroes were connoisseurs with an international perspective—people who doted on the world's best food and drink with an obsessiveness that twenty years earlier might have made them seem suspiciously sensual (and in the case of men, homosexual). Fictional secret agent James Bond was the most flagrant example and ultimate role model. He was British, which in the 1960s was the pinnacle of suavity, and he knew how to savor all the cultures on earth with savoir faire—fussing over fine wine and ordering foreign food with finesse. Then, too, there were John and Jacqueline Kennedy in the White House. After eight years of dowdy Ike and Mamie who ate meat and potatoes, and before that, even worse, the Trumans, who liked such hillbilly fare as barbecue and fried chicken, here was a refined couple who served champagne and vintage wine with dinner of *selle d'agneau* and *foie gras en gelée avec salade verte*. The Kennedys even employed a French chef, René Verdon, who prepared what the gastronomic press extolled as an "all-French" menu for British Prime Minister Harold Macmillan when he came to the White House for lunch: trout garnished with sauce Vincent followed by roast beef with artichoke shells filled with fondue of tomatoes and giant asparagus; and for dessert, vacherins with raspberries and chocolate ice cream garnished with whipped cream and candied violets. "The White House was geared to a new plateau of excellence," Deane and David

"Dine, wine, break bread with us; partake with us of our favorite dishes from kitchens all over the world."

—Mary and Vincent Price,
in the introduction to
*A Treasury of
Great Recipes*, 1965

Heller wrote in their biography, *Jacqueline Kennedy*. Of course, Jackie spoke French, which not only enabled her to pronounce the names of the food served in the White House, but also endeared her to the French themselves, which among Francophilic gourmets was probably the highest possible badge of distinction. "Vive Jacqueline!" the crowds in Paris yelled during the Kennedys' triumphal state visit in 1961. "Vive les Kennedys," echoed American gourmets, who at last had a First Family who didn't make them feel as if they were citizens of a nation composed entirely of hamburger-with-ketchup-eating bumpkins.

The watershed event in America's discovery of international cuisines was the New York World's Fair of 1964. Here were tastes of some of the great foods of the world, and not only for high-flown gourmets. International cuisine had become something that every broad-minded American wanted to at least sample. (Bring the kids and eat in a tree house at the African Pavilion!) No longer the domain solely of the nonconformist or the effete epicure, food with an international flavor was popping up in motel dining rooms and even at some ambitious family dinner tables all over the country. And at the World's Fair, anyone who was curious could sample the goodies of the world in exotic eateries ranging from a Polynesian Pavilion with dance and drum recitals to the dazzling Granada Restaurant at the Spanish Pavilion, where fairgoers learned about such Iberian delicacies as boned partridge, paella Valenciana, and sangria, the fruit-spiked wine punch that caught on with adventurous epicures everywhere. Among the other dishes that seemed to leap from their pavilions into the repertory of American cooks with even the slightest gourmet aspirations were Belgian waffles, Swiss fondue, Thai coconut-chicken curry, Malaysian satay, Swedish meatballs, Mexican turkey mole, Greek moussaka, and African chicken-peanut stew.

And what about the American pavilions at the World's Fair? They were a sorry spectacle indeed, at least from the point of view of those Americans yearning to become enlightened epicures. There was, for instance, a Greyhound (bus) Pavilion, which offered the Food Service of

Tomorrow exhibit in which visitors were invited to cook their own meat-and-potatoes meals in just seconds using prototypical microwave ovens. Or you could chow down on cheap chuck-wagon suppers at the Texas Pavilion, fried bologna sandwiches at the West Virginia Pavilion, or Tad's $1.19 steak dinners at the Wisconsin Pavilion. To be fair, there were exhibits that featured some interesting regional Americana, but few gourmets paid

much respect to the New England johnnycakes or Maryland crab or New Orleans gumbo being offered. Even these folksy dishes seemed rather pedestrian compared to the likes of murgh curry and tandoori specialties from India and mint tea with petite pastries from Morocco. For many discriminating gastronomes, America's position among the cuisines of the world was best represented by "Festival '64, the American Restaurant," which purported to offer "America's contributions to gourmet cookery," including stuffed ham and pumpkin pie. This professedly gourmet dining room, sponsored by the American Gas Association, was, alas, located in the Festival of Gas Pavilion.

Certainly not all gourmets looked down their noses at American cookery. James Beard was always a champion of well-prepared regional Americana; and nearly half of the Prices' *Treasury of Great Recipes* come from such American institutions as the Blue Fox of San Francisco, Locke-Ober's of Boston, even Chavez Ravine of Los Angeles (the Dodgers' ball park, which inspired the Prices' recipe for "stuffed frankfurters"), as well as from the avant-garde Four Seasons of New York. Eventually, after it became a fad in the early eighties, even Julia Child embraced American food and did a television show about it. But the attitude of many gourmets, especially back in the sixties, was that Americans, by and large, ate terribly. Inundated by instant mixes and jiffy recipes, without a creditable haute cuisine establishment to set standards, obsessed with nutritional trivia taught in home economics classes, and afflicted with palates debased by years of eating food that was too sugary, too fatty, and just plain bogus, America appeared to be a culinary wasteland in the eyes of many gourmet cooks.

Indeed, the impetus behind much gourmet cookery was a strong streak of American self-loathing. As the sixties wore on, and as conflicts between a swelling counterculture and an ever-more-entrenched establishment began to deepen (over the Vietnam war, civil rights, drugs, long hair, etc., etc.), the culinary battle lines became clearer, too. On one side were TV dinners, Wonder bread, Hamburger Helper, Cool Whip, and Richard Nixon in the White House eating his allegedly favorite snack of cottage cheese and ketchup, or daughter Tricia's notorious tuna noodle casserole made with condensed soup, or one of Pat Nixon's equally ill-famed gelatin salads. All these travesties were considered symptoms of what Waverley Root and Richard de Rochemont, authors of *Eating in America* (1976), vilified as "the increasing deterioration of taste in the nourishment of the Machine Age and the decreasing interest of our industrially produced mass-distributed foods." Storming these barricades were those whose palates were not (in Root and de Rochemont's words) "irremediably atrophied"—gourmets as well as a growing health-food movement who had discovered a world of enlightenment, sophistication, and nonindustrialized peasant honesty in such foreign-born pleasures as Szechuan beef, Beaujolais wine, and pita bread.

A strange sociogastronomic phenomenon had occurred by the end of the 1960s. Once considered the self-indulgent pleasure of the spendthrift voluptuary, gourmet cooking had developed a cachet among the socially conscious. Most gourmets were not health foodists, and they disdained sprouts and tofu nearly as much as TV dinners, but there were some aspects of their appreciation of international cuisine that made their tastes run parallel to counterculture values. To serve tawny rice pilaf instead of pure white mashed potatoes was a way to ally oneself with the culturally uncorrupted (and non-white) peoples of the Third World. To study the cuisines of Africa or Southeast Asia was to reject plastic, flavor-impoverished, bleached-white, industrially produced American groceries. Ita Jones, author of a counterculture cooking column in the sixties called "The Grub Bag," observed, "The loss of art in American life is a tragedy. Many of us forget that the art of living, the art of loving, and the art of eating are things which don't befall us but are learned." Ms. Jones's solution to America's deprivation was to learn to cook foods from other countries; and in a column called "The American Hamburger," which she condemns as flavorless fodder for ignoramuses, she suggests an enlightening substitute—"The European 'kotlette,' the juicy original product our hamburgers are faint copies of."

Such positioning of gourmet cookery as a club against the culinary booboisie was not really new. Back in 1949, Morrison Wood had written in his introduction to *With a Jug of Wine*, "If you are looking for recipes such as Miss Sally Arbuthnot's celebrated (in Round Corners, Nebraska) corn chowder, or Aunt Arbethera's scalloped chicken, or the chocolate meringue pie that won first prize at the Sulpha County Fair, don't waste your time going on. . . . However, if you're seeking new taste thrills, if you'd like to become a renowned host or hostess, if you'd like to cook your way into a man's (or woman's heart), or if you have an adventuresome spirit and yearn to experiment or try something new—you've bought yourself a piece of goods."

By the 1960s the enemy, for those who fancied themselves a cut above middlebrow America, was no longer Aunt Arbethera or the meringue pie from the county fair. The enemy had become big American business—General Foods, Campbell's, Jell-O, etc.; or to use a favorite term of the time, the *establishment*. Although a lot of culinary iconoclasts were very much part of the establishment in other areas, gourmet cooking had become one of the ways they let the world (or at least their dinner guests) know that their tastes and experience were broader and more international than the average American supermarket shopper's corn dogs and Dream Whip. No one rendered the gourmet's spiteful view of

"How shall we tell our fellow Americans that our palates have been ravaged, that our food is awful, and that our most respected authorities on cookery are poseurs?"

—John and Karen Hess,
The Taste of America,
1977

typical American taste better than John and Karen Hess in their vitriolic book *The Taste of America* (1977). Describing a woman they saw on television who said that her children enjoyed eating junk food, the Hesses scoff, "If she is a typical American, and she sounds like one, her very first mouthful of nourishment was a synthetic, sweetened bottle formula; she was weaned on starchy baby foods loaded with sugar and monosodium glutamate, and she grew up on soda pop, candy, corn flakes, ketchup-doused hamburgers, and instant coffee. . . . The truth is that good food in America is little more than a memory. . . . The American traveler now can find tastier victuals in such countries as Turkey or Morocco than he can find at home." Not all gourmets were as mean as the Hesses, and just about the time they were stomping on American taste in the mid-seventies, a revival of interest in regional American cooking and eating (even among worldly gourmets) was getting underway; but the Hesses' rancor in contrasting loathsome American eating habits to admirable foreign ones (the cookbooks for which are variously described as "remarkable," "fascinating," "serious," "discriminating," "wonderfully exciting," and "highly sophisticated") does stake out one extreme position of what it used to mean to be an American gourmet.

Recipes

Beurre d'Ecrevisses (Lobster Butter)

Lusty Aïoli (Garlic Mayonnaise)

Coquilles Saint-Jacques Provençale

Escargots de Bourgogne (Snails!)

Bold Gourmet's Seviche

French Onion Soup

Bouillabaisse Magnifique

Incredibly Rich Lobster Thermidor

Polynesian Chieftain Fried Shrimp

Bistro Coq au Vin Rouge

Julia's Poulet Rôti

True Boeuf Bourguignonne

Venerable Sukiyaki

Cassoulet to Make Your Reputation
    as a Chef

Trader Vic's Indonesian Lamb Roast

Life-Affirming Moussaka

Ham and Eggs Hawaiian

Clémentine's Crêpes Parysis

Soufflé au Grand Marnier

Tropic Isle Baked Bananas with
    Rum Sauce

Pears of Bacchus

1964 World's Fair Sangria

Beurre d'Ecrevisses (Lobster Butter)

MAKES ½ CUP

*S*amuel Chamberlain described La Bresse in southern Burgundy as "truly a little principality of *La Gourmandise*, a temple of sane and subtle cooking," known especially for delicious chicken and crayfish. The latter, he wrote, had the power to "open up an enchanted vista in your kitchen." Because the Chamberlains spent so much time in Maine, they adapted the regional French recipes that called for crayfish to young lobsters. Crayfish butter—or in this case, lobster butter—was an essential provision in any true gourmet's repertoire. It is wonderful to spread on hot broiled fish steaks or fillets just before serving, or simply gobbed onto a chunk of warm French bread before a meal.

Shells from a 1-pound lobster (or a dozen crayfish)
¼ pound (1 stick) butter

Dry the shells on a cookie sheet in a 350-degree oven for 12 to 15 minutes. Pound them in a mortar until pulverized. Place them in the top of a double boiler with the butter and 2 tablespoons of water. Heat over simmering water 15 minutes, stirring occasionally. Strain the liquid into a bowl. Place the pulverized shells in a strainer over the bowl and pour about 2 tablespoons of boiling water over them to retrieve all the butter. Refrigerate until the butter layer hardens on top. This crust is the lobster butter; skim it off and discard any liquid below. Keep the butter in a jar, refrigerated.

"*Virile*, highly aromatic, and given to color" is how *Bouquet de France* raved about the cooking of the Mediterranean. The book's recipe for aïoli was so virile that it was presented with a warning that those who convert to it as a more robust mayonnaise might find themselves ostracized from civilized company for a day. Aïoli *is* powerful stuff, certainly no substitute for the mayonnaise you use in egg salad or on a bologna sandwich (Mistral, the Provençal poet, is said to have scorned mere mayonnaise as "marmelade." But then, what did he know about bologna sandwiches?) However, for a cold supper of hard-boiled eggs and spiced beef along with salt-roasted potatoes and steamed artichokes (hold the hollandaise), aïoli makes the meal. When preparing it, have all the ingredients except the water very cold.

Lusty Aïoli (Garlic Mayonnaise)

MAKES 1⅓ CUPS

1 egg yolk
¼ teaspoon salt
Pinch of white pepper
6 garlic cloves, mashed to a pulp
1¼ cups olive oil
1½ to 2 teaspoons lemon juice
1 tablespoon tepid water

Mix the egg yolk, salt, and pepper into the garlic pulp and place this mixture in the bowl of a blender. Turn the blender on high speed and add ¼ cup of the olive oil drop by drop. Gradually add lemon juice and water as the blender continues to run. Still blending at high speed, drizzle in the remaining olive oil. Refrigerate to store.

WARNING: True aïoli must be made with raw eggs, which are considered risky nowadays because of the salmonella scare. You can make safe, bogus aïoli by mashing garlic into bottled mayonnaise thinned with olive oil, but that's just the kind of housewife shortcut strategy that true American gourmets abhorred.

Coquilles Saint-Jacques Provençale

*I*n the early 1970s Joseph Wechsberg, writing for *Gourmet*, reminded readers that Lyon is known to French people as the gastronomic capital of France, and that the Lyonnaise claim to have mastered *l'art de bien manger*, the art of eating well. The reason for Lyon's fame, Wechsberg went on to say, is that good eating around Lyon was not the prerogative of the idle rich: Everyone ate well there, most notably in small, family-run bistros known as *bouchons*. One such establishment was Christian Bourillot, whose patron, Monsieur Bourillot, proclaimed, "There are those who practice *la cuisine gadget*, using tricks, but they don't last long in Lyon." *Gourmet* provided readers with his recipe for coquilles Saint-Jacques, a buttery dish of sautéed scallops that became immensely popular as an hors d'oeuvre in American restaurants, which frequently cosseted the scallops in a creamy, cheesy sauce. This Lyonnaise version is simplicity itself, other than the fact that it requires using two pans at once: You mustn't crowd the scallops into a single pan.

> 2 pounds sea scallops, rinsed and cut in half if very large
> Salt and pepper
> ½ cup flour
> ½ pound (2 sticks) butter
> ½ cup minced parsley
> 1 tablespoon finely minced garlic
> Lemon wedges as garnish

Sprinkle scallops with salt and pepper. Dust them with the flour, shaking off any excess.

Divide butter in half and melt each half in a large skillet over moderately high heat until it is golden. Divide the scallops between the pans and sauté them for 2 to 3 minutes, or until lightly browned and cooked through. Divide the parsley and garlic in half and toss half of each into each pan, tossing about 30 seconds longer. Transfer the scallops to a heated serving dish and serve garnished with lemon wedges.

To average American eaters who weren't gourmets, escargots were the ultimate totem of epicurean eccentricity: Imagine eating the creepy-crawlies from your lawn! When you found them in the gourmet shop, they barely looked like food in their elaborate package, the snails in a separate can and the shells heaped into a tall see-through plastic canister. To eat them properly, one needed special ovenproof snail dishes, tiny two-pronged forks to extract the snails, and snail clamps to hold the shells. Once all the tools were assembled and the will to eat them established, the recipe was as simple as ABC. And the results were far more accessible than most snail-o-phobes ever imagined: basically garlic-butter with briny snail taste, all mopped up with crusty French bread.

Escargots de Bourgogne (Snails!)

48 snail shells
48 snails
12 tablespoons butter
6 tablespoons minced parsley
8 garlic cloves, pulverized
1/4 cup minced shallots
Pinch of grated nutmeg
Salt and pepper
French bread, uncut

Wash and drain the snail shells. Drain the canned snails (but do not rinse).

Cream together the remaining ingredients except the bread, using only a pinch of salt (canned snails are salty).

Preheat oven to 400 degrees.

Place one snail in each shell, then pack each shell full of garlic butter. Arrange the shells in snail dishes with the open ends up and heat them 10 to 12 minutes, until they are bubbling hot.

Serve with French bread, which should be torn from the loaf, all the better to mop up the juices in the snail dishes.

Bold Gourmet's Seviche

SERVES 4 TO 6

*I*f we were sociologists, we would divide midcentury American gourmets into two basic categories: those who sought elegance and those who sought honesty. The latter relished peasant food: odoriferous, garlicky, messy fare that seemed to thumb its nose at the uptight Americans who ate such sanitized aliment as frozen fish sticks and TV dinners. In their workshirts and peasant blouses, turquoise jewelry and free-breathing sandals, these robust counterculture gourmets discovered food from the Spanish-speaking world beyond the Tex-Mex clichés of tacos and refried beans. Chicken mole, for instance, was an excellent way to be different because it was a main dish made with—would you believe?— chocolate! (To be accurate, it was unsweetened cocoa.) Another shocker that gained favor among those with courageous palates was seviche. Long before America's discovery of sushi, the idea of eating fish raw was no less weird than eating pork or turkey raw. The gourmet was quick to point out, of course, that the overnight lime juice marinade in effect "cooked" the fish. Nonetheless, to order seviche in a restaurant or to serve it to company was the proclamation of a culinary sensibility on the cutting edge of adventure. This recipe is adapted from *The New York Times Cocktail Party Guide* (1970).

1 pound fresh fillet of haddock, sliced into thin strips
3 long, hot green chili peppers (about ¼ cup)
3 long, hot red chili peppers (about ¼ cup), or 1 teaspoon hot red pepper flakes
1 medium onion, cut into paper-thin slices (about 1 cup)
1 cup lime juice
1 teaspoon salt
Chopped cilantro

Place the strips of fish in a crockery bowl. Cut the peppers in half, remove and discard their seeds, then cut them into thin strips and add the strips to the fish. Add onion, lime juice, and salt. Mix well. Cover and chill overnight.

Serve sprinkled with cilantro.

$\mathcal{F}$ew revelations from the Gallic kitchen have found such widespread and long-lasting acceptance among Americans as French onion soup—one of those honest rustic dishes that somehow expressed the general excellence of French eating habits. In many American kitchens, particularly in restaurants aiming to make a reputation on their unstinting generosity, the fairly elegant basic recipe (this one adapted from *Mastering the Art of French Cooking*) is thrown into catastrophic imbalance by massive extra amounts of cheese in the liquid, creating a great, unwieldy wad of rubbery goo with barely any room for onion broth. In proper equilibrium, there seems never to be quite enough cheese or bread, making their presence a special treat.

French Onion Soup

SERVES 4 TO 6

- 5 cups thinly sliced yellow onions
- 3 tablespoons butter
- 1 tablespoon olive oil
- 1 teaspoon salt
- ¼ teaspoon sugar
- 2 quarts beef broth
- 3 tablespoons flour
- ½ cup dry white wine or dry white vermouth
- Salt and pepper
- 6 to 8 rounds oven-toasted French bread
- 3 tablespoons Cognac
- 1½ cups grated Swiss cheese

In a covered saucepan, cook the onions in butter and oil over low heat 15 minutes. Uncover the pan, raise the heat to medium, and stir in salt and sugar. Cook 25 to 30 minutes more, stirring frequently, until the onions are dark golden brown. As they brown, bring the broth to a boil in a separate pot. Sprinkle flour onto the onions. Stir almost constantly over medium heat 3 minutes more. Remove from heat. Pour the boiling broth onto the onions. Stir in the wine and add salt and pepper to taste. Return to heat and simmer, partially covered, 30 minutes more.

To serve, place pieces of hard-toasted French bread in 6 or 8 tureens. (For an extra-gourmet touch, use the recipe for Sophisticated Garlic Bread, page 34). Pour the soup over the bread. Stir about ½ tablespoon of Cognac into each bowl. Top each serving with grated cheese.

Bouillabaisse Magnifique

SERVES 6

*T*he most famous of all dishes from Mediterranean France, bouillabaisse is nothing but offhanded fisherman's stew made from the fish that were available; and yet its mystique was such that gourmets fussed and worried endlessly over exactly which species it ought to contain. It was impossible to get some of the authentic ingredients such as sea-devil and hog fish in America, but Samuel Chamberlain suggested that red snapper, whiting, and small eels made a good substitute. Chamberlain got this recipe for bouillabaisse from the Restaurant Isnard in Marseille—"one of the admitted shrines of bouillabaisse." Depending on which fish you use, its flavor will range from mild to luscious. We recommend a combination of mild and strong-flavored fish. In particular, eel is a great way to give it oomph.

> 2 garlic cloves, finely chopped
> ½ cup finely chopped onion
> 2 large tomatoes, peeled, seeded, and chopped
> ⅓ cup olive oil
> Pinch of thyme
> 1 bay leaf
> 1 tablespoon chopped parsley
> 1 tablespoon chopped fennel
> 4 pounds fish: red snapper, whiting, eel, or other small, firm fish, including 1 "chicken" lobster (a 1-pounder) in its shell
> 1 teaspoon salt
> ½ teaspoon freshly ground pepper
> Pinch of saffron
> Toasted garlic bread (page 34), in slices

In a large heavy saucepan over medium heat, sauté the garlic, onion, and tomatoes in olive oil. Add seasonings.

Clean and cut the fish into coarse slices. Scoot aside the onion and tomato mixture in the saucepan and put the lobster and firmer fish into the bottom of the pan, the softer fish on top. Add enough boiling water to barely cover. Add salt, pepper, and saffron. Bring to a brisk boil and cook 15 minutes, until the fish is cooked through.

Place garlic bread in the bottom of a wide shallow serving dish. Pour the broth over it. Remove the fish from the pan and serve in a separate dish.

$\mathcal{A}$side from their increasing rarity and their inherently delicious flavor, lobsters were especially fit for the gourmet's kitchen because their gentle-flavored meat so nicely lent itself to deluxe preparations involving wine, sherry, cheese sauce, seasoned bread crumbs, and flaming folderol. In addition, the intricate exoskeleton (if kept intact when extracting the meat) suggested many fabulous presentation ideas. The swankiest of all lobster dishes was the one allegedly created for Napoleon during the month of Thermidor on the First Republic's new calendar, and involved stuffing the sherry-sweetened meat back into the lobsters' shells.

Incredibly Rich Lobster Thermidor

SERVES 4

- 2 lobsters, 1½ pounds each
- 2 tablespoons olive oil
- ½ cup chopped onion
- 1 cup sliced mushrooms
- 4 tablespoons butter
- 2 tablespoons flour
- ¼ teaspoon salt
- Pinch of cayenne
- ½ cup milk
- ½ cup heavy cream
- 2 tablespoons dry mustard
- 3 tablespoons freshly grated Parmesan cheese
- ½ cup cooking sherry
- ¼ cup fresh bread crumbs

Steam or boil the lobsters 17 to 20 minutes until done. Halve each and carefully remove the meat from their bodies and claws. Keep the shells warm in a low oven.

Sauté the onions and mushrooms in olive oil until the onions are tender. Remove from heat.

In a saucepan, melt 2 tablespoons of the butter over medium heat. Stir in flour, salt, and cayenne. When smooth, add milk and ¼ cup of the cream. Stir constantly until mixture comes to a boil. Add onions and mushrooms. Stir in remaining cream, mustard, cheese, and sherry. Simmer, stirring constantly, until the mixture is reduced to a thick, creamy consistency, 3 to 5 minutes. Cut the lobster meat into small pieces and add it to the creamy mixture. Stuff the shells with creamy lobster. Sprinkle the shells with bread crumbs and dot with the remaining butter. Put under a broiler about 1 minute, until browned.

Polynesian Chieftain Fried Shrimp

SERVES 4

*T*hese shrimp were served at the Polynesian Pavilion of the 1964 World's Fair in a dining room designed to resemble a South Seas longhouse, its doorway flanked by two giant wooden tiki gods. Thumping war drums provided background music, and every customer received a colorful plastic lei.

1 pound large raw shrimp in their shells
¾ teaspoons salt
1½ teaspoons curry powder
¼ teaspoon powdered ginger
3 tablespoons lemon juice
3 tablespoons cornstarch
1 cup flour
1 teaspoon baking powder
½ to ¾ cup milk
1 cup finely grated, unsweetened coconut (available
   in health food stores)
Vegetable oil for frying
Sweet-and-sour sauce

Remove the shells of the shrimp, but leave their tails intact. Use a sharp knife to slit their backs and remove the intestinal vein. Rinse them under cold running water and pat dry.

In a medium bowl, mix salt, curry powder, ginger, and lemon juice. Add shrimp, stir to coat, and refrigerate 2 hours, tossing once or twice. Drain and reserve the marinade.

Dip the shrimp in cornstarch. Shake off excess.

Make a batter of flour, baking powder, ½ cup milk, and reserved marinade, adding more milk if batter is too thick to dip the shrimp. Dip the shrimp in the batter, then in the coconut.

Heat 1 inch of oil in a deep skillet or frying kettle to 370 degrees. Fry the shrimp, a few at a time, for 3 to 5 minutes, or until golden brown and the shrimp are cooked. Drain on paper towels. Serve immediately with sweet-and-sour sauce of choice for dipping.

The first postwar English-language guide to the restaurants of Paris was the work of James Beard and Alexander Watt, published in 1952: *Paris Cuisine*. In addition to light-hearted descriptions of their favorite restaurants, the two bons vivants offered recipes representative of the best French kitchens, among them two different versions of a dish that would soon become one of the hallmarks of American gourmet taste: coq au vin. Popular not only because of its flavor, but also because it is easy enough to make so that even beginners feel a sense of accomplishment, coq au vin depends on wine for its flavor (très sophisticated!), and is a basically forgiving recipe for which every French chef and nearly every American gourmet could devise their own special twist. Beard and Watt offered one from Air France, which eagerly provided *Paris Cuisine* with recipes that the airline's chef had developed in a pioneering effort to serve first-class food even in an airplane. Air France's coq au vin recipe allegedly kept its flavor for 2½ to 3 hours in a vacuum container, thus allowing flyers to—in the words of Beard and Watt—"enjoy *les plaisirs de la table*" even in the air. The recipe that follows is *not* the long-lasting trans-Atlantic coq, but is based on the better one Beard and Watt got from the chef at Paris's *Le Cochon d'Or*. It yields a very well-cooked chicken that wants to fall off its bones. If you like it firmer, you can reduce the simmering time at the end by 5 to 10 minutes.

4 slices of bacon, diced
6 tablespoons butter (2 of which are softened)
1 roasting chicken, 3 to 3½ pounds, cut as for fricassee
1 garlic clove, peeled and mashed
12 small onions, peeled
6 medium mushrooms, sliced
¼ cup brandy
½ teaspoon dried thyme
1 teaspoon freshly ground pepper
½ teaspoon salt
1 bay leaf
2 cups red burgundy wine
2 tablespoons flour
1 cup beef broth
Chopped fresh parsley

Bistro Coq au Vin Rouge

SERVES 4

continued

In a heavy stockpot or casserole, cook the bacon until its fat is rendered. Lower heat and add 4 tablespoons of butter. When the butter melts, add the chicken pieces and brown them on both sides 8 to 10 minutes. Add garlic, onions, and mushrooms.

Heat brandy. Ignite it and add to the stockpot.

When the brandy flames burn out, add thyme, pepper, salt, bay leaf, and burgundy. Bring to a boil, cover, and simmer for 20 minutes.

Mix flour with remaining 2 tablespoons (softened) butter to create a paste. Stir the paste into the simmering liquid. Add beef broth. Cover, return to a simmer, and cook 25 minutes longer.

Serve sprinkled with fresh parsley.

*J*ulia Child's long-abiding gift to American gastronomy was not the importation of laborious French recipes, but the lesson that even the simplest dishes deserved special attention. No food was so basic that it could not become elegant and delicious if cooked with panache. (There isn't a simpler entrée than roast chicken, and an excellent one can be made by simply putting it into a 475-degree oven and pulling it out an hour later. But in Julia's kitchen, no dish was quite so effortless.) Julia's *poulet rôti*, trussed and buttered and basted, became nothing less than a gourmet's affidavit. "You can always judge the quality of a cook or a restaurant by roast chicken," advised *Mastering the Art of French Cooking*, which included a series of detailed diagrams showing how to truss a chicken with mattress needles and white string. "We bought poultry needles, threaded them, and, studying the diagrams of *Mastering the Art of French Cooking I*, pierced thighs in one direction and wings in another, struggling to keep the thread taut and the knots tight," wrote Betty Fussell about the culinary education she got from Julia Child. "It was a job, but we were determined to out-French the French." In fact, trussing isn't really necessary to create a simple-but-elegant roast chicken; what is necessary is plenty of butter.

Julia's Poulet Rôti

SERVES 3 TO 4

    1 chicken, 3 to 4 pounds, at room temperature, patted dry
    6 tablespoons butter, softened
    Salt and pepper
    2 tablespoons butter, melted
    1 tablespoon olive oil
    1 tablespoon minced shallot or scallion
    1 cup canned chicken broth

Preheat oven to 500 degrees.

Work 2 tablespoons of the butter under the skin of the chicken. Rub 2 tablespoons of the butter inside the cavity of the chicken, and the remaining 2 tablespoons of butter over the outside skin of the chicken. Sprinkle with salt and pepper. Place chicken breast side up in a V-shaped roasting rack in a roasting pan. Cook 15 minutes.

continued

Reduce heat to 375 degrees and baste bird with a combination of the melted butter and olive oil. Turn breast side down. Roast 20 minutes. Baste again and turn breast side up again. Roast 10 to 15 minutes more, testing for doneness by cutting deep into the flesh between the body and leg. If the juices run clear, the chicken is done. Remove it from the oven and let sit at room temperature 10 minutes before carving.

Remove all but 2 tablespoons of fat from the roasting pan. Stir in minced shallot and cook slowly over medium heat for 1 minute. Add the broth and boil vigorously, scraping up chicken pieces from the bottom of the pan with a wooden spoon. Boil until the liquid is reduced by half. Season to taste with salt and pepper. Use as gravy for carved chicken.

True Boeuf Bourguignonne

SERVES 4 TO 6

"*I* have had boeuf bourguignon served to me in some of the top restaurants across this country, from New York to California," Morrison Wood wrote in *A Jug of Wine.* "Usually the dish includes various vegetables such as carrots, turnips, tomatoes, and whatnot. I've even had it prepared with prunes stuffed with almonds. But none of these dishes is true *boeuf bourguignonne.* The real *boeuf bourguignonne* is simply Burgundy beef, or beef stewed in Burgundy. The only extraneous flavors which mingle with it are onions, which have already been cooked, set aside, and added later, and the delicate flavor of mushrooms." One shouldn't use expensive French Burgundy, Wood goes on to say, Pinot Noir from California is fine; and for maximum enjoyment he suggests sharing the dish with "your favorite feminine or masculine companion." When we first tested this recipe, what delighted us the most about it was the color—the lusty dark, nearly purple brown of the beef and wine—a long-forgotten hue reminiscent of many a happy bistro meal from the 1960s.

10 large pearl onions, blanched and peeled (or frozen)
2 to 4 tablespoons bacon drippings
2 pounds lean chuck, cut into 1-inch cubes
1½ tablespoons flour
½ teaspoon salt
¼ teaspoon freshly ground pepper
¼ teaspoon dried marjoram
¼ teaspoon dried thyme
½ cup beef bouillon (homemade or low-salt)
1 cup American burgundy (not imported) wine
½ pound small fresh mushrooms, washed (about 24)

In a deep heavy skillet, sauté the onions in 2 tablespoons of bacon drippings until brown. Remove the onions and reserve. Sauté the beef cubes in the same drippings, adding more bacon drippings if necessary, until beef is browned on all sides. Sprinkle with flour and seasonings. Add bouillon and wine. Stir well. Bring to a boil, lower heat to a bare simmer, and cook uncovered for 3¼ hours. If necessary to keep beef barely covered, add more bouillon and wine (in a ratio of 1 to 2).

Return browned onions to skillet. Add mushrooms. Stir well. Simmer 1 hour longer, again adding more bouillon and wine if necessary. Sauce should be thick and dark brown.

Serve with crusty French bread, tossed green salad, and your imported Burgundy.

Venerable Sukiyaki

SERVES 6 TO 8

*P*robably the most unlikely number one hit song in 1960s America was "Sukiyaki," by Kyu Sakamoto. Originally a Japanese tune titled "Ue O Muite Aruko" ("I Look Up When I Walk"), it was recorded as an instrumental in England by jazzman Kenny Ball. But because his record company figured nobody could pronounce the title, they renamed it with the single Japanese word everybody did know: *sukiyaki*. *Newsweek* commented that this would be like releasing "Moon River" in Japan with the title "Beef Stew," but the song hit number ten on the U.K. chart in January 1963; and when, as a lark, American disk jockey Rich Osborne of KORD in Pasco, Washington, tracked down Kyu Sakamoto's original vocal version and played it on the air, an amazing thing happened: His audience loved it. Audiences all across America loved it! "Sukiyaki," sung entirely in Japanese, became the first foreign language song to hit number one on *Billboard*'s Hot 100 chart (not counting 1958's one-word hit, "Tequila"). It stayed number one for *three weeks* in June. This was only months before the opening of the World's Fair in New York, at which tourists could enjoy the pleasure of real sukiyaki, eaten Japanese-style, sitting cross-legged on straw mats at low tables.

America's relish for sukiyaki—the dish, not the song—was originally promoted by soldiers stationed in Japan after World War II and during the Korean War, who sometimes advertised their international savoir faire by advising that the proper pronounciation was not *soo-kee-ya-ki*, but *s'kee-ya-ki*. Among American hosts and hostesses looking for a meal that was exotic to cook and serve, but not weird to eat, the sweet-and-salty combination of beef and veggies was a favorite throughout the 1950s and 1960s. Prepared in a chafing dish or electric skillet at the table, sukiyaki is both informal and sophisticated, hence an exemplary meal for gourmets of the modern persuasion. This recipe is from the House of Japan building at the World's Fair. It requires a very large skillet or wok; or it can be halved.

2 pounds sirloin, partially frozen
4 tablespoons sesame oil
½ cup beef broth
½ cup soy sauce
¼ cup sugar
1 tablespoon dry sherry
2 cups thinly sliced onions
1 cup sliced celery
1 cup drained, sliced bamboo shoots
1½ cups sliced fresh mushrooms
1 cup shredded fresh spinach
4 scallions, sliced
1 pound vermicelli, cooked and drained

Cut the steak into paper-thin pieces, about 2 × 3 inches.

Heat oil over high heat in a large skillet. Add the meat and quickly brown it on all sides.

Combine broth, soy sauce, sugar, and sherry in a bowl. Add half this mixture to the beef. Push the beef to one side of the skillet. Add onions and celery. Cook 2 to 3 minutes, stirring. Add the remaining soy mixture, bamboo shoots, mushrooms, and spinach. Cook 3 minutes more. Add scallions. Cook 1 minute more. Heap vermicelli on one side of a platter and sukiyaki on the other. Serve immediately.

Cassoulet to Make Your Reputation as a Chef

SERVES 8

*F*ew books summarize the gourmet point of view as succinctly as *Twelve Company Dinners*, written by Margo Rieman in 1957 as a step-by-step, hour-by-hour guide to the preparation of twelve refined menus for the ambitious host who wants to serve company something sophisticated. "Almost any young wife can prepare a casserole for guests, but the idea of a whole dinner causes her to break out in a cold sweat," Ms. Rieman observed, reassuring her readers, "It Can Be Done," just so long as you have a wire whisk, a French chef's knife, and a good bottle of wine to serve with whatever you prepare. Meal Number Two in her scheme, entitled *Menu to Make Your Reputation as a Chef*, was built around cassoulet, the French provincial stew with white beans, preserved goose, and regional sausages. Most of its essential ingredients were not available in American supermarkets, but that didn't stop resourceful cooks from creating innumerable native versions of the dish. In fact, cassoulet became like paella (Meal Number Three): a hallmark of the adventurous mid-1950s cook. *Twelve Company Dinners* says that authentic cassoulet "takes about eight hours to prepare, with constant doing of this and doing of that—much too elaborate for the

Menu to Make

Your Reputation

as a Chef

average cook." Black bean cassoulet, on the other hand, can be made in a trice, with minimal this-and-that.

1 pound black turtle beans
4 cups red wine, or more if needed
½ pound garlicky, full-flavored sausage
   (cooked or uncooked)
2½ pounds boneless beef chuck, cut into 2-inch cubes
½ cup olive oil
2 medium onions, chopped
2 garlic cloves, chopped
½ teaspoon dried rosemary
1 bay leaf
Dried basil
Dried oregano
Dried tarragon
1 teaspoon salt
½ teaspoon freshly ground pepper
Cayenne

Wash beans well and put them in a pot with 4 cups of cold water and 2 cups of the red wine. Bring to a boil for 2 minutes, turn off the heat, and let the beans soak 1 hour.

Bring the beans to a simmer and let them cook over the lowest possible heat until they are almost tender, about 2½ hours.

Cut the sausages in half and place them in a large casserole with ¼ inch of water over medium heat, frying them until they are browned. Remove them from the casserole and wipe out all but a tablespoon or two of the grease. Raise the heat and brown the beef, then remove the beef and wipe out any remaining grease. Lower the heat to medium-low and pour ¼ cup olive oil into the pan. Sauté the onion and garlic until the onion is lightly golden, about 5 minutes.

To the cooked onions in the casserole, add browned meat and sausage, rosemary, bay leaf, a pinch each of basil, oregano, and tarragon, salt, pepper, dash of cayenne, and remaining 2 cups of red wine. Cover and let simmer over medium-low heat for 1 hour.

Preheat oven to 300 degrees.

Add beans to the casserole with the remaining ¼ cup olive oil and bake, covered, for 3 hours. Add more wine as casserole cooks if the cassoulet seems dry.

Trader Vic's Indonesian Lamb Roast

SERVES 4 TO 6

*A*t our house, whenever we want to convince dinner guests that Trader Vic's in San Francisco really is a good place to eat, we serve them Indonesian lamb roast, a recipe the Trader said was "the most delightful thing in our restaurant as far as lamb is concerned. I think the lamb industry should give us a blue ribbon, because we serve more lamb in our restaurant than any other restaurant in this country, and it's because of this recipe." About the marinade, he wrote, "It's a mixture of screwball spices, but it tastes good."

⅓ cup finely chopped celery
⅓ cup finely chopped onion
1 garlic clove, minced
¾ cup peanut oil
¼ cup red wine vinegar
2 teaspoons A.1. steak sauce
2 dashes of Tabasco
3 tablespoons honey
1 teaspoon dried oregano
3 tablespoons curry powder
2 bay leaves
½ cup Dijon mustard
Juice and peel of 1 large lemon (2 to 3 tablespoons juice)
12 loin lamb chops or 2 racks, trimmed of fat
   (about 3 pounds)

Sauté celery, onion, and garlic in oil. Add all the other ingredients except lamb and simmer briefly. Cool and chill. Marinate the meat in this mixture for 4 hours, refrigerated.

Preheat oven to 400 degrees. Drain meat but reserve marinade. Wrap the exposed bones of the chops with foil, leaving the meat exposed, and arrange it in a greased shallow baking pan. Brush the meat with the marinade. Bake 10 to 15 minutes for rare chops, 20 to 30 minutes for racks. Turn once and baste frequently while cooking. To crisp the meat, finish it under the broiler for 1 to 2 minutes. To use any leftover marinade as sauce (it isn't really necessary; this meat should be quite juicy), bring it to a boil momentarily and remove the bay leaves before spooning it onto the lamb.

*I*n the gourmet's quest to rediscover the gustatory ecstasies that puritanical Americans seemed to have repudiated, Greece was a happy hunting ground. Thanks to Melina Mercouri's performance as a zesty, earthy Greek prostitute in the movie *Never on Sunday* (1960) and Anthony Quinn's as a zesty, earthy Greek peasant in *Zorba the Greek* (1964), Greece developed a reputation as a land whose people relished life with gusto. The Greeks, as we came to idealize them in the 1960s, were a life-affirming race who sang folk songs and danced barefoot on the sandy beach, and wore colorful peasant skirts or handsomely tattered fishermen's sweaters. When they ate they gleefully smashed plates and wine glasses on the floor and shouted "oopah!" when flaming goat cheeses were presented at the table. Their hearty cuisine, which many American travelers tasted for themselves during ever-more-popular package tours to southern Europe, the Mediterranean, and the Aegean Sea, became a symbol of down-to-earth pleasure; and by the late 1960s, Greek-style moussaka was ensconced as a gourmet standard—just as Greek fishermen's caps and sweaters became a familiar uniform among guys (and gals) who wanted to show they weren't button-down types. Not only was moussaka joyous and exotic (anything with eggplant was exotic); it was convenient company food: a one-dish meal that could be assembled and even baked well before guests arrived, then heated before serving. In fact, one of moussaka's enthusiastic champions was the pianist Liberace (an accomplished cook), who recommended serving it on those evenings when there was a show on television that everybody wanted to watch: "The table is already set with everything that is needed. The guests are seated facing the screen, the program is tuned in, and dinner begins." Oopah!

Life-Affirming Moussaka

SERVES 6 TO 8

continued

3 medium eggplants
Salt
⅓ cup chopped onion
1 pound ground lamb
2 tablespoons olive oil
½ teaspoon allspice
½ teaspoon salt
½ teaspoon freshly ground pepper
1 cup tomato sauce
3 eggs, lightly beaten
2 cups half-and-half
2 tablespoons chopped fresh parsley
1 cup dry bread crumbs
½ cup crumbled feta cheese
Vegetable oil for frying
4 tablespoons butter, melted

Wash the eggplants, then pare their skin off in ½-inch strips lengthwise, leaving ½-inch of peel between the strips. Cut them into ½-inch slices. Sprinkle the slices generously with salt and place them between lengths of paper towels, weighted down with heavy plates. Let stand 1 hour. Rinse and drain off moisture. Pat dry.

Preheat oven to 350 degrees. Grease a broad 3-quart baking dish.

Sauté the onion and lamb in olive oil until the lamb is cooked through. Stir in the allspice, salt, pepper, and tomato sauce. Cover and simmer slowly 20 to 25 minutes. Drain excess oil.

In a separate skillet over high heat, briefly brown eggplant slices on both sides in about ¼ inch of vegetable oil, adding oil to skillet as needed. Drain eggplant on paper towels.

Combine eggs, half-and-half, parsley, ½ cup of the bread crumbs, and the feta cheese.

Place one layer of eggplant at the bottom of the baking dish. Top it with a layer of the lamb mixture. Repeat until all the lamb is used and finish with eggplant on top. Pour the egg mixture over the eggplant, sprinkle with remaining crumbs, and drizzle with melted butter. Bake 1 hour, until mixture is set and golden brown on top.

*A*rguably, this is the dish from which all ersatz Polynesian cookery descended—the first exotic meal served at Trader Vic's first Oakland restaurant, Hinky Dink's. The Trader had learned to cook it from his French-Canadian father, whom he described as "a helluva cook," in *Trader Vic's Helluva Man's Cookbook* (1976). He wrote that ham and eggs Hawaiian was the traditional Sunday morning breakfast around his house when he was growing up. The recipe is for two servings: Multiply as you wish.

Ham and Eggs Hawaiian

SERVES 2

- 5 tablespoons butter
- 2 slices canned pineapple
- 1 ripe (but not overripe) banana, split lengthwise
- 2 thick center ham slices
- 6 eggs
- Salt and pepper

Melt 1 tablespoon of the butter in a heavy skillet over medium heat. Fry the pineapple slices 2 to 3 minutes on each side. Remove them to a warm serving platter. Add another tablespoon of butter to the pan and fry the banana halves until browned. Remove them to the serving platter. Add another tablespoon of butter; fry the ham slices until slightly browned. Remove them to the serving platter. Add the remaining butter to pan and, when it has melted, crack the eggs into the juices in the skillet. Cover and fry the eggs in the juice until they are cooked to desired degree. Slide the eggs onto the serving platter. Season with salt and pepper to taste.

Clémentine's Crêpes Parysis

SERVES 4

"*O*ne of the most unctuous and succulent dishes we have ever encountered," raved Clémentine's biographer, Phineas Beck, about these ham-and-cheese pancakes that the Burgundian cook managed to make with ingredients she found in the "super-American Super-Market." Making thin, elegant crêpes was an essential talent for gourmet chefs; a smooth, lumpless sauce béchamel was equally important ... and considerably more difficult. Monsieur Beck's recipe, which follows, was a simple white sauce augmented by what he called "refinements reminiscent of the elaborate old recipes."

For four people, you will want twelve crêpes, which should be made *after* preparing the sauce béchamel.

SAUCE BÉCHAMEL

2½ cups milk
4 peppercorns
½ bay leaf
½ small white onion, sliced thin
4 thin slices of carrot
4 parsley sprigs
3 tablespoons butter
2 tablespoons flour
Salt and white pepper

CRÊPES PARYSIS

12 to 15 crêpes (page 36)
12 to 15 slices of very thinly sliced ham (about 8 ounces)
½ cup freshly grated Parmesan cheese
Butter

In a heavy enameled saucepan, heat the milk, peppercorns, bay leaf, onion, carrot, and parsley over low heat. Bring to the slowest possible simmer, but do not boil. Simmer 15 minutes. Strain the milk and clean the saucepan well.

In the same pan, over low heat, melt 2 tablespoons of the butter and very slowly sift in the flour. Stir constantly with a wooden spatula about 3 minutes until the roux is thick and smooth. Remove from the heat. Whisk in 2 cups of the warm, seasoned milk. Simmer, whisking constantly, about 2 minutes, or until the sauce is medium-thick. Season to taste with salt and white pepper (but use salt sparingly; the ham you will wrap inside the crêpes is salty). Finish with 1 tablespoon butter.

Prepare crêpes.

Preheat oven to 350 degrees.

To make crêpes parysis, layer each crêpe with a thin slice of ham. Sprinkle with Parmesan cheese. Drizzle the open crêpes with sauce béchamel and roll them into loose tubes. Place them in a greased shallow baking dish. Dot generously with butter. Bake 8 to 10 minutes, until bubbling hot.

Soufflé au Grand Marnier

SERVES 4 TO 6

*M*ary and Vincent Price called this soufflé the "aristocrat of desserts . . . simple ingredients transformed by the magic formula of a kitchen wizard." They found their wizardry at Tour d'Argent in Paris, the dining room of which is pictured in their *A Treasury of Great Recipes*: "Imagine yourself sitting at this table, enjoying a glorious meal, impeccably served, with all Paris spread out beyond the window! That is dining at the Tour d'Argent, one of the gastronomic thrills of a lifetime."

¼ cup confectioners' sugar
5 egg yolks
3½ tablespoons flour
1¾ cups hot milk
1 tablespoon butter
6 tablespoons Grand Marnier
3 ladyfingers
6 egg whites, at room temperature
Pinch of salt
2 teaspoons butter
2 teaspoons plus 1 tablespoon granulated sugar

In a saucepan, beat confectioners' sugar with egg yolks until sunny yellow. Beat in flour, then gradually beat in hot milk. Continue beating over medium-low heat until the mixture is thickened. Do not boil. Remove from the heat, add the butter, and cool.

Stir in 3 tablespoons of the Grand Marnier.

Cut ladyfingers in half lengthwise and soak them in the remaining 3 tablespoons of Grand Marnier.

Preheat oven to 400 degrees.

Beat egg whites with a pinch of salt until stiff. Fold them into the egg yolk mixture.

Butter a 2-quart soufflé dish and sprinkle it with 2 teaspoons of granulated sugar. Put in half the soufflé mixture. Place the ladyfingers on top and cover them with the remaining soufflé mixture. Place the soufflé in the lower third of the hot oven. Reduce the temperature to 375 degrees. Bake 30 minutes. Sprinkle the top of the soufflé with 1 tablespoon of granulated sugar. Bake 10 minutes longer. Serve immediately.

$\mathcal{L}$ike pineapples, bananas added a certain exotic *je ne sais quoi* to almost any dish. For a gourmet dessert, they were far too humble to serve plain; but Trader Vic invented a way to turn them into something prodigious, yet without the flaming pageantry that frequently accompanied fancy banana preparations in Polynesian restaurants. It is an elementary recipe, but a combination of flavors that cannot be improved—reminiscent of butter rum Life Savers.

Tropic Isle Baked Bananas with Rum Sauce

SERVES 6 TO 8

2 egg yolks
½ cup sifted confectioners' sugar
¼ cup half-and-half
¼ teaspoon salt
1 tablespoon Jamaica (dark) rum
8 ripe (but not overripe) bananas
2 tablespoons butter, melted
½ cup brown sugar
¼ teaspoon ground cloves
2 tablespoons grated orange peel
1 cup orange juice
¼ cup heavy cream

Beat the egg yolks until they are lemon-colored; add sugar, half-and-half, and salt. Mix well. Place in the top of a double boiler over simmering water and beat until the mixture thickens, about 5 minutes. Stir in rum and continue beating until smooth. Cover and chill.

Heat oven to 350 degrees. Peel the bananas and place them in a shallow baking dish. Brush them with melted butter and bake 10 minutes. As bananas bake, mix brown sugar, cloves, orange peel, and juice. Spoon this mixture over the bananas and return the bananas to the oven for 20 minutes more.

As the bananas bake, beat the cream stiff and fold it into the chilled sauce.

Remove the bananas from the oven and top them with chilled rum sauce. Serve immediately.

Pears of Bacchus

SERVES 8

*I*t is fun to imagine the befuddled expressions on the faces of ordinary eaters invited to dinner at the home of a friend who was a gourmet when, after facing a plate of snails or a fish with its head still attached, they were presented with dessert of pears in red wine. Where was the cake? The pie? The ice cream and cookies? Gourmets frequently skipped such commonplace sweets at the end of a meal in favor of interesting cheeses, perfectly ripe berries, or pears in red wine. Poached pears are hardly haute cuisine, but they were a regular feature on the dessert menus of most French bistros, and therefore a standard offering among home cooks who favored French-accented gastronomy but didn't want to go to the trouble of a soufflé or a tarte poire Williams. They also provided the host at home with an opportunity to serve more wine (always desirable at the epicure's table) and to be, as *Twelve Company Dinners*' author, Margo Rieman, put it, "refreshingly different."

> 3 cups dry red wine
> 1½ cups sugar
> 8 pears
> 2 inches of vanilla bean
> 1 cinnamon stick
> Zest of 1 lemon
> Red food coloring
> Whipped cream (optional)

In a large pot big enough to hold all the pears snugly, mix the wine and sugar. Stir over medium heat and bring to a boil. Boil 5 minutes. As it boils, peel the pears, leaving their stems on.

Add the vanilla bean and cinnamon stick to the syrup, then set the pears in the syrup and add enough boiling water to barely cover them. Reduce heat to the lowest possible simmer and poach the pears 25 to 30 minutes, or until they are just tender. Add a few drops of food coloring if the pears do not turn a pleasant blushing pink as they cook. To do this, spoon some of the syrup into a cup, add a few drops of coloring, then return the colored syrup to the pot, making sure you don't pour it directly on a pear.

Using two spoons, carefully remove pears to a serving bowl sized so the pears can stand up snugly.

Bring the poaching liquid to a hard boil and cook 15 to 20 minutes. Pour 1 to 1½ cups of the thickened liquid over the pears. Refrigerate, covered with plastic wrap, until serving time. Serve cool with dabs of whipped cream, if desired. Eat them with a sharp knife and fork.

*M*ichael and Ariane Batterberry, authors of the exhilarating social history *On the Town in New York*, described the Spanish Pavilion in the Park Avenue Ritz Tower as "a member of the city's loftiest restaurant aristocracy" in the mid-1960s. Its proprietor, Alberto Heras, who opened it after a rousing success with his Spanish Pavilion at the 1964 World's Fair, gave the Batterberrys his famous recipe for sangria, as follows. It wasn't long before Americans discovered that sangria didn't have to accompany only paella or arroz con pollo at an Iberian-themed dinner party. It was a way of converting the serving of wine—which could be awfully solemn—into a merry event well suited to nearly any kind of party food.

1964 World's Fair Sangria

SERVES 4

1 bottle red Spanish wine
2 tablespoons sugar
1 lemon, cut into slices
½ orange, cut into slices
1 shot glass (1 ounce) Spanish brandy
1 shot glass (1 ounce) Cointreau
2 cups ice cubes
1 cup cold club soda

At least an hour before serving, pour the wine into a large pitcher. Add the sugar and mix well. Stir in lemon and orange slices, brandy and Cointreau. Chill until ready to serve. Just before serving, add the ice cubes and club soda, stirring just enough to chill very well. Pour sangria only—leave fruit and ice in the pitcher.

_ 3 _

TV CUISINE

Once upon a time the only practical way to learn the nuances of haute cuisine was to sail to Europe and eat there, or at least go to a high-priced restaurant in America and eat a facsimile of continental food. If you could not afford either of those experiences, you were pretty much out of luck—doomed to know only about ordinary American things to eat. Television came along and put gourmet cuisine into nearly everybody's home. On programs designed as gastronomic lessons, during cooking segments of variety and talk shows, as well as in half-hour advertisements and thirty-second spots for miraculous kitchen gadgets, the viewing public learned culinary skills heretofore the exclusive domain of skilled chefs. Anyone with a television set had access to the epicurean enlightenment that was once the prerogative of the privileged few.

Thanks to television, it was no longer necessary to go to France to know about boeuf bourguignonne; nor was it necessary to go to a French restaurant, nor even to sign up for a cooking class nor read a French cookbook; moreover, you didn't really have to eat it to get familiar with it! All you had to do was flip channels until you found James Beard, Dione Lucas, Julia Child, or Graham Kerr preparing it on their television program. Expert chefs and connoisseurs galore appeared on TV to dish out advice about how to cook snails and pronounce soufflé, how to twirl spaghetti on a fork, how to sip wine, poach salmon, and flambé a crêpe. Earnest gourmets learned these lessons step-by-step as they watched experts show them how to cook; countless others sat back in their easy chairs and vicariously enjoyed the spectacle of chopping, slicing, dicing, lip-licking, and swooning that was most on-the-air cooks' routine. Television turned cooking into popular entertainment and made it

Julia Child on the set of "The French Chef," 1964

possible for a chef to be a celebrity nearly as famous as a movie star.

In the early years of network broadcasting, food was treated as it had been for decades on the radio: as the dominion of practical housewives whose main interest was swapping family-pleasing recipes and time-saving techniques. In the late 1940s, every day of the week from four to four-thirty in the afternoon, CBS television affiliates in twenty-four cities from New York to Chicago (but no further west) carried a program called the "Homemakers Exchange," hosted by a prim, authoritative home economist named Louise Leslie, who delivered household hints from her all-electric Hotpoint kitchen and home laundry. She showed ladies how to make pots shine with S.O.S., how to make rugs look like new with a Lewyt "No-Dust-Bag-To-Empty" vacuum cleaner equipped with Speed Sak and Swish-Wonder Carpet Nozzle, how to brighten upholstery with Super Renuzit, and how to cook food with 15 percent less shrinkage by wrapping it in Wear-Ever Aluminum Foil. In the rustic across-the-backyard-fence tradition of America's radio homemakers, who had been disseminating domestic tips and trusty recipes on the airwaves to farm wives since the 1920s, Miss Leslie addressed viewers as her "television neighbors," and shared secrets for such down-home vittles as turkey pot pie, butterscotch nut rolls, and vanilla crumb refrigerator cake.

It was apparent from the very beginning of the medium that television would be a fantastic way to sell household products by actually showing viewers just how wonderful the products were, as Miss Leslie did every week with S.O.S. and Super Renuzit. It was an especially good medium for selling groceries. *Here is Television, Your Window to the World*, a 1946 instructional book for those who wanted jobs in broadcasting, worried considerably that there was no really effective way to peddle soap products on television because studio lighting (then) was too crude to illustrate the difference between a spanking-clean white shirt and one that was tattletale gray; but the book rhapsodized about what a dream it was to sell vegetable shortening: "Simple!" the lesson begins: "actual demonstrations of how to prepare cookies, pies, and cakes with a close-up of the finished product." *Here is Television, Your Window to the World* punctuated its instruction with a picture of a can of Spry, looking lovely in front of a mammoth studio camera. The CBS "Homemakers Exchange" built its repertory of recipes around this basic principle of product usability; in fact, during one three-month period at the end of 1950, Miss Leslie demonstrated recipes for prune cupcakes, prune dumplings, prune sherbet, baked prune whip, prune apricot compote, prune confections stuffed with fondant, even prune ham rolls and "minted prunes"—all using Sunsweet "Tenderized" prunes, which, not surprisingly, happened to be a sponsor of the show.

Miss Leslie was no globe-trotting connoisseur, and most of the recipes she shared on the "Homemakers Exchange" were old-fashioned, but the show's theme was distinctly modern, and very much in the same forward-looking spirit that inspired many to take up fancy cookery as a way to separate themselves from a dowdy past. The "Homemakers Exchange" taught that up-to-the-minute people found The Good Life by filling their homes with the latest products. Anyone who had his own television set in 1949 was already at the vanguard of consumerism, and a natural customer for the latest in cooking gear; and for companies with appliances and groceries to merchandise, a cooking show broadcast by the new medium was sheer magic. Like a tireless traveling salesman that people welcomed into their homes, television actually showed members of the audience precisely how each appliance would make them happy. At least once during every "Homemakers Exchange" program, Louise Leslie could be counted on to open her Hotpoint no-defrost refrigerator to fetch a resplendent perfection salad or Knox gold pineapple mold (Knox gelatin was a sponsor, too), reminding the audience that her fridge saved so much time it was "like getting an extra Sunday every week!"

In the early days of television, when air time was cheap, many kitchen product manufacturers ran fifteen-minute and half-hour advertisements touting Wonder Shredders, Chop-O-Matics (precursor of the Veg-O-Matic), Juicerators (endorsed by Johnny Carson, Merv Griffin, and Bess Myerson), electric skillets, deep-fat

"Whether watching a late late show, a football game, a major live news event, or educational programming, nothing excels good food and good TV in the comfort of your own home."

—TV Guide Cookbook

fryers, and chafing dishes. What is interesting about these early program-length advertisements (and is still interesting about their modern-day progeny, now broadcast in the wee hours mostly on cable channels) is how educational they were. Aside from selling products, they demonstrated sometimes elaborate and esoteric cooking techniques that few ordinary homemakers would ever have a chance to learn anywhere else. In this way, the advertisements contributed untold nuances to the elevation of America's culinary consciousness in the 1950s. One of the most enlightening series of product pitches began in May 1949, when Betty Furness began demonstrating Westinghouse Speed-Electric ranges and refrigerators in long commercials set in what she called the "magnificent Westinghouse kitchen, where wonders are performed." Furness did not present herself as an especially accomplished cook or an expert like Miss Leslie, but it was clear that her having a Westinghouse Commander, complete with color-glance controls, miracle-sealed oven, warmer drawer signalette, and super-corox coils ("get red-hot in 30 seconds!") produced what the Westinghouse Home Economics Institute acclaimed as foods that "taste better, look better, and are better for you . . . in a cleaner, cooler kitchen!"

Perhaps the silliest instructive gastronomic show ever to run on television was known as "The Continental." No food was eaten or cooked on the program, and it wasn't designed to be didactic, but it was a unique education in how to preside over the dinner table like an epicure. Telecast Tuesdays and Thursdays at 11:15 P.M. on CBS during the first three months of 1952, it featured Renzo Cesana as

"The Continental"—a suave, Italian-accented bachelor who looked straight into the camera and yearningly addressed each member of his audience (presumably female) as if she were his date for the evening. He welcomed her to his apartment, removed her stole, and escorted her to a table set for two, where he proffered a single rose. By candlelight, he sipped champagne and whispered sweet nothings to the camera for fifteen minutes until fade-out. Here was a rare opportunity for television viewers to study how a sophisticated and romantic dinner was conducted. Watch Señor Cesana uncork the champagne and pour it. See his candelabras cast enchanting shadows on the polished silverware and gleaming china. Listen to him weave the dinner conversation around such romantic subjects as his bucolic fiefdom (he said he was a member of the landed gentry), the pleasures of fine wine, and his connoisseurship of all things beautiful. He didn't serve any food or eat anything during the program—after all, it would have been impolite for the host to chew during what was essentially a fifteen-minute monologue. "The Continental" was just too weird for audiences and went off the air quickly; but its fame as a pinnacle of preposterousness lived on in television's gastronomic folklore. Poor Renzo Cesana was forever after typecast as a candlelight lothario for whom fine dining was a prologue to seduction; in fact he came to call his performance as the unctuous host "my Frankenstein's monster"; and as late as the 1970s, Dan Ackroyd was doing Renzo Cesana bits on "Saturday Night Live."

Food's big breakthrough on television, and the initial successful coupling of gourmet cookery with the medium, was the appearance of James Beard. After some success doing cooking demonstrations on NBC television's "Radio City Matinee" and a show called "For You and Yours" in the mid-forties, Beard got his own regular segment on a Borden Dairy Company variety and talk show called "Elsie Presents" in 1946. The show began with Harriet Van Horne at a desk giving viewers shopping tips, gossip, and theater criticism. Then a giant puppet of the sponsor's mascot, Elsie the Cow, appeared and announced, "Elsie Presents James Beard in 'I Love to Eat'!" and Beard spent the last half of the show (fifteen minutes) showing viewers how to cook something. The program was a success because Beard formulated a charming blend of instruction and fun—the pattern for nearly every successful TV chef who came after him. Prior to Beard, no one knew quite how to make a cooking show on television entertaining; so recipes were swapped and read aloud and prepared step-by-step, as they had been on the radio, and home economists in pince-nez glasses told housewives how to conserve left-over bacon fat. Beard was no recipe-swapper or home economist. He was a performer—his first career goal was to be an opera singer. When that failed on the West Coast, he came to New York in 1937 and gained fame not as an actor, but as a caterer, at Hors d'Oeuvre, Inc. He remembered coming back to New York after the war and being offered a job by NBC to create a food show: "At last—a chance to cook and act at the same time."

For Beard, serving good food was always more than a matter of sustenance or proper nutrition; it was a performance. "Put on a fine show!" he goads readers of his autobiography *Delights and Prejudices.* "Like the theater, offering food and hospitality is a matter of showmanship, and no matter how simple the performance, unless you do it well, with love and originality, you have a flop on your hands." As a cooking teacher, Beard put on that kind of show when he gave lessons in his Greenwich Village townhouse—sharing wine with students, eating the mistakes as well as the successes, encouraging them to be original, unafraid of trying something new and crazy. "I think if I have done nothing else," he told us, "I have taught people to enjoy making food." That attitude made him terrific on television, where even the most daunting recipes were transformed into enjoyable romps with pots and pans and acres of garlic. Beard loved to be outrageous, once making the rounds of prime-time variety programs with a specially made skillet six feet long and three feet wide and cooking crêpes in it with a blowtorch. Surely, if he could flame the biggest crêpes suzettes on earth with ease, anyone at home could make normal-size crêpes and enjoy their own flaming dessert.

Shortly after Beard became a regular on NBC, Dione Lucas, author of *The Cordon Bleu Cookbook*, began appearing weekly on CBS in a program originally titled "To the Queen's Taste" (later, "Dione Lucas' Cooking Show"). Ms. Lucas addressed viewers from the magnificently accoutered kitchen of her Cordon Bleu restaurant and cooking school in New York, guiding them step-by-step through basic lessons for dishes from omelets (her *specialité*) to mousse au chocolat, always extolling creative cooking as a fine and noble art. A British-accented diplomate of the Ecole du Cordon Bleu in Paris, Lucas was clear and meticulous as a teacher, and her recipes were precise; but unlike James Beard before her, she was not an entertainer; and unlike Julia Child fifteen years later, she made little attempt to handhold her audience and help them relax when facing a daunting recipe; and she was certainly no culinary comedienne. Still, she made her mark on television cookery: Her show lasted a year and a half on the network, and several years after that in local markets. She played the role of television's supreme European epicure; and for those pioneers of the gourmet revolution who sought authentic and precise

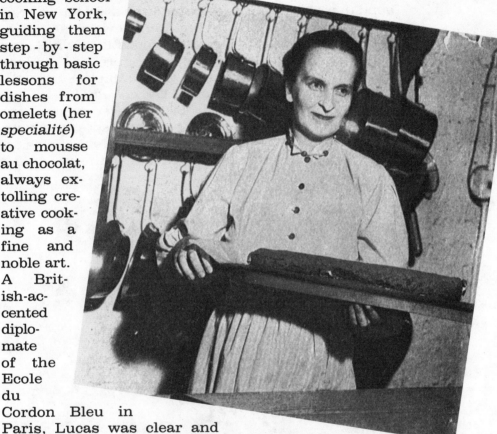

Dione Lucas in her Cordon Bleu kitchen

instruction more than entertainment, she remained a beacon of culinary excellence.

James Beard was America's best-known chef throughout the fifties and into the sixties, not only because of his own television appearances but also because he was popularized by the food industry, which found there were profits to be made by associating products with the James Beard brio. On television as well as in print he endorsed innumerable foodstuffs, wines, and utensils; and he served as company figurehead in advertisements for Omaha Steaks, Camp Maple Syrup, the French National Association of Cognac Producers, and the Taylor Wine Company. Beard never seemed shy about putting his imprimatur on sponsors' products, which was another reason he fit so well on television, which, after all, exists to sell products. In the post-Nader years of the seventies, he took plenty of

James Beard on behalf of Gourmet Stripes kitchen linens

guff from anti-business critics for being too cozy with big food companies; some worried that he had become more of a pitchman than a pure-souled culinary artiste; but the relationships with products rarely bothered him. After all, they helped feed his enormous appetites; and he enjoyed the position of authority they confirmed. Although there were some endorsements he came to regret (privately), Beard always liked being in the spotlight they provided.

More important, Beard's television persona as willing and eager spokesman for various foods never seemed to bother the millions of home cooks who respected him and learned from him. In fact, the opposite is true. Until the 1960s, most Americans generally liked and trusted big companies, especially big food companies, which have supplied decades' worth of recipes, free cooking brochures, reassurances from spotless test kitchens, and lovable mythical product mentors (from Elsie and Betty Crocker to the California Raisins); and have also been proud sponsors of favorite television programs. Traditionally, Americans have also respected whoever was elected spokesman for a multimillion-dollar food corporation. Because of his lifetime alliance with such a wide variety of people's favorite things to eat, Beard earned a position that to many consumers and cooks seemed far more important than mere epicure. He became a pop culture icon, the ultimate product pitchman and, in the eyes of many Americans, the definitive chef.

By 1960, cooking demonstrations were such a fundamental part of television, especially on talk shows, that the Knox gelatin company published a brochure called "On-Camera Recipes," the cover of which shows a woman making a gelatin mold in a TV kitchen behind a bank of lights and cameras. The woman is not a celebrity and the recipes in the brochure do not come from a television show. But the design of each page is a series of stills, framed in television-shaped rectangles, that show exactly how to make each dish. "Every recipe here was continuously photographed as it was carried out," the brochure tells readers. "Just like the recipes that you see demonstrated on television."

A large amount of television cookery in the fifties was nothing other than indirect advertising. Companies hired chefs to appear on programs and demonstrate recipes that required viewers to buy whatever it is they were selling. This practice continues to thrive today, but as television viewers grew more sophisticated and skeptical, particularly in the wake of the TV quiz show scandals of 1958, a large number of them became wary of what they saw on television and developed a hunger for more honest programming that at least seemed independent of commercial consideration and free of slick Madison Avenue hucksterism.

Along came Julia Child. No one acted more honest than she. First of all, she appeared on PBS, the noncommercial, "educational" network; and the only thing she seemed to be selling was the glory of French cuisine. Beginning in 1962 and airing for a decade (then followed by "Julia Child & Company"), "The French Chef," as the show and she were called, was a revelation. Here was "serious" cooking that was nonetheless casual, carefree, and sometimes flat-out hilarious. The chef herself could be hypnotically butterfingered and frequently seemed unpolished and unprofessional—which made her appear all the more true-to-life, and made the recipes she demonstrated seem within reach of anyone with the will to try them. Mrs. Child was not a trained, well-modulated actor as Beard was. She did not know how to hit her mark on the stage at every turn and how to deftly camouflage flubs and bloopers and exactly fit every recipe into the time-slot alloted. She often dripped things and made soufflés that listed and styled plates of food that would never pass muster in a four-star kitchen. In fact, like so many cultured people in the early days of television, she looked down her nose at the very medium itself, revealing in her introduction to *The French Chef Cookbook* (1968) that she kept her own ugly little television set hidden away in an unused fireplace in her Cambridge house. Still, no TV chef was ever so naturally telegenic, so charming in her awkwardness, and so farcically irrepressible. Viewers watched her talk to her eggs, caress a dead fish, address the camera as an old friend, make mistakes and recover with aplomb, and always enjoy herself while whisking, chopping, tossing, and imparting the perspicacity of French cooking.

Julia Child had two audiences. There were the true

"We pulled the television set out of hiding and turned it on at 8:30. There was this woman tossing French omelettes, splashing eggs about the place, brandishing big knives, panting heavily as she careened around the stove, and WGBH-TV lurched into educational television's first cooking program."

—Julia Child on watching herself in the pilot episode of "The French Chef" believers who read and relished *Mastering the Art of French Cooking* and used it so intensively they had to buy second copies when their first one grew unreadable because of all the spilled sauce, melted butter, and crumbs. For these people, Julia Child was (and remains) a god whose presentation of French food and techniques was nothing less than the definition of modern gourmet cooking at its best. They would likely have been her acolytes even if "The French Chef" never had gone on the air. The television program brought her a

much bigger, different audience that tuned in just because she was so much fun to watch. No doubt many of these viewers were converted, bought her (and other TV chefs') books, and began cooking gourmet food themselves; but there were plenty of viewers who had little intention of cooking what she demonstrated, who nonetheless simply loved to watch her cook. She was such a character! A jovial clown with an upper-crust whinny who acted looped (but was only loopy) as she hooted her way through recipes that worked or didn't (it hardly mattered) and lurched through her TV kitchen and made a big mess of it just as we all do at home. Like "The Continental" ten years before her, the video personality Julia Child projected was so original that she too became a Dan Ackroyd character on "Saturday Night Live," in a now-famous sketch where she winds up lying on the floor in a pool of her own blood (having hacked off her thumb), but nonetheless unflappable and crying out her trademark salutation, "Bon appetit!"

Although many viewers tuned in only to enjoy her antics (and discovered good food as a fringe benefit of the fun), Julia Child was an inspiring television teacher and a major force behind the pop culture infatuation with

French food in the sixties. Americans have always had a fondness for didactic self-improvement schemes, from *How to Win Friends and Influence People* to *Dress for Success* and *Thin Thighs in Thirty Days*; and "The French Chef" was the culinary version: a fast, workmanlike instructional half-hour without a trace of one-upmanship or snobbery. As in her book, every single step of the cooking process was documented and demonstrated so that even a completely inexperienced cook could try to follow it. And to help the detailed instruction go down easy, the soundtrack pulsated with the breathlessly buoyant, reassuring voice of Julia herself (nearly every viewer felt familiar enough to call her by her first name), crooning over the beauty of a poaching egg or the aroma of onions sizzling in butter, laughing off her mistakes, slamming a big old fish around the counter or dropping it on the floor, and gaily extolling the results as the program rushed to its conclusion. Thanks to "The French Chef," amiably eccentric cooking teachers became a staple of the public television airwaves and countless home cooks diligently turned themselves into American gourmets.

Graham Kerr, "The Galloping Gourmet": "Whatever you do, don't lose the aroma."

One of the most charismatic eccentrics to follow in Julia Child's wake was Graham Kerr, who called himself The Galloping Gourmet because he fairly galloped through his cooking demonstrations, talking nonstop, winking at the camera, and enjoying hearty quaffs from his ever-present glass of wine. Kerr was an Englishman born into the hotel industry who had honed his culinary skills in New Zealand, which he loved because "New Zealanders are a great practical people who are not in the least bit concerned with status." On his cooking show, "The Galloping Gourmet," which began on Canada's CBC and was syndicated in the United States in 1969, Kerr showed all of Julia Child's enthusiasm plus the spice of insouciant youth, which in the 1960s was the dearest coin of the cultural realm. His repartee was laced with light-hearted double entendres about food's seductive powers; and he fairly burst with suggestions for using food and cookery to make life fun. He introduced his viewers to an organization he called S.P.O.D.E., the Society for the Propagation of Delicious Eating, which practiced his modern, four-couple version of the progressive dinner, for which one couple provides the home and main course, another the appetizers and drinks, a third the dessert and cheese, and a fourth the after-dinner drinks and coffee. He suggested that after one successful S.P.O.D.E. dinner the quartet of couples separate and each organize another dinner, with three new couples. "In this way from 4 couples you involve at the second dinner 16 couples, then 64, then 256, then 1,024, then 4,096, then 16,384, then 65,536, then 262,144." He breathlessly concluded, "the tenth dinner should net over one million recipes from nearly three million people! At this point I leave you."

Kerr wasn't avuncular like James Beard or neighborly like Julia Child. What he was, was sexy—not overtly sensuous, but playful enough to make cooking seem like a swinging, and perhaps even slightly naughty activity. For example, about dessert he offered these nuggets of philosophical badinage: "I prefer to regard a dessert as I would imagine the perfect woman: subtle, a little bittersweet, not blowsy and extrovert. Delicately made up, not highly rouged. Holding back, not exposing everything and, of course, with a flavor that lasts." Abetted by his accent (which was the height of mod in the 1960s), Kerr created a new image of the culinary bon vivant, considerably less serious and sophisticated than Julia Child. After all, he wasn't talking about *mastering* the art of cooking; he was simply showing viewers how to have fun and eat well. Like *Cosmopolitan* and *Playboy* magazines, the Galloping Gourmet succeeded in the Age of Aquarius because he helped define a new code of behavior: youthful, enthusiastic, and relentlessly intimate (viewers learned all about his off-camera wife/producer Treena). If you watched his show on television, you didn't gain mastery of many classic recipes or the rules of haute cuisine, but you did see how to enjoy cooking and how to share its pleasures with a lover or with friends. As presented by the Galloping Gourmet, fine food was not a goal in itself (as it seemed when Julia Child cooked it); it was a way to have a more enjoyable social life. Because of this beguilingly flippant attitude, the Galloping Gourmet became a great popularizer, reassuring viewers that good eating and skillful food preparation did not require laborious technique or diligent study. "I'm an anti-snob," he once proclaimed. "I'm not in love with food—it's an entertaining game of skill."

Recipes

Homemakers Exchange Checkerboard
   Sandwiches
Deviled Eggs for the Den
Oysters Rockefeller, Cordon Bleu
WRCA Watercress Salad
Salade Niçoise
"My Specialité, the Omelette!"
Chicken Kievski
Chicken with 40 Cloves of Garlic
Pot-au-Feu
Liver and Bacon Fromage
Galloping Gourmet Fillet of Fish
   Macadamia
Mrs. America's Almond Rice Parisian
"I Love to Eat" Ratatouille
Babas au Rhum the Hard Way
Elemental Chocolate Mousse
High-Rise German Pancakes

Homemakers Exchange Checkerboard Sandwiches

SERVES 4 AS HORS D'OEUVRE

*H*ere is the end of an era. Louise Leslie of the CBS "Homemakers Exchange" broadcast this recipe on her television program in late 1950. The crafty concept of checkerboard sandwiches was a hangover from the 1930s, when loaves of bread were first widely available factory-sliced; the novelty of their precision became the basis for all kinds of architectonically marvelous tea-time sandwiches. (Wonder bread was the first such brand.) The very notion of dainty, cleverly fabricated tea sandwiches seemed old-fashioned by 1950, when housewives were more in the market for time-saving snacks that involved no such elaborate construction. Miss Leslie's sponsor, the O & C food company, did provide the one up-to-date flourish for the recipe: canned fried onion rings mushed into the cheese. If you are an antique-food collector and have a vintage can of O & C in your collection, we suggest you break it open and delight in the thought that you are having an authentic taste of history. We have found that Durkee onion rings, the brand currently available in our market, work just fine. This recipe is now so passé that serving it to modern guests seems a tour de force of retro hipness.

3 slices of white bread (not a spongy brand)
3 slices of whole wheat bread (not a spongy brand)
3 tablespoons butter, softened
¼ pound Cheddar cheese spread (we use most of a 5-ounce jar of Kraft Old English Spread)
1 can (2.8 ounces) Durkee fried onion rings

Trim crust off the bread.

Beat together the butter and cheese spread until smooth. Stir in the onion rings.

Spread a slice of whole wheat bread with the creamed mixture and place a slice of white bread on top. Spread the white bread with the mixture. Top it with another slice of whole wheat.

Repeat the process, this time starting with white bread and having a whole wheat middle layer.

Trim each pile evenly and cut it into 4 even strips. Spread the sides of the strips with the cream cheese mixture, then reattach them in such a way that you create two loaves, each with a checkerboard pattern at the ends. Wrap each loaf in wax paper and chill.

Just before serving, slice each loaf into ¼-inch slices.

"Today's hostess need not be harried," *TV Guide* advised home cooks in 1960. "After spreading out the food (the kind you may eat with your fingers . . .), she has time to join her guests for an evening of television." Recipes suggested for an evening of television included small sandwiches, stuffed celery, two-bite "finger pies," ice cream (you don't have to take your eyes off the TV screen as you spoon it up out of the bowl), and a whole assortment of hard-boiled egg snacks—because half an egg was wieldy enough to eat without utensils. The old faintly fancy standard, deviled eggs, was proposed as especially suitable for *afternoon* television watching, "when the girls drop over."

Deviled Eggs for the Den

SERVES 4 TO 6

6 hard-boiled eggs
¼ cup mayonnaise
¼ teaspoon salt
⅛ teaspoon pepper
1 teaspoon prepared mustard
1 tablespoon pickle relish
Paprika

Split the eggs lengthwise and carefully remove their yolks. Mash the yolks with the remaining ingredients except the paprika and pile this mixture back into the whites. Garnish with a dusting of paprika.

Oysters Rockefeller, Cordon Bleu

SERVES 2 TO 3

*D*ione Lucas usually showed American television viewers how to make continental specialties; but New Orleans was practically French, and its famous appetizer, oysters Rockefeller, was in the pantheon of expensive restaurant dishes for which ambitious home cooks wanted the secret. Ms. Lucas's recipe is not the original one from Antoine's, but it is ingratiating. What a treat it is to have a dab of whipped cream *before* a meal!

8 to 12 large oysters on the half shell
¾ cup sour cream
2 garlic cloves, minced
Salt and pepper
1 cup chopped cooked spinach, well drained
3 tablespoons freshly grated Parmesan cheese
1 tablespoon bread crumbs
1 tablespoon butter
¼ cup heavy cream, whipped

Remove oysters from their shells. Mix ¼ cup of the sour cream with half the garlic and a dash each of salt and pepper. Put a heaping teaspoon of this mixture in the bottom of each shell. Cover with the raw oyster. Combine the remaining sour cream and garlic with the spinach and top the oysters with it. Mix the grated cheese with bread crumbs and sprinkle it on top. Dot each oyster with butter and put them in a baking pan under a broiler about 4 inches from the heat. Broil 3 to 4 minutes, just until the oysters begin to curl. Remove and put a tablespoon of whipped cream on top of each oyster. Return them to the broiler just long enough to brown the whipped cream.

*L*ettuce is a litmus test for gourmets. It is a truism among those with sophisticated palates that iceberg lettuce is not good (flavorless, coarse, common) and green salads ought to be made with green things that are "interesting." It wasn't until fairly recently that such curiosities as radicchio, mâche, limestone lettuce, and dandelion leaves gained widespread favor among aspiring gourmets; but for many years watercress, with its mustard tang, was an approved alternative to bland lettuce. In 1958, Josie McCarthy, resident cook on New York's WRCA, collected the most requested dishes from her TV appearances in a book called *Josie McCarthy's Favorite Recipes*, a compendium of such imaginative (but unintimidating) dishes as "lemonade fried chicken," "steamed zucchini with salami," "fish fillets thermidor," and this recipe for watercress salad—an unconventional alternative to the usual bowl of iceberg lettuce. Ms. McCarthy, more a descendant of the pedagogical, old-fashioned radio homemakers than a stylish gourmet TV chef, assured her viewers that "salad greens are noted for their rich supply of vitamins and minerals needed by the body every day."

   1 cup fresh rye bread crumbs
   3 tablespoons olive oil
   1 small garlic clove, minced
   1 tablespoon drained prepared horseradish
   1 bunch watercress, washed, chilled, and dried
   French dressing (the pink stuff)

Combine the rye bread crumbs, olive oil, and garlic in a skillet. Cook over medium-high heat, stirring almost constantly, 10 to 12 minutes, until crisp and dry. Cool. Add horseradish and mix thoroughly.

Place the watercress in a salad bowl or on salad plates. Sprinkle with the horseradish-crumb mixture. Serve with French dressing.

Salade Niçoise

SERVES 4 AS MAIN COURSE

*I*n his memoirs, *Delights and Prejudices*, James Beard revealed that he was someone who much preferred eating and cooking outdoors to working in a kitchen. He often appeared on television to offer viewers ideas for barbecues, picnics, and nice-weather food that provided maximum outdoor eating pleasure from minimum indoor effort. One such hearty summertime salad he liked to recommend was salade niçoise—a natural for American palates accustomed to ordinary tuna salad but seeking something dressier. He served it with chunks of corn bread and finished things off with his favorite dessert, fresh berries—a menu that is the best of both worlds, fresh-picked American and interesting gourmet.

> 8 to 12 warm, boiled redskin potatoes
> 1 cup vinaigrette salad dressing
> 1 head romaine lettuce, washed and torn into large pieces
> 2 cups green beans, blanched 3 minutes,
>   drained, and cooled
> 2 cans (7 ounces each) oil-packed albacore tuna,
>   drained and flaked
> 3 tomatoes, skinned, seeded, and quartered
> 4 hard-boiled eggs, quartered
> ½ cup Kalamata olives
> ½ cup green olives, pitted and sliced
> 2 to 6 anchovy fillets, to taste
> Chopped parsley as garnish

Slice the potatoes about ¼ inch thick and marinate them in ¼ cup of the salad dressing. Arrange romaine lettuce around the outside of a large serving platter. In the center of the lettuce circle, arrange the beans on one half of the plate and the marinated potatoes on the other, with tuna in the center. Arrange the tomatoes and eggs atop the lettuce around the edge of the plate; and in a circle just inside them, arrange both kinds of olives. Arrange anchovy fillets atop the potatoes and beans. Sprinkle remaining dressing over the salad and garnish with parsley.

Why was it that Americans had come to think of eggs as only breakfast food? That is what Dione Lucas often wondered as she instructed viewers in the basic techniques and elaborate variations of her favorite dish, the omelet. The making of an omelet (as opposed to scrambled eggs) was probably the most frequently practiced entry-level feat of skill among aspiring gourmets; and a seasoned omelet pan hanging from an overhead rack in the kitchen was a sure sign of someone who cared about fine food. It was important, Dione Lucas advised (before the invention of nonstick surfaces), that the pan be cast iron or aluminum rather than stainless steel or copper; and it had to be seasoned before use. That meant cleaning it and heating it with oil, and never, ever letting water touch it! She also advised that omelets, unlike soufflés, should *not* be made with freshly laid eggs, which might curdle in the pan. Eggs two to three days old were ideal. Her recipe for an *omelette fines herbes* contains not only herbs but onion and garlic, too. She even suggests adding small croutons of fried bread to the mélange.

"My Specialité, the Omelette!"

SERVES 1

3 eggs
1 teaspoon cold water
Pinch of salt and pepper
1 teaspoon minced parsley
1 tablespoon minced chives
1/8 teaspoon crumbled dried tarragon
1 thin onion slice
1 very small garlic clove
1/4 cup small croutons (optional)
1 tablespoon butter

Beat the eggs with water. Add salt and pepper and beat well, but not until frothy. Combine herbs and chop them fine with the onion and garlic. Add croutons, if desired.

Heat the pan until a small piece of butter sizzles briskly without browning. Melt the butter. Swirl in the herb mixture. Drop in the eggs. Stir quickly with a fork and shake the pan until the eggs begin to set. Stir more slowly on the top of the set eggs for another minute. Leave the eggs to set for a few seconds. Fold the omelet in half and turn out at once onto a serving dish.

Chicken Kievski

SERVES 4
(2 HALVES PER PERSON)

*W*henever James Beard appeared on television, he liked to show how easy it was to make difficult-seeming food. One of his early demonstrations was chicken Kievski, known to devotees of continental cuisine as chicken Kiev. Actually, it is a fairly uncomplicated dish; but there is no denying the high drama of the diner's first incision into the meat, which sends a geyser of warm herbed butter spouting out onto the brown rice or into the semolina gnocchi that Beard recommended as the breasts' companion.

4 boned and skinned chicken breasts, each cut in half
8 tablespoons butter, softened
1 tablespoon lemon juice
2 garlic cloves, minced
1 tablespoon chopped fresh chives
1 tablespoon dried tarragon
½ cup flour
3 eggs, beaten
2 cups soft bread crumbs
Vegetable oil for frying

Place chicken breast halves between wax paper and pound them, taking care not to break the flesh. Breasts should be fan-shaped, about 5 inches across. Refrigerate the flattened breasts.

Cream together the butter, lemon juice, garlic, chives, and tarragon. Refrigerate about 1 hour, or until the butter is firm enough to shape into 8 tapered fingers.

Roll each piece of chicken around a finger of butter, tucking in the ends of the meat to make a neat little package. The chicken should stick to itself, but use a toothpick if necessary. Roll the chicken in flour, dip it in eggs, then roll it in bread crumbs. Refrigerate at least 1 hour.

Heat about 1 inch of oil in a deep skillet to 360 degrees. Fry the breasts until golden brown, about 5 minutes per side, turning very carefully with tongs so as not to break the coating. Season with salt and pepper to taste. Serve with brown rice, gnocchi, kasha, or other dark grain.

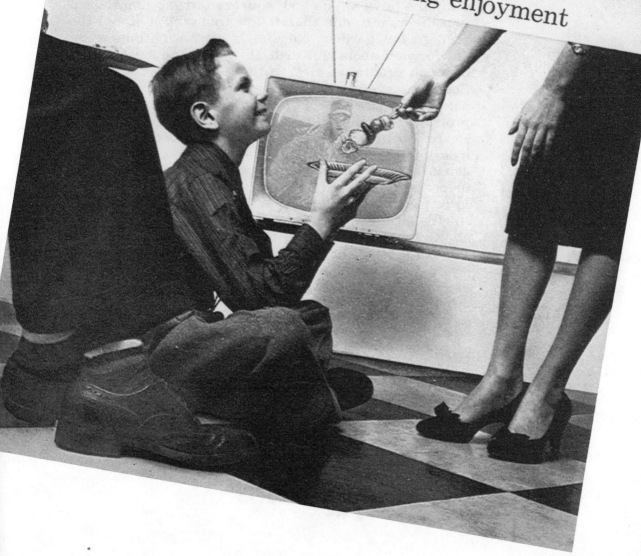

TV Snacks
add to viewing enjoyment

Chicken with 40 Cloves of Garlic

SERVES 6 TO 8

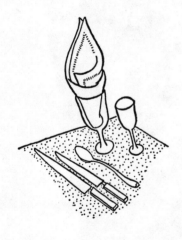

*F*launting one's love of garlic was as much the sign of a gourmet by the mid-1950s as eating chocolate-covered ants and knowing how to inhale a wine's bouquet. To this day, garlic appreciation is one of the ways that people announce their venturesome palates; love of garlic, like love of chocolate, is considered a mark of supreme sensuality. In the winter 1990 edition of the *Simple Cooking* newsletter, John Thorne wrote about the Provençal dish *Poulet aux Quarante Gousses d'Ail*, "You pick up a clove, suck off the juices that cling to it, bite away the husk at one end, squeeze the succulent mash into the mouth, and then follow this with a bite of the rich, greasy, garlicky chicken. If there is nothing sexually forward about this dish, then food and love have no common ground at all." In the next edition of *Simple Cooking*, several readers wrote to complain that in his panegyric Thorne forgot to mention America's foremost proponent of chicken with forty cloves of garlic, James Beard. Beard relished this dish, not only because he was a dark-meat man (dark meat is more succulent) and because he adored the flavor of garlic, but because the immense amount of garlic in the recipe seemed so shocking to conventional American palates. When he presented the finished dish on "The Garry Moore Show" after first showing how much garlic went into it, he dared the host to have a bite. Lo and behold! Long, slow baking in a covered casserole rendered the garlic mild and the chicken delicious. It was kitchen magic . . . and terrific television. This recipe is from *The New James Beard*.

⅔ cup olive oil
8 chicken drumsticks
8 chicken thighs
4 celery ribs, cut into 4-inch-long strips
2 cups chopped onion
6 parsley sprigs
1 teaspoon dried tarragon
½ cup dry vermouth
2½ teaspoons salt
¼ teaspoon freshly ground pepper
Grated nutmeg
40 garlic cloves, unpeeled
Rounds of freshly sliced French bread

Put the oil in a shallow dish and add the chicken pieces, turning to coat them evenly with oil.

Preheat oven to 375 degrees.

In a heavy 6-quart casserole, combine the celery, onions, parsley, and tarragon. Lay the oiled chicken pieces on top. Pour on the vermouth. Sprinkle with salt and pepper and a dash of nutmeg. Tuck the garlic cloves in and around the chicken pieces. Cover the casserole tightly with aluminum foil, then the lid. Bake 90 minutes without removing the lid.

Serve chicken, pan juices, and garlic cloves with French bread. Diners should squeeze the buds of garlic from their husks onto the bread, then spread the garlic like butter.

Pot-au-Feu

SERVES 6 TO 8

A glorious show-off dish: "The host starts the proceedings as usual by spearing out the beef and placing it on a platter," *Mastering the Art of French Cooking* suggests. "Then he finds a sausage, and after that a big piece of pork. Finally, to wild acclaim, he brings out a chicken." This was exactly the kind of zany behavior at which Julia Child, the French Chef, excelled on television, creating in this case a meal that was as friendly seeming as any ordinary pot-au-feu, yet spectacular enough for a grand dinner party, and sure evidence that someone had labored long and hard and skillfully in the kitchen. The recipe in *Mastering the Art* makes enough pot-au-feu for 12 to 16 people and requires an enormous kettle. We have adjusted the recipe to yield 6 to 8 servings.

> 2 carrots, peeled and quartered
> 2 peeled and quartered onions, each stuck with
>   a whole clove
> 1 scraped parsnip
> 1 celery rib
> 1 leek
> 2½ cups beef broth
> 2½ cups chicken broth
> 1 large herb bouquet containing 4 parsley sprigs,
>   1 bay leaf, ¼ teaspoon thyme, 2 garlic cloves,
>   and 4 peppercorns tied in cheesecloth
> 2 pounds boneless rump pot roast
> Optional: raw or cooked beef bones, meat scraps,
>   poultry carcasses, necks, gizzards
> 2 pounds pork butt
> ½ stewing hen (3 to 4 pounds)
> Vegetable garnish: carrots, onions, turnips, leeks:
>   1 to 2 of each per person, tied in cheesecloth
> 1 pound lightly smoked country or Polish sausage
> Salt and pepper to taste
> Parsley

In a large kettle over medium heat, combine the carrots, onions, parsnip, celery, and leek with broths, herb bouquet, beef, and optional bones and scraps. Add enough water to cover the beef. Bring to a simmer. Partially cover and simmer slowly 1 hour, occasionally skimming off fat from the surface.

Add the pork and chicken and more water as needed to cover all the meat. Bring the kettle quickly back to a simmer. Simmer 3½ hours more, skimming occasionally. Add the vegetable garnish 1 hour before the end, and the sausage 30 minutes before the end. Before the 3½ hours is up, taste and season the broth.

To serve, drain the meats and retrieve the cheesecloth with the vegetable garnish. Arrange these vegetables on a large, hot platter and moisten them with a ladleful of cooking stock. Decorate with parsley. Place the meats in a large casserole for presentation and carving at the table, or carve them in the kitchen and arrange them on a platter. Strain, degrease, and season enough cooking stock to fill a large serving bowl as gravy. Serve with additional sauce such as tomato coulis or velouté.

"The Gourmet" starred David Wade (*right*), whom Gregory Peck once called "The Rembrandt of the Kitchen." In this episode, celebrity guest Reginald Denny showed Wade how he cooked lobster tails in cream sauce.

Liver and Bacon Fromage

SERVES 4

*N*ot all early television chefs told viewers how to cook sophisticated food, as did Julia Child, Dione Lucas, and James Beard. In 1954, Martha Dixon became host of the "Copper Kettle Show," a how-to-cook program on WJIM-TV in Lansing, Michigan. Mrs. Dixon told viewers, "I believe culinary artists are made—not born;" and to prove her point, she created a repertoire of television recipes that fairly bristled with deluxe flourishes, but were frequently as easy to make as a casserole. Some of her way-out specialties included *tromp la langue* mock chicken made from steak and veal, Chinese egg rolls, company creamed tuna (one can serves four!), and a dozen different kinds of voluptuously stuffed potatoes. Familiar as it might have tasted, nothing cooked on the "Copper Kettle Show" ever seemed plain or ordinary; even a blue-plate dish of liver and bacon got the high-falutin touch and became, in her words, "liver and bacon fromage"—a gourmet dish based on the Law of the Cheeseburger, which says that any meat is improved when topped with melted cheese. In this case, the paradigm is even better: a *bacon* cheeseburger.

6 bacon slices
3 tablespoons flour
½ teaspoon salt
⅛ teaspoon garlic salt
⅛ teaspoon pepper
1 pound beef liver, sliced ½ inch thick
⅓ cup grated American cheese

Fry the bacon until crisp in a large skillet. Remove and drain on paper towels. Pour off all but 2 tablespoons bacon fat from the skillet.

Mix together the flour, salt, garlic salt, and pepper. Dredge the liver well in this mixture and brown it on both sides over medium heat in the bacon fat. As the second side cooks, crumble the crisp bacon into bits and mix it with the grated cheese. Sprinkle the bacon-cheese mixture over the liver, then cover the pan. As soon as the cheese melts, remove the liver to a serving platter.

After breezing onto the airwaves in the late sixties as the "Galloping Gourmet," Graham Kerr produced a series of "Television Cookbooks" that included typeset recipes from the show as well as handwritten comments, which he said he added while sitting at the dining table in his television studio set because "the printer is screaming for action. As usual you see—we gallop!" Kerr made cooking into such a merry activity, assuring viewers, "[I] dislike food that is cooked for status alone, am not over impressed by any one national cuisine." Across the page that offered his extra-luscious variation of fish *amandine*, using Australia's native macadamia nuts, he scribbled, "I added extra lemon juice to the pan juices.—G.K."

Galloping Gourmet Fillet of Fish Macadamia

SERVES 2

1 egg yolk
4 tablespoons clarified butter, melted
2 tablespoons lemon juice
2 swordfish steaks, 6 ounces each
½ teaspoon cracked white peppercorns
Salt to taste
¼ cup grated macadamia nuts
2 tablespoons dry sherry
1 tablespoon chopped parsley

Mix together the egg yolk, 2 tablespoons of the melted butter, and 1 tablespoon of the lemon juice.

Season the fish steaks with peppercorns and salt. Brush them with the yolk mixture and press the grated nuts into each side.

Warm the sherry.

Place 1 tablespoon of the butter in a frying pan over medium heat. Add prepared fish steaks and fry 3 minutes per side. Add the heated sherry and set it alight. When the flame extinguishes, place the fish on a serving dish and sprinkle it with parsley. Add the remaining tablespoon of butter and the remaining lemon juice to the frying pan. Heat, stirring to scrape up any nut pieces, and spoon this mixture over the fish. Serve immediately.

Mrs. America's Almond Rice Parisian

SERVES 6

*M*ike Douglas, the Philadelphian known for his lilting way with a song, had a nationally syndicated television talk show through most of the 1960s. Although no great cook himself, Douglas shared his show every week with a different co-host; and one of the co-host's duties was to demonstrate how to cook his or her favorite recipes on the air. When Marilyn Mitchell, Mrs. America, appeared on the show, she gave Mike and the viewers at home an exhibition of the talents that won her her crown by whipping up a platter of rice that she elevated from an everyday starch to a Parisian delicacy by including almonds and mushrooms. It is quite a homely dish—all shades of brown—but unmistakably foreign, and tasty in a suburban sort of way.

½ cup rice
½ cup sliced almonds
½ cup sliced mushrooms
3 tablespoons butter
1 can (10¾ ounces) undiluted French onion soup
¾ cup hot water

In a heavy-bottomed pot, brown the rice, almonds, and mushrooms in butter about 10 minutes, stirring frequently. Add soup and water. Stir. Bring to a boil. Reduce heat. Cover and cook 20 minutes, or until all the liquid is absorbed and the rice is tender.

"*I* strongly believe that the vegetable has never had its due in this country and I am determined to do something about it," James Beard proclaimed in 1949. Throughout his career, he introduced Americans to interesting vegetable dishes, including caponata from Italy, oriental eggplant, fiddlehead ferns, stir-fries, beer-batter tempuras, and vegetable soufflés. Shortly after he began his career as a caterer, he discovered the Provençal specialty, ratatouille, which he recalled preparing both cold and hot in the late 1940s. Although making it on television had none of the drama of his flaming barbecue demonstrations, or of the largest crêpes in history (which he did for Jack Parr on "The Tonight Show"), its bright medley of colors made it a natural prop as a tablemate for more thrilling dishes as color television was popularized.

"I Love to Eat" Ratatouille

SERVES 6 TO 8

1 large onion, sliced
2 garlic cloves, chopped
½ cup olive oil
2 green peppers, seeded and cut into thin strips
1 large eggplant, peeled, and diced
4 small zucchini, cut into ¼-inch slices
8 to 10 very ripe tomatoes, peeled, seeded, and chopped
1 teaspoon dried basil
1½ teaspoons salt
1 teaspoon pepper

In a deep saucepan or kettle, sauté the onion and garlic in olive oil until the onion is transparent. Add peppers, eggplant, and zucchini. Blend well. Reduce heat, cover pan, and cook 8 to 10 minutes, until the eggplant softens. Add tomatoes and seasonings and continue simmering, covered, 10 minutes. Remove the cover and let the mixture cook down, stirring often. Correct seasonings. Serve hot, or cold with lemon juice or vinegar and additional olive oil.

Babas au Rhum the Hard Way

12 BABAS, 2 PER SERVING

To make one's own babas au rhum was a feat of skill as impressive as baking a baguette from scratch. "Babas and savarins always seem to delight guests," advises *Mastering the Art of French Cooking*, "and they are not difficult to make if you have any feeling for doughs and baking." For some reason, many American cooks were terrified of dough and baking and shunned any recipe that called for yeast to rise. But yeast never had a better propogandist than Julia Child, who made it look like such fun to punch and slap dough around the kitchen.

DOUGH

> 1 package active dry yeast
> 3 tablespoons lukewarm (105 to 115 degrees) water
> 2 eggs, at room temperature
> 2 tablespoons sugar
> 1/8 teaspoon salt
> 1 1/2 cups flour
> Additional flour and milk or water as needed

SYRUP

> 1 cup sugar
> 2 cups water
> 2/3 cup dark rum

To make the babas, dissolve the yeast in the water and let it stand 5 to 10 minutes, until foamy.

In a large mixing bowl, blend together eggs, sugar, and salt. Add the flour and the dissolved yeast mixture. Mix with a wooden spoon. When the dough becomes too hard to stir, begin kneading it in the bowl with your hands. It will be very sticky at first, but will gradually detach itself from the bowl and your hands. Slap and pull and knead it for about 5 minutes, until it becomes elastic and smooth. If it is too stiff, knead in milk or water in droplets. If it is too soft, knead in flour by teaspoons.

Cover the dough in the mixing bowl with plastic wrap and let it rise 1 1/2 to 2 hours in a warm place, until light and spongy and doubled in bulk.

Butter 12 baba molds or muffin cups about 2 inches deep and 2 inches in diameter. Divide the dough into 12 portions and place one portion in each of the prepared molds or muffin cups. Cover lightly with plastic wrap. Let rise another 1 to 1½ hours, until dough is about ¼ inch above the rim of the molds and has doubled in bulk.

Preheat oven to 375 degrees.

Bake babas in the center of the oven for 15 minutes, until they are nicely browned and pull away from the sides. Unmold babas onto a cake rack to cool to lukewarm.

As babas cool, make the syrup by combining the sugar and 1 cup of the water in a saucepan. Bring to a boil, then remove from heat. Add remaining 1 cup water and stir until sugar is completely dissolved. Stir in rum. Let cool to lukewarm.

Arrange lukewarm babas in a dish that holds them snugly so they won't roll around. Prick the tops in several places with a toothpick. Pour lukewarm syrup over them and let them stand 30 minutes, basting frequently with syrup. They should imbibe all the syrup and become swollen, moist, and spongy, but still hold their shape. Drain the soaked babas on a rack for 30 minutes.

Serve with berries and/or whipped cream.

Elemental Chocolate Mousse

SERVES 8

Yes, there was a time when mousse was exotic, and seemed like a great indulgence, a thrilling alternative to dowdy old pudding. Mousse was especially popular as a dessert among early television chefs, who broadcast their lessons live, because even though it didn't have the spectacular appearance of a high-rise soufflé, it was indestructible and wouldn't collapse on the set. Since those early days, mousse itself has become rather plain-seeming, and dozens of sinful, decadent, preposterously rich, liquored-up versions have come and gone. Dione Lucas's absolutely basic recipe from the late 1940s recaptures early mousse's charm.

> ½ **pound dark sweet chocolate (not milk chocolate)**
> ¼ **cup cold water**
> 5 **eggs, separated**
> 2 **tablespoons dark rum**

Break the chocolate into small pieces and place it in the top of a double boiler with the cold water. Stir over simmering water until the chocolate dissolves and becomes silky smooth. Remove from heat and let stand in a pan of cool water, stirring occasionally. When the chocolate is cooled to room temperature, beat in the egg yolks and rum. Beat egg whites stiff but not dry, then thoroughly fold them into the chocolate mixture. Spoon into 8 small soufflé cups or glasses and chill at least 4 hours.

NOTE: It is possible to make chocolate mousse using gelatin rather than raw eggs, and thereby avoid any risk of salmonella from the eggs. However, it was raw-egg mousse—silk-smooth and cream-rich—that was the gourmets' choice, made with very fresh eggs and the finest quality chocolate. Samuel Chamberlain called a similar recipe in *Clémentine in the Kitchen* a "delectable substance"; and his daughter Narcisse's recent revision of the book rejoiced, "This is the simplest recipe for chocolate mousse you are likely to find and also very likely the best."

A recipe James Beard liked for his television appearances because there was usually enough time to make these pancakes from scratch, get them in the oven at the beginning of the show, and serve them before the final credits. Their appearance coming out of the oven is nothing short of spectacular—a soufflé-like demonstration of eggs' lifting power. Beard recalled eating them in Portland when he was a young man; and he suggested they be served not only for special breakfasts, but at brunch, and even as dessert after a light supper (in which case he advised flaming them with rum or Cognac). This recipe makes a pancake big enough for two.

High-Rise German Pancakes

SERVES 2

3 eggs
½ cup milk
½ cup flour
½ teaspoon salt
Pinch of cinnamon
Pinch of nutmeg
1½ tablespoons sugar
4 tablespoons butter, 2 of them melted
2 tablespoons confectioners' sugar
½ lemon

Preheat oven to 425 degrees.

Beat the eggs with milk. Sift together the flour, salt, cinnamon, nutmeg, and sugar, and whisk this mixture into the eggs. Beat in the 2 tablespoons melted butter.

Heat 2 tablespoons of butter in a 12-inch ovenproof nonstick skillet until it bubbles, but do not let it brown. Pour the batter into the hot butter then immediately put the pan into the hot oven. Bake 15 minutes, reduce heat to 375 degrees, and bake 5 to 7 minutes more, until the sides are golden brown, high and dry, and the center is soft but set. Slide the pancake onto a heated plate. Sprinkle it with confectioners' sugar and spritz it with the juice from the ½ lemon.

— 4 —
GOURMET
RESTAURANTS:
Suave, Snob, and Slob

*I*n the beginning, there was the Pavillon. Opened by Henri Soulé in 1941 as a spin-off from his acclaimed French Pavilion at the 1939 World's Fair, and especially hallowed in its early years as a citadel of civilization because its chef and many of its staff were exiles from occupied France, the Pavillon was the epitome of classical gourmet dining. There was simply nothing else like it. Among international cognoscenti, it was unanimously recognized as the best restaurant in the United States; and Joseph Wechsberg, who profiled Henri Soulé for *The New Yorker*, proclaimed it "the *world*'s most distinguished restaurant." It was as genteel as the Twenty-sixth Street Delmonico's in its *haut monde* heyday of the 1880s, as snooty as the Waldorf when Oscar Tschirky ruled the dining room at the turn of the century, and ever so much more elegant than the famed "lobster palaces" where newly minted millionaires went to stuff themselves in the Gay Nineties. The Pavillon established standards of exquisite food, opulent decor, and preferential service that were the paradigm of haute cuisine in America for at least two decades. Wechsberg described entering the place as an experience similar to finding oneself in the champagne party of a lavish production of *La Traviata*. "Few set designers would have the means of creating the brillance of this set with its chandeliers and mirrors, the symphony of colors with its shades of red, green, and chartreuse and the superbly populated stage with many stunning Violettas. A beautiful show, efficiently produced and effectively displayed, a composite impression made of lights and mirrors and flowers, of tinkling

The Pump Room of Chicago, famous for its Caviar Wagon and costumed staff, and most of all for dinners served on flaming swords.

glasses and the muted clatter of cocktail shakers, the subdued voices of men and the laughter of women, the scent of *beurre noisette* and Miss Dior."

To its friends, it was sometimes known as "Soulé's Bar and Grill. But arrivistes and curiosity-seekers with money that was too new or tastebuds that were callow were not welcome at the Pavillon. Half the tables in its dining rooms were permanently reserved for regulars, who included the Duke and Duchess of Windsor as well as assorted Hearsts, Fords, expatriated European connoisseurs, and privileged American *bec fins* visiting New York. Hungry ordinaries who came for lunch frequently waited until one-thirty, at which time they could expect that unoccupied famous people's tables might be made available. For its favored clientele, the Pavillon was an exclusive club, its East Fifty-fifth Street entrance described by Mr. Wechsberg as "flanked by two Rolls-Royces, a Cadillac, a Bentley, and a Lincoln Continental, all with liveried chauffeurs and low license numbers." Here was epicureanism as—let us be frank—the height of snobbery. This was an aspect of gourmet dining, not new to the Pavillon but perfected there, that became enshrined in the customs of many Pavillon imitators in New York, where getting a good table (not in Siberia) and being treated politely were luxuries enjoyed only by favored customers. In her review of one such establishment, Lafayette ("the rudest restaurant in town"), Gael Greene wrote, "In our greatest restaurants, only fool's luck or expertise count if you are unknown." In many of the city's lavish French dining rooms that descended from the Pavillon, Greene found that neither luck nor expertise had any effect on the punctilious restaurateurs who kept Soulé's brand of *haut snobisme* alive.

Soulé, a short and Napoleonic perfectionist, was known for the fresh roses in his restaurant, which florists spent six hours each day arranging, and which complemented plush red damask banquettes and murals that showed the chestnut trees on the Champs Elysées. The food (from what *The New York Times* declared "the best kitchen in town") included sole from the English Channel, turbot from Dieppe, loup de mer from the Mediterranean, and fresh salmon from the Adour—all just hours away from their home waters (and displayed, unabashedly, on a cold buffet right alongside the astronomical invoice from the fishmonger); grouse, partridge, duck, and pheasant in their seasons; an illustrious Chateaubriand with sauce béarnaise, and such awesome desserts as "Bombe Pavillon" (coffee and vanilla ice cream topped with a compote of fruits and served in flaming kirsch) and pear Hélène sprinkled with crystallized violets and garnished with chocolate sauce. At the Pavillon, Americans could also enjoy the epicurean novelty of cheese served at the end of the meal—"noble cheese," according to Mr. Wechsberg, whose essay, "Dining at the Pavillon," concluded, "A slight mist of happiness seemed to descend between the chestnut trees of the Champs Elysées. This, I knew, was going to be another long-remembered evening whose very memory would help sustain life in its grimmer moments." Thus spoke the inveterate connoisseur of fine cuisine.

Henri Soulé, "Temple Keeper" of the Pavillon

The Pavillon was the gourmet's Mecca through the 1950s; then in 1960 chef Pierre Fra-

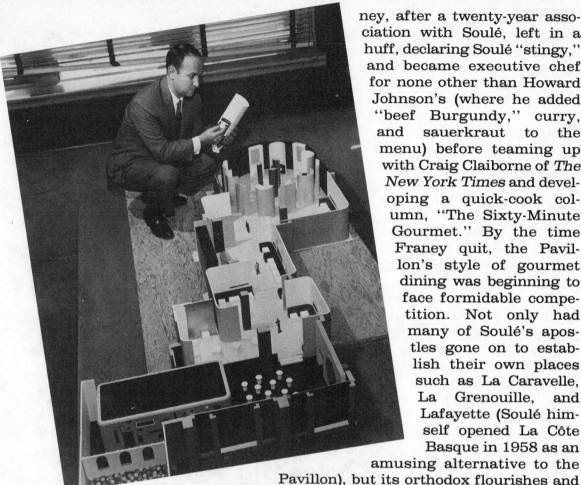

Joseph Baum studies a
scale model of a Restaurant
Associates showpiece.

ney, after a twenty-year association with Soulé, left in a huff, declaring Soulé "stingy," and became executive chef for none other than Howard Johnson's (where he added "beef Burgundy," curry, and sauerkraut to the menu) before teaming up with Craig Claiborne of *The New York Times* and developing a quick-cook column, "The Sixty-Minute Gourmet." By the time Franey quit, the Pavillon's style of gourmet dining was beginning to face formidable competition. Not only had many of Soulé's apostles gone on to establish their own places such as La Caravelle, La Grenouille, and Lafayette (Soulé himself opened La Côte Basque in 1958 as an amusing alternative to the Pavillon), but its orthodox flourishes and full dress swagger had begun to seem fusty, stiff, and—one of the worst adjectives to apply to anything in the 1960s—old. Brillat-Savarin, whose maxims were fundamental truths for America's most serious connoisseurs, had written, "No man under forty can be dignified with the title of gourmet"; and indeed, the Pavillon had become a place for superannuated taste-in timeworn tradition. As the tenets of gourmet life grew fashionable and appealed to an ever-younger segment of upwardly mobile society, the glories of the Pavillon lost their sparkle; and its notorious arrogance toward outsiders made it simply inaccessible for many middle-class citizens who wanted to cultivate their palate. Besides, the newfangled gourmets of midcentury America weren't so interested in the overniceties of Monsieur Soulé's stuffy private club; they were hungry for something different—for entertainment, high style, and *modern* meals.

Although the Pavillon's antediluvian ways of haute cuisine persisted, and continue to hold sway in at least a few ornate palaces of epicureanism in nearly every American city, the rules of fine restaurant dining began to get rewritten in the fifties by a company called Restaurant Associates. Under the guidance of Joe Baum and Jerry Brody, operational director and president, this management firm reconceived what eating out could be. By doing so, they gave a new currency to the idea of swank eating places and infused them with the same kind of excitement that was rejuvenating home cooking. They did not by any means democratize the concept of gourmet dining, but they did popularize it; and as was happening to cooks in upscale home kitchens all over America, the concept of the restaurant gourmet became a fashionable image to strive for.

The genius of Restaurant Associates was to realize that dining out could be a form of recreation. They didn't just serve superb food in luxurious surroundings, they put on a show; they created restaurants that were as much *mise en scène* as they were *salles à manger*. Their most extravagant application of this principle was The Forum of the Twelve Caesars, which opened in New York in 1958—a restaurant with a theme established by twelve seventeenth-century paintings of the Caesars, from Julius to Domitian, by Camilio Procaccini, that hung on its brocaded walls. Everything about the Forum was imperial. Working on the prodigal scale of a CinemaScope costume epic, Restaurant Associates boasted that it spent two years studying the classics to ensure that everything was accurate, impressive, and unprecedentedly sumptuous. The basic idea—itself an audacious break with the ordinary Francophilic gourmet ritual—was to emulate the splendors enjoyed by the elite citizens of ancient Rome, i.e. gastronomic rarities and treasures plucked from the entire known world, which were deemed to be anything rich and spicy and spectacular. To help guests feel important, tables were especially low; on the other hand, to engender feelings of power, silverware was extra large, and the fork was to the right of the knife—"an expression of heartiness." Drinks were doubles; wine was served in goblets, coffee in capacious cups; wine buckets were gladiators' helmets; waiters were liveried in Phoenician purple and red; the barman wore a toga. *Gourmet* found it "hard to believe that there has ever been such completely perfect service anywhere—even in the palaces of the Caesars themselves."

The Forum of the Twelve Caesars was dramatically expensive: Dinner for two could cost nearly fifty dollars, which was three to five times the price of most polite bourgeois restaurants; but in addition to the stage effects and unstinted luxury, customers got some dazzlingly good (not to mention utterly original) food. The Latinate menu, tied with a purple ribbon and secured by a golden seal, written in prose that was a feat of classical erudition, offered such arcane dishes as "Truffle-stuffed quail, Cleopatra—wrapped in Macedonian vine leaves, baked in hot ashes," "Epigrams of venison, sauce vitae," and "Pheasant of the golden house on a silver shield in gilded plumage, roasted with an exquisite sauce." For dessert there were "Crêpes triomphantes" (with nut cream, orange liqueur, chocolate sauce, vanilla ice cream), a "Crown of chestnuts" puréed and glacéed, and "Est! Est! Est!—a Forum whimsy" constructed of cream, meringue, and melba.

Serving such food was no simple matter of setting it down in front of customers. Everything came out of the kitchen with a flourish—enthroned on a rolling cart, impaled on a sword and presented to the diner as though he were a pagan chieftain inspecting the severed head of an enemy, or set on fire. Throughout the mealtime, flames at tableside preparations leapt ten feet into the air from every section of the high-ceilinged dining room, creating an atmosphere that one review described as "a Neronian weekend orgy."

Joe Baum had begun to hone his pyrotechnical skills in 1952 in his first job with Restaurant Associates, running the Newark Airport's Newarker Restaurant, where he transformed what might have been a sedate grill-room overlooking the airstrip into a culinary spectacle. "The Newarker is a success because that magic ingre-

Dinner as dinner theater:
flambeéd dessert and coffee
at The Pump Room in
Chicago

dient, imagination, is part of every *plat*," Tom Marvel wrote in *Gourmet* in July 1956, praising the restaurant's "flaming foods in all their glory." The Newarker became famous for the dramatic, high-proof serving fires that engulfed shashlik, prime steak chunks with wild rice, skewered scallops wrapped in bacon, baked Alaska, and brandied coffee. "We invented the sparkler for dessert, God help me," Baum told Gael Greene, moaning about "the ooze of copycat restaurants and the flaming Fujiyamas used everywhere—without charm or even the saving grace of humor."

Humor was the truly revolutionary and very American thing about The Forum of the Twelve Caesars. Gourmet dining in the manner of the Pavillon was traditionally serious, even solemn business; it was usual for connoisseurs of important restaurants to panegyrize their haute cuisine with the same reverential hush customarily tendered important paintings in art museums. Joseph Wechsberg began his book *Dining at the Pavillon* (1962) with this rhapsody: "In the land of Brillat-Savarin, Auguste Escoffier and Fernand Point, where the philosophy of good eating is regarded as an abstract science and cooking a major art, the celebrated practitioners of *la grande cuisine* easily (and deservedly) eclipse cabinet ministers, field marshals, multimillionaires and members of the Académie Française." *Philosophy of good eating . . . abstract science . . . major art . . . practitioners of la grande cuisine:* In the light of such an apotheosis, the extravagances of The Forum of the Twelve Caesars could easily be understood as something other than forthright. With all its deference to the treatises of Apicius (the Roman cookbook author who invented pâté de foie gras and was identified by Pliny as "the greatest spendthrift of all"), the restaurant appeared to be more a monumental burlesque, a great tongue-in-cheek parody of haute cuisine's pretensions. "Could anyone possibly think I was serious?" Joe Baum asked. Among his menu's purple prose you could find such items as "Fiddler crab lump à la Nero," "Mushrooms of the sincere Claudius" (Claudius was assassinated by poison mushrooms), and "The noblest Caesar of them all" (Caesar salad). Amazingly, some reviews of The Forum of the Twelve Caesars did seem to take it all in utter earnest; but this was inevitable considering the high prices and the fact that there were simply no modern precedents for Restaurant Associates' unique combination of grade-A food and ironic whimsy. For all its folderol, classical enlightenment, high prices, and truly refined cookery, The Forum invited customers to enjoy themselves in a way they never could in a stodgy, old-fashioned French restaurant. And therein lay the acumen of Restaurant Associates.

At one of its most elegant creations, a restaurant dubbed The Tower Suite, every customer was made to feel he or she was being taken care of by a personal maid and butler. To instill this mental impression, Restaurant Associates devised a novel flourish. Each member of the serving staff was instructed to approach the customer at the beginning of the meal and introduce himself: "Hello, my name is Rodney. I will be your waiter this evening." It was a ravishing innovation in service— the height of refinement; and it allowed a diner to feel like a millionaire, or at least as if he were eating in a millionaire's home. Like Baum's thrilling flaming specialties at the Newarker and the Forum of the Twelve Caesars, the waiter's self-introduction was eagerly adopted by many other restaurants that wanted to exude upscale airs; and as the winds of gourmet dining swept through nearly every level of public dining above truck stops and hash houses, waiters' announcement of their names became a familiar—and annoying—conceit of vast numbers of modern eateries aiming to prove to customers that they offered personal service.

Each Restaurant Associates eating place had a theme, and not all were aimed at polished gourmets. The creations included Zum Zum, at which the culinary scheme was "German beer stube"; Charley O's (an Irish pub); the Hawaiian Room in the Hotel Lexington (where familiar Polynesian fare was augmented by genuinely exotic *nasi goreng* curry from Indonesia, Javanese skewered meat, and lobster Cantonese); Fonda del Sol (olé!); and Paul Revere's Tavern and Chop House (colonial Americana). Each place was carefully planned as a dining experience that extended beyond the food to decor and ambience. On a level of restaurant dining below that of serious epicureanism, these places helped estab-

"I imagined diners at the Tower Suite to be visiting a rich uncle in the city," said Restaurant Associates' George Lang. "No menu was needed because waiters introduced themselves. And there would be mid-meal sorbet to refresh the palate. Because I am a musician, I named that course 'intermezzo.'"

lish the concept that eating out could be about more than food; it could be living theater.

This idea was abetted in the 1960s by the growth of outlandish "fun" restaurants that were also singles bars, led by Warner LeRoy's Maxwell's Plum, where urban swingers ate breast of capon in champagne sauce and flaming strawberries Romanoff under such startlingly original decor as a Tiffany-like glass ceiling, hanging plants, and flickering gas lamps. Like the waiter's self-introduction from the Tower Suite, the outlandish decorative cues trickled down from Maxwell's haute rococo to become the common "fern bars" of the seventies—symbols of a restaurant where the food wasn't really *serious*, but was nonetheless a cut above plate lunch. By the end of the decade in Chicago, a company called Lettuce Entertain You under the direction of Rich Mellman had picked up the gauntlet of fun theme dining and began opening stupefyingly accoutered restaurants with new gastronomic gimmickry: salad bars of unprecedented variety, flamboyant boozy drinks with outrageous ingredients and names to match ("Climb Every Mounds Bar"—a coconut and chocolate rum libation), and atmosphere designed to make dining out a swinging party. In Chicago, and nearly all over America, this formula for fun is still a mighty success.

There was nothing particularly *fun* about Restaurant Associates' most significant gourmet creation, The Four Seasons; but it did share one quality with the Forum of the Twelve Caesars as well as lesser Restaurant Associates landmarks. It exuded a powerful sense of thematic mission. It was a tour de force like The Forum, but this time a tour de force of *good taste* rather than of hedonism. Its concept, Joe Baum recalls, came to him while reading a collection of haiku poetry: He determined he would make a restaurant that changed as the world turned. Elemental. Elegant. Timeless but radically modern. Entirely different from the romantic nostalgia for France that infused the Pavillon! The space itself was an intoxicating spectacle of modernist authority, elevated above Park Avenue between Fifty-second and Fifty-third Streets in Mies van der Rohe and Philip Johnson's Seagram Building, which was a towering black-and-bronze culmination of Bauhaus less-is-more precision. Two large square rooms were connected by a travertine marble corridor with a lofty view of the building's lobby. One room had a marble pool of bubbling water (which could be, but was not, frozen over for the winter season) and quivering brass chain draperies on the windows (actually, a slight mistake—no one expected the air currents to cause the chains to ripple); the other room was cozier, paneled in French walnut and decorated with an overpowering Richard Lippold brass rod sculpture suspended above its bar. Miró tapestries adorned the entryway; and in the corridor between the two rooms hung a grand tapestry that Pablo Picasso had painted as a theater curtain for the ballet *The Three-Cornered Hat.*

Like the quartet of trees (one at each corner of the pool), the beds of flowers, the waiters' uniforms, and the table settings, the menu at The Four Seasons was changed, completely, four times a year. Written with the advice and counsel of James Beard, the menu presented guests with a selection of dishes that were almost shockingly minimalistic, at least compared to the over-sauced and fussy ones served by nearly every other first-class restaurant in New York at the time. There was a great emphasis on seasonal rarities: fiddlehead ferns, snow hare, autumn venison, winter crabmeat cakes from Maryland, exotic mushroom salads and hot rhubarb compote in the spring. Wishing to revivify America's appetite for vegetables, which he felt got short shrift even in gourmet restaurants, Joe Baum pioneered serving baby ones (an invention usually attributed to California cooks of the 1970s)—carrots, peas, beans, asparagus, etc., obtained in the spring on special order from local truck farmers and arranged as small bouquets in baskets that were shown to diners for their approval and selection. As a token of the kitchen's audacity (and much to James Beard's chagrin), garlic was banished from everything, even snails, for a short while in the beginning (but was returned, without fanfare, to the kitchen in the early sixties). Hardly any of the signature dishes of the Four Seasons menu would be familiar to denizens of a place such as the Pavillon: moussaka orientale, crisped shrimp with mustard fruit, coriander prosciutto with pineapple, chocolate velvet cake and cappuccino soufflé at dessert. "This sort of thing is bound to disappoint the man who is strictly and solely impressed by the traditional cuisine of France," wrote Ted Patrick and Silas Spitzer. "But gourmets who have an adventurous viewpoint approve this striking out in new directions."

The Four Seasons was defiantly *not* a French restaurant, and yet it aimed for the pinnacle of excellence. This was a significant innovation—to spend top dollar for utterly original meals rather than the classics and for such apparently humble (but in fact exquisite) dishes as Vermont Cheddar cheese soup and Amish ham steak rather than pâté de foie gras and quenelles éminences. The Four Seasons, the most expensive restaurant in America, was—astonishingly—an *American* restaurant. Much of what it served and many of its cooking techniques owed something to Old World traditions, but the arrogant modernity of the setting and service and the tradition-be-damned audacity of its kitchen (miniature croissants with dinner! snow pea pods, and not in a Chinese restaurant! bite-size cherry tomatoes!) were new-world brash.

Most serious American gourmets in the sixties made a pilgrimage to New York—to savor the Pavillon in its final days or try its swank French progeny, and to discover the chic originality of The Four Seasons and the giddy grandeur of The Forum. With no disrespect meant to New Orleans and San Francisco, which had their own restaurant traditions, New York City was sanctified in the gourmet canon as America's culinary beacon in the sense that it was the city where styles were set, and where gourmet dining was defined. New Orleans food and San Francisco food, also Chicago and Los Angeles food, were, at their best, expressions of regional character; New York food, at its most celebrated, was detached from mid-Atlantic traditions, and was more an expression of contemporary gastronomic trends. (All of which is still true.) Of course nearly every other city of any size in this country had its *serious* palace of gourmet cuisine; and some have been (or continue to be) first-rate: Detroit's London Chop House and Mr. Paul's, Charley's Café Exceptionale of Minneapolis (defunct), the Maisonette of Cincinnati, Bern's Steak House in

Tampa, Ernie's and the Blue Fox of San Francisco, and Ernest Byfield's original Pump Room in Chicago. Great as some such places are or may have been in their heydays, each was unique—an outpost of fine dining, not part of a scene, as were the uppermost restaurants of New York.

All of this is not to say that New York was the only place where important and influential things were happening in restaurants in the sixties. In fact it can be argued that what happened in New York mattered little outside New York, and only to a small number of earnest gourmets around the country. The more significant events, in terms of sheer numbers of people affected and meals sold and the elevation of America's gourmet consciousness, happened in the dining rooms of Holiday Inns all across the country. There were 200 Holiday Inns in 1962, 1,400 by the end of the decade. From their kitchens (as well as from the kitchens of other burgeoning motel chains in the sixties) emanated an entire new style of restaurant eating that quite literally covered America. "The brightest ray in the whole spectrum of eating is the motel," rejoiced Ted Patrick and Silas Spitzer in an article about "The Future of American Restaurants" in 1960, the same year Pierre Franey left Le Pavillon for Howard Johnson's. "This once tawdry part of the American scene has become quite a

thing of beauty and elegance. And in the competition for the touring customer, the forward-looking motel owner has learned there is no lure comparable to a fine restaurant. It is our prediction that in the next few years some of the best restaurants in the United States will be found in, or as adjuncts to, motels." Indeed, by 1970 Golden Anniversary celebrants in the hinterlands were dining on duck à l'orange at their local Ramada or Treadway Inn, vacationing families were learning about the merry ritual of the intermezzo sherbet course (an immensely popular affectation among sweet-loving Americans) between the lobster tails and the chateaubriand, and prom kids and their dates sat in banquettes at panoramic windows in chain motels and hotels that were the tallest building in town, dining on flaming baked Alaskas. The time had arrived when anyone and everyone could be a gourmet.

It didn't *all* really begin in Holiday Inns, but they are the proper place in which to anchor any exegesis of the kind of food and style of eating known as "continental cuisine" because they are where continental cuisine was perfected. To our knowledge, no one has ever decisively fixed the limits of this ambitious cuisine-without-a-country, and it is difficult to try to do so with any kind of precision; but as the Supreme Court said about obscenity, you know it when you see it: expensive food from another continent (usually Europe, but possibly South America or Asia) chosen from a menu speckled with accents *acute* and *grave* as well as *le, la,* and *les* and perhaps even some umlauts and upside-down exclamation points. The food is served with considerable fuss (frequently prepared tableside over Sterno, or with high-proof combustion effects) by a waiter in a tuxedo at a table with cloth napkins by candlelight and accompanied by wine from a bottle with a cork. In a continental restaurant, pepper is dispensed from a majestic mill, lofted above the food with much ceremony by the waiter; salads are frequently made as you watch, in great hardwood bowls that can be made to spin on their pedestals; desserts and coffees arrive engulfed in flames. Continental kitchens are unbounded by the idiosyncrasies of a single nation's cuisine. Customers can choose some of what they like from several countries. They can even choose some foods that do not really belong to the traditional cooking of any known country, but are staples of any worthy continental chef, such as tournedos Mexicana (steaks with chili sauce), carpet-

bagger steak (stuffed with oysters and/or mushrooms, cheese, ham, or crabmeat), surf 'n' turf, twice-baked potatoes, and coconut hot fudge snowballs for dessert.

Continental cuisine proliferated dramatically because the sixties were halcyon days for the food processing industry, which began supplying restaurants with ready-to-defrost gourmet entrées and whole meals that not only eliminated the need for a skilled chef, but also provided the restaurateur with such fringe benefits as perfect portion control (no waste) and uniform plate coverage. Suddenly kitchens with only unskilled staff or a chef who knew but one cuisine could offer customers great dishes from all over the world. John and Karen

Hess's *The Taste of America* quotes *Quick Frozen Foods*, an industry magazine, as gloating, "Breaded shrimp, oysters, crab meat specialties, lobster Newburg, and pompano are packed in attractive packages with four-color illustrations and tend to make a chef proud of preparing a gourmet entrée." Some meats were available partially cooked, with grill marks already on them; and the half-baked loaf of bread was popularized, eliminating the need for a baker but providing restaurants the opportunity to pamper customers with a "hot-from-the-oven" loaf presented on a wooden board with a cutting knife and a ramekin of whipped yellow unguent that resembled butter. For thousands of motel dining rooms, small town chophouses, and eventually even truck stops, it had become easy to serve elaborate-seeming foods that were once the signature of a gourmet chef. In addition to being easy to serve, the other thing that put this new generation of instant, no-fuss gourmet food onto menus across the land was that people were hungry for it.

The notion of continental restaurants had great appeal to novitiate gourmets eager to taste the delicacies of the world. Like a one-country-per-day tour of Europe, it was the most efficient way to broaden one's awareness, providing an eclectic *menu dégustation* of foreign (or foreign-seeming) taste experiences. "Modern civilization has made exotic foods from all over the world easily available to us," rejoiced *Gusto International* ("a magazine for the modern epicure") in 1969, lauding not any one cuisine but the "ennobling experience" of eating veritable bouquets of things from Italy, Paris, Copenhagen, and Cathay all in one sitting.

Although the world was their oyster, continental restaurant chefs elevated a small number of showy but eater-friendly dishes to classic status within the repertoire of this jet-age cuisine. In nearly any continental restaurant, you could be certain of finding at least one *plat du jour* that had been given the cordon-bleu treatment, that is, turned into a fried ham and cheese sandwich. Beef Wellington became another continental standard, much to the horror of gourmet purists who scoff at the fact that the beef must be cooked twice (es-

Sybarites just plopped things into their genteel mouths, sucked and savored, then swallowed.

sentially steamed inside its crust the second time). What such criticisms fail to appreciate is the sheer abundant luxury of beef Wellington that once made it so appealing to gourmets. (It is now thoroughly passé; although only last year we saw it featured on the menu of the finest restaurant in a small town in southwestern Iowa.) Here was maximum richness on a single plate: the buttery pastry crust, the moist duxelles and lush foie gras, and the beef itself, a tender tenderloin to begin with, enfeebled to utter plushness by its second turn in the oven. Such softness and ease of eating were important elements of most continental dishes: lobster tails instead of whole, messy lobsters; creamy stroganoffs; buttery chicken Kiev; plenty of au gratins, deboned birds, and bite-size shellfish in Newburg sauce. The principle of such fork-tender foods was that true luxury dining ought to require minimal effort from the diner. Trenchermen tore at their food, sawed it with a knife, spit out pits and bones. Sybarites didn't have to engage in such arduous labors; they just plopped things into their genteel mouths, sucked and savored, then swallowed.

Almost more important than the food and pageantry in many continental restaurants was the view. "I find it difficult to rate restaurants by the food they serve," Jerome Klein wrote in *Alitalia Views to Dine By* in 1961, explaining that the purpose of his book—a guide to hundreds of dining rooms around the world with terrific views—was to reveal "the rare spots where you and I may find an atmosphere that is rich beyond belief; where we may sit down and view the world, at our pleasure, from a table. This sheer luxury is available to us in many lands for the price of a meal." In many American restaurants conceived and built during the sixties (chain motel dining rooms in cities especially), the guiding principle of the spectacular view was narrowed somewhat to a view from high above a skyline. Eating many stories up in the air was not only intrinsically scenic, providing a view of tall buildings, the sunset, etc.; it also suggested the soaring view from a jet, which was considered a swank way to travel; and most important of all, it symbolized the *exaltation* of the dining experience—elevating one's tastebuds above the humdrum and mun-

dane. If the restaurant slowly rotated high in the sky, providing a 360-degree view, that made the event seem even loftier.

"There was always a tower in the mind of man—a wanting to rise high above his surroundings. Point by point, that desire had jutted civilization's claims from earth to sky." So rhapsodized Harold Mansfield and George Gulacsik in their book, *Space Needle USA*, which is about the building of the tower at the 1962 Seattle World's Fair. Man's yearnings to rise high, the authors assert, reached its modern climax in the Space Needle, the featured attraction of which was a restaurant called the Eye of the Needle that spun in circles and served Pacific northwestern specialties as well as rich continental cuisine. "Our appetizers and salads become your lift-off on a memorable meal," the Eye of the Needle menu advised, telling customers, "The scene from your commanding table on the rim of the slowly circling disk will add delight to the outstanding foods." The bill of fare included such continental delicacies as crab en brochette wrapped in bacon and swaddled in béarnaise sauce, breast of chicken "Taj Mahal" (in a lightly spiced "Indian sauce with almonds"), coupe tropical (whipped vanilla ice cream and chocolate mousse "surmounted" with banana and pineapple), and kirsch-marinated strawberries in a meringue ring with a rosette of whipped pink ice cream on top.

The best view of all, and the ultimate outpost of unconditionally ersatz continental cooking was in airplanes, particularly on international flights. By the mid-sixties, the role of flight attendant had consummated its evolution from airborne nurse (which is how the job began in 1933) to waitress, and modern stewardesses were instructed by the airlines that "today's commercial airliner is the equivalent of a dining room." In 1964 *Venture*, a deluxe hard-cover magazine aimed at enlightened tourists, blithered that soon "travelers on trans-Atlantic jets flying at twenty-five-hundred miles an hour will barely have time to have lunch aloft. Today's airlines, already worried about tomorrow's meal service, have estimated that by the time a passenger drinks a glass of champagne, he will have traveled 495 miles. One hors d'oeuvre is equal to 16.5 miles, an entire meal, 4,118, which means that passengers on the New York-Amsterdam run will have to stop eating somewhere about the salad."

Modern subsonic jets presented no such dilemmas. As airlines began boasting of their luxurious cuisine to attract a bigger share of the growing market, international travelers found themselves faced with lap-size trays of sacher torte reminiscent of Vienna, paella "in the classic tradition of Spain itself," according to Iberian Airlines advertisements, and brioches vaguely similar to what they'd find in Paris. Even on domestic flights, United Airlines passengers in 1962 ate meals that the menu advised were prepared by Chef John Wolfsheimer, member of the American Culinary Association, whose offerings included crabmeat salad with vin rosé dressing, pot roast of beef bourguignonne, Italian green beans, and a Holland roll (all as parts of one meal). In 1968, as part of its "Foreign Accent Service" on flights from New York and Chicago to California, TWA actually dressed its flight attendants in outfits meant to evoke the atmosphere of Italy (togas), France (gold mini skirts), Park Avenue (black lounging pajamas), and England (flannel "serving wench" attire) and had them dish out meals to match, including Italian "Medaglione à la Rossini," French "Quiche de Marseilles," American lobster thermidor, and English "Windsor-style" lamb chops. On international flights, Alitalia began serving an astonishing entrée called Suprema de Pollo Farcita Leonardo, which was a boneless and skinless breast of chicken packed full of pâté de foie gras, diced ham, and truffles, all sopped in brandy, and covered with sweet, thick cherry wine sauce. According

to the airline's executive chef, this was not strictly an Italian dish, but rather a continental one prepared in the Italian style.

Continental cuisine was a rare term in the fifties; but by the time Craig Claiborne put out his *New York Times Guide to Dining Out in New York* in 1964, he listed several "continental" eateries among his choice restaurants, lauding their cosmopolitan specialties such as stuffed cannelloni, chicken Kiev, curried chicken, and paella. But quickly, as the gourmet revolution trickled down the socioeconomic ladder and continental cookery was installed in motel dining rooms across the land, the term was disowned by serious gourmets. By the end of the decade Claiborne had discontinued the category *continental* in his guidebook and had expunged the term from descriptions of restaurants so categorized earlier, substituting the word *international*, a more acceptable way to characterize food from many different lands with no single discernible national character of its own.

As the concept of continental cuisine lost its glamour, the very image of gourmet dining underwent a crisis. The term "gourmet" had become overburdened with connotations of pretension and extravagance, the pinnacle of which was Craig Claiborne and Pierre Franey's notorious page-one *(New York Times)* dinner for two at Chez Denis in Paris in 1975 that cost $4,000 and resulted in a hail of angry mail from readers irate about their self-indulgence. The other problem that had affixed itself to the idea of gourmet restaurant dining was that, more and more, *gourmet* meant *phony*. There were far too many dining rooms in motels, hotels, the tops of bank buildings, and elsewhere (including airplanes) boasting of gourmet cuisine that was in fact nothing but pre-frozen and half-baked institutional food. Pretentious, self-indulgent, phony: These were truly horrible epithets in the post-Aquarian years of the early seventies, particularly as many eaters were discovering natural and healthy food and going back to honest peasant cooking.

As Warren Belasco noted in his book, *Appetite for Change*, "The age of truly plastic food seemed close at hand." All that appeared to be wrong about the direction of the American "food establishment" was summarized

"The dirty secret of American luxury dining is precooked frozen food."

—John and Karen Hess in *The Taste of America*

by gourmet cooking, which strived to position itself so high on the food chain, detached from the simple fruits, seeds, and grains most people recognized as sustenance. The original impetus of gourmet cooking after World War II had suffered a stunning inversion. Having begun as a crusade to shake off culinary intolerance and to explore all the gastronomic pleasures of the globe, gourmets found their principles subverted and suddenly symbolic of artifice, plastic mass culture, and even imperialism. As fast as many had rushed to embrace the gourmet way of life in the fifties, they ran from it in the seventies.

To earnest gastronomes, leery of the overused term *gourmet*, the very notion of *continental cuisine* came to epitomize the bastardization of fine dining and the proliferation of pseudoepicureanism among people with crude palates. Calvin Trillin, joking about the meaning of the term, suggested the continent in question must be Antarctica, because so much continental food is made from frozen ingredients. John and Karen Hess scoffed, "In the restaurant field as in home cooking, the gourmet hacks have persuaded the public that foreign and fancy are synonymous with good. An extraordinary example of this was the dinner thrown by President Cottage-Cheese-and-Ketchup [Richard Nixon] for Comrade Brezhnev at the White House. The menu was printed in mangled French, and the recipes seemed to correspond. The plate of resistance (if we may) was *Supreme of Lobster en Bellevue*, an aspic unknown to haute cuisine." In 1967 *Playboy* magazine advised its readers, "If *le, la,* or *les* appear in front of most dishes and *à la mode* keeps popping up the way truffles should in a truffle omelet, chances are the proprietor is unnecessarily padding his bill of fare (also perhaps, his table checks) in hopes of attracting linguistically uninformed customers who judge French cuisine by word count, not how it tastes." Despite such enlightened criticism, for many Americans eager to pamper their palates and lift their culinary standards from canned spaghetti and fish sticks into the realm of excellence, continental restaurants with plenty of French articles on the menu were citadels of fine dining.

Recipes

Vermont Cheese Soup, Park Avenue
Albert Stockli's Crisped Shrimp with
    Mustard Fruit Sauce
Golden Eggs of Crassus
Bar Room Chef's Salad
Clove Sorbet
Poularde Pavillon
West Side Poitrine de Volaille
    à l'Estragon
Original Chicken Cordon Bleu
Duck à l'Orange Treadway
Baked Stuffed Shrimp, Surf 'n' Turf Style
Filet Mignon Caesar Augustus
Beef Stroganoff Imperiale
Beef Wellington to Impress All Who Dine
Steak Diane
Pomme de Terre Macaire
Sauerkraut with Champagne
Peppermint-Stick Snowballs with
    Fudge Sauce
Four Seasons Cappuccino Soufflé
Ecole Cordon Bleu Chestnut Cream Tart

Vermont Cheese Soup, Park Avenue

SERVES 4

A creation of Restaurant Associates' head chef Albert Stockli for the menu of The Four Seasons, which in 1965 Vincent Price called "the one restaurant that epitomizes New York today . . . sophisticated, urbane, expensive." The soup, however, is none of these things. It is rib-sticking food with rustic charm—a reflection of Stockli's culinary beginnings in Switzerland. Price was so in awe of the great chef's imagination he once called him the "Luther Burbank of the kitchen."

3 cups chicken broth
1 leek, chopped (white part only)
1 celery rib, chopped
½ medium onion, chopped
2 tablespoons cornstarch
2 tablespoons cold water
1 cup shredded sharp Vermont Cheddar cheese
⅛ teaspoon ground white pepper
⅛ teaspoon grated nutmeg
Salt
1 egg yolk
½ cup heavy cream
¼ cup dry white wine

Combine the chicken broth, leek, celery, and onion in a saucepan. Bring to a boil, reduce heat, and simmer, covered, 45 minutes. Strain into a clean saucepan.

Mix the cornstarch with the cold water to form a paste. Stir the paste into the soup and cook until the soup is slightly thickened. Add cheese. Cook, stirring, until cheese melts. Add pepper, nutmeg, and salt to taste. Lower heat.

Beat the egg yolk with cream. Stir in ½ cup of the hot soup to warm the egg mixture, then beat the egg mixture into the soup very rapidly. Cook 2 minutes, but do not boil. Add wine and serve.

As a young man Albert Stockli had served as a chef on fishing boats in the South Pacific. In the 1950s, he and James Beard worked together to create a menu for Restaurant Associates' Hawaiian Room restaurant, which *Gourmet* called "fun, exotic, and really delicious." Formerly a typical ersatz Polynesian restaurant, the modernized Hawaiian Room offered many authentic or at least truly novel Asian and South Pacific dishes, including mustard greens soup, elaborate curries, flaming goat meat on swords, and Polynesian broiled shrimp. At the end of the decade, as Stockli, Beard, et al., worked to create a bountiful menu for what was to become the R.A. flagship, The Four Seasons, Stockli devised the vaguely oriental sweet and hot combination of crisply fried shrimp with mustard-spiced fruit. It is now a gourmet classic; and the reputation of Stonehenge, a country inn in Ridgefield, Connecticut, that Stockli himself once operated, is based to a large degree on this one dish (as well as trout from a trout pond and the fact that Liz Taylor and Mike Todd honeymooned there in the 1950s).

Albert Stockli's Crisped Shrimp with Mustard Fruit Sauce

SERVES 4 AS A
MAIN COURSE,
8 AS AN HORS D'OEUVRE

1 pint assorted apricots, pears, cherries, tangerines, peaches, plums preserved in heavy syrup
2 tablespoons Dijon mustard
2 tablespoons butter
3 tablespoons flour
1 cup hot milk
1 cup heavy cream
1 teaspoon salt
1½ cups flour, plus flour for coating shrimp
1½ teaspoons baking powder
2 eggs, beaten
1 cup milk
16 jumbo shrimp or prawns in shells
1 tablespoon lemon juice
Vegetable oil for cooking

To make sauce: Combine the fruits in their syrup with 1 tablespoon of the mustard. Let stand overnight. Drain fruits and chop them very fine, almost to a paste, reserving syrup. There should be about 1½ cups of fruit.

In a saucepan, melt the butter. Gradually stir in the flour and continue cooking until mixture begins to bubble. Remove from heat and stir in hot milk. Return to

continued

heat and stir vigorously 1 minute, until smooth, thick, and bubbly. Cover. Cook on very low heat 3 minutes, stirring often. Stir in cream, the remaining tablespoon of Dijon mustard, ½ teaspoon salt, ¾ cup of the chopped fruit, and enough of the reserved syrup to make a smooth sauce. Keep warm.

To make batter: Sift and measure flour, baking powder, and ½ teaspoon salt. Combine 2 eggs and milk. Add to dry ingredients and whisk to make a thick batter. Strain if lumpy.

To make shrimp: Poach shrimp with lemon juice in barely simmering (but not boiling) salted water for 5 minutes, until just cooked. Drain and remove shells, leaving tails intact. Deeply slit them down the back and remove the vein. Stuff them with the remaining ¾ cup of chopped fruit, about 2 teaspoons per shrimp. Set aside.

Heat oil in a deep skillet or deep fryer to 370 degrees.

Roll stuffed shrimp in flour. Dip each in batter, then use tongs to put them in the oil, a few at a time so as not to crowd them. Fry until golden brown and crisp, 3 to 4 minutes. Drain on paper towels and serve hot with mustard fruit sauce and additional Dijon mustard, if desired.

The Forum of the Twelve Caesars found ways to make even boiled eggs seem imperial. The strategy at work in this dish, named after the Roman Marcus Licinus Crassus (who was richer even than the Greek Croesus, and whose severed head was filled with molten gold by the Syrians who killed him in 53 B.C.) is that it is called *eggs*, and it is eggs that you see when it arrives at the table, but underneath the eggs is a lode of the ambrosial flavor combo that once symbolized the height of gourmet eating: lobster meat, butter, and sherry. If you are not a restaurant, we recommend making the preparation of this dish a group effort, with one person in charge of the lobster sauce and another (or two) doing the eggs: It involves a lot of delicate work that is simply too much for one cook preparing what are supposed to be merely a warm hors d'oeuvre. At the Forum, these eggs were served *after* cold hors d'oeuvre and *before* "Roman Ramekins" of truffled cream and mousse of pike, the whole fresh truffle (roasted in ashes), and the *plats principals* that followed.

9 eggs
3 tablespoons butter
½ pound lobster meat, chopped very fine
2 tablespoons sherry
½ cup tomato purée
1½ teaspoons paprika
Salt and pepper
Oil for frying
¾ cup plain bread crumbs
6 pieces of crustless white toast

Place 8 of the eggs in cold water in a saucepan and bring the water to a boil. Boil the eggs precisely 3½ minutes, then run them under cool water until they are cold. Gently crack each egg all around and very carefully peel away the shell—the yolk will still be runny inside and the white will be very fragile. (You need only 6 eggs for this recipe, but the 2 spares are insurance against peeling mishaps.) Set the eggs aside while you make the lobster sauce.

In the butter, sauté the lobster meat with sherry, tomato purée, paprika, and salt to taste for 2 minutes. Remove from heat.

continued

Heat 1 inch of oil in a deep skillet to 360 degrees.

Season the bread crumbs with salt and pepper. Beat the 1 remaining egg. Dip each boiled egg in the seasoned crumbs, then into the beaten egg, then in the seasoned crumbs again. Use a slotted spoon to ease the eggs into the hot oil. Boil each about 1 minute, turning once gently, until barely crisp all around. Carefully remove the eggs with a slotted spoon to a paper towel.

To assemble the dish, cover each piece of toast with warm lobster sauce and put a single golden egg on top.

CAUTION: For the proper effect, the eggs in this dish must be soft boiled. Runny yolks, alas, aren't cooked enough to eradicate the possibility of salmonella; however neither can we recommend using hard-boiled eggs, which make the little effigies of Crassus's head appear to be stuffed with egg salad rather than molten gold.

*I*n the late 1970s a television mini-series called "The Moneychangers" featured Lorne Greene playing a millionaire. In one of his first scenes, viewers see him at lunch as he muses out loud, "Which shall I have today, Caesar salad or chef's salad?" That line was all that was needed to make sure the audience knew he was rich. As much as champagne and caviar, these two salads signify the high life because each in its own way is lavish enough to be a main course. At its worst, chef's salad is nothing more than cold cuts on top of lettuce, smothered in Thousand Island dressing. At its best, as it has been for many summers in the Four Seasons' Bar Room, it is a distinguished warm-weather meal, needing only a chewy crusted loaf of bread on the side and a bowl of fresh berries to follow. The unusual and truly luxurious tuna-flavored dressing, which was revealed in *The Four Seasons* cookbook, is good for just about any cool salad of vegetables or greens. These measurements yield about 1½ cups—enough for this salad, with a bit left over for tomorrow's.

DRESSING

> 4 egg yolks
> 1½ tablespoons Dijon mustard
> ¾ tablespoon tarragon vinegar
> 1½ teaspoons kosher salt
> ½ teaspoon freshly ground pepper
> 1 cup olive oil
> 1 can (3¼ ounces) oil-packed albacore tuna (reserve oil)
> ½ cup sour cream
> 2 teaspoons lemon juice

Bar Room Chef's Salad

SERVES 6

continued

SALAD

2 carrots, peeled and julienned
1 zucchini, seeds discarded, julienned
3 celery ribs, julienned
1 red pepper, peeled and julienned
1 green pepper, peeled and julienned
1 piece of daikon radish, about 6 inches long,
   peeled and julienned
1 cup coarsely chopped cabbage, red and/or white
12 ounces boiled ham, julienned
12 romaine lettuce leaves
Small bunches of arugula, watercress, dandelion,
   and mâche
12 ounces mortadella, julienned
2 tablespoons freshly grated Parmesan cheese
12 thin slices of Genoa salami
3 pimientos, quartered
18 niçoise olives

To make the dressing, combine the egg yolks with mustard, vinegar, salt, and pepper. Beat until thick and creamy (or use a blender). Add olive oil in a slow stream, beating (or blending) until well blended. Stir in oil from tuna, sour cream, and lemon juice. Chop tuna well and fold in.

To arrange the salad, mix together carrots, zucchini, celery, peppers, radish, cabbage, and ham. Add enough of the dressing to thoroughly coat these ingredients and toss them lightly.

Arrange lettuce leaves on a large serving dish. Place dressed vegetables in the center of the dish and decorate the sides with small bunches of arugula and other greens. Scatter mortadella over the vegetables. Sprinkle with Parmesan cheese.

Fold Genoa salami in half, then quarters. Open up each folded piece so three layers are on the bottom and one on top. Use these to garnish the platter, along with pimientos and olives.

NOTE: This Four Seasons recipe is from the days when eating raw eggs was considered safe. Now it is not; and there is really no way to make the dressing—actually a glorified mayonnaise—without raw yolks. Hence, although it is utterly delicious, we are duty-bound to present it here only as a historical artifact.

Between courses of a long and elaborate feast, gourmets customarily paused to refresh their palates. A soupçon of cool, faintly sweetened sorbet was the traditional restorative; but alas, many continental restaurants with aspirations to be grand didn't quite understand how important it was to serve something subtle. And so they interrupted meals with bowls of cloddish sherbet in pastels bright and sweet as candy Chuckles. We remember looking forward to an entrée of surf 'n' turf in one such establishment in Philadelphia in the early seventies; but before it arrived, we were presented with a great, frozen heap of rainbow sherbet that lacked only hot fudge, whipped cream, and a cherry on top. When we asked, "What's this?" the waiter instructed us, "For cleaning up your palate!" And since that day, we have been leery of any midmeal sorbet. One place where we are happy to make an exception is The Four Seasons, where they understand exactly what a midmeal bracer ought to be: barely frozen ice, hardly sweet, with a zest that reawakens tastebuds. Their recipe for clove sorbet is best when prepared a day ahead and frozen (in an ice cream machine) just before a meal. That way it can be served chilled, but not solid, so it melts into an icy liquid as soon as it hits the tongue.

Clove Sorbet

SERVES 8 (ABOUT 4 CUPS)

- 1 cup sugar
- 3 cups water
- ⅓ cup whole cloves
- 1 cup dry white wine
- 2 tablespoons lemon juice

In a saucepan, stir together sugar and 2 cups of the water. Bring to a boil and boil 5 minutes. Cool completely. This is the simple syrup and can be made days in advance.

Place the cloves and the remaining cup of water in a pot. Bring to a boil and cook 2 minutes. Let cool overnight. Strain and discard cloves.

Combine clove water with cooled simple syrup, wine, and lemon juice. Pour into an ice cream freezer and freeze according to directions.

Poularde Pavillon

SERVES 3 TO 4

*M*any of the dishes by which customers knew the Pavillon were not at all fancy. Monsieur Soulé, *le patron*, made a glorious peasant beef stew; and one of his personal favorite dishes was sautéed baked potatoes—hot spuds scooped out of their skins, mashed into a pulp with butter, then flattened in a skillet with more butter and fried. Those who knew him well frequently told stories about his favorite summertime snack—hot dogs from a roadside stand near his country home. This famous Pavillon recipe for chicken in champagne sauce isn't exactly peasant food, but it is simplicity itself. Aspiring swank restaurants prepared their own imitation of Poularde Pavillon, offering customers much pomp and circumstance as the captain carved it and waiters bustled about making the champagne sauce; but at the Pavillon, nearly all the work was done in the kitchen, and the rolling carts were used mostly to finish dishes and to dramatically add butter to the *purée de pommes de terre* that frequently accompanied the chicken. Joseph Wechsberg reported that Soulé's *chef de cuisine*, Clement Grangier, was known to mutter, "Some people who order this dish never drank such a wine" while pouring vintage champagne into one of his distinguished sauces.

1 roasting chicken 3 to 4 pounds, at room temperature and patted dry
3 tablespoons butter, softened
½ teaspoon salt
1½ cups dry French champagne
2 cups heavy cream
2 tablespoons finely chopped shallots
2 tablespoons minced mushrooms
1 parsley sprig, chopped
1 bay leaf
Pinch of dried thyme

Preheat oven to 350 degrees.

Rub 1 tablespoon of butter inside the chicken and under its skin. Rub 1 more tablespoon of butter on the outside of the bird and sprinkle with salt. Place in a small 2-quart casserole with 1 cup of the champagne. Roast 45 minutes, basting every 8 minutes and turning the chicken until it is an even golden brown on all sides. Remove the chicken and keep it warm on a hot plate as you prepare the sauce.

Degrease the juices, then add cream, shallots, mushrooms, parsley, bay leaf, and thyme. Simmer over medium heat on top of the stove, stirring frequently, until sauce has reduced by a third, about 10 minutes. Strain into a clean saucepan. Place over medium heat and add remaining 1 tablespoon butter and the remaining ½ cup champagne. Spoon sauce over chicken when serving.

West Side Poitrine de Volaille à l'Estragon

SERVES 6

*L*ucky New Yorkers (and knowledgeable tourists) who wanted to explore French cuisine had their choice: the exalted haute establishments of the East Side such as Le Pavillon and Baroque, or a whole community of informal bistros on the West Side in the Forties and Fifties between Seventh and Ninth Avenues. These little places were treasured by aficionados of real French food; and to this day their names evoke the inexpensive neighborhood delights that made New York's reputation as an eater's paradise: Café Brittany and Brittany du Soir, Pierre au Tunnel, René Pujol, A La Fourchette. *All Around the Town*, a "New York Cookbook" written in 1972 by Ceil Dyer and Rosalind Cole, advised readers, "There, in small, unpretentious, intimate settings where the chefs, barmen, waiters and waitresses keep up a mellifluous chatter in French, the food is always good and often exceptional, the prices are sensible, and the ambience is the next best thing to a trip to France." *All Around the Town* got this recipe for scrumptious

chicken rolls from Theo and Yvette Le Guelaff of Chez Napoleon on West Fiftieth Street, where "the cuisine is country French but with a highly personal touch."

6 chicken breasts, split, boned, and skinned
5 tablespoons butter
6 tablespoons chopped shallots
6 chicken livers, chopped
3 tablespoons flour
1 egg, lightly beaten
½ cup fresh bread crumbs
½ cup dry white wine
2 teaspoons chopped fresh tarragon
1 cup brown sauce (page 27)

Pound chicken breasts evenly flat, between 2 sheets of wax paper.

Heat 3 tablespoons of the butter in a heavy sauté pan and sauté the shallots and chicken livers until tender. Divide the liver-shallot mixture among the chicken breasts and roll them up around the mixture, jelly-roll fashion. Dip the rolled breasts first in flour, then in beaten egg, then in bread crumbs. Place them on a flat dish and refrigerate until ready to cook.

Preheat oven to 400 degrees.

Place breasts in a deep ovenproof casserole. Melt the remaining 2 tablespoons of butter and pour it over the chicken rolls. Brown the rolls in the oven, about 15 minutes.

Combine white wine, tarragon, and brown sauce in a saucepan. Cook over medium heat until reduced by a third, about 10 minutes. Pour over browned chicken rolls. Cover rolls and bake 15 to 20 minutes, or until chicken is tender, basting occasionally.

Original Chicken Cordon Bleu

SERVES 4

*V*eal, chicken, or even occasionally beef or turkey cordon bleu seemed to have special appeal to many American gourmets in search of continental sophistication because it was boneless (hence easy to eat), fried (like chicken or chicken-fried steak), topped with cheese like a cheeseburger (but of course, ever-so-much classier), and frequently smothered in creamy, wine-laced gravy. It became an especially favored dish among restaurateurs because although the first steps in its preparation involve some work, nearly everything can be done well in advance, leaving the dinnertime kitchen staff with nothing to do but heat it up, sauce it, and arrange it on a plate. By the mid-1960s, food processing companies were selling already-made and precooked cordon bleu entrées to restaurants, thus eliminating the need for any work at all.

4 large boned and skinned chicken breast halves (about 1½ pounds)
2 ounces thinly sliced smoked ham
2 ounces Swiss cheese, cut into 4 equal "fingers"
¼ cup flour
½ teaspoon salt
¼ teaspoon pepper
1 egg, beaten
¾ cup fresh bread crumbs
2 tablespoons butter
1 tablespoon vegetable oil
¼ cup chicken stock
½ cup white wine, heavy cream, or additional chicken stock

Lay the chicken breasts between pieces of wax paper and use a mallet to pound them to between ¼- and ⅛-inch thickness. Take care not to pound holes in the chicken.

Layer each breast with the ham, then place a finger of cheese in the center. Roll up to completely enclose the ham and cheese. Chicken may adhere to itself but if not, secure it with toothpicks.

Lightly dredge the chicken in seasoned flour, then dip in egg, then coat with bread crumbs. Place on a baking sheet and chill at least 15 minutes, or up to 4 hours.

Heat the butter and oil in a large skillet and sauté the chicken over medium-high heat until browned, about 10 minutes, turning carefully with tongs or a spatula.

Add 2 tablespoons of the chicken stock to the skillet, cover and simmer 10 to 15 minutes, until chicken is cooked through. Carefully remove chicken to a warm platter.

Add the remaining stock to the skillet and cook 1 minute, stirring up browned bits clinging to the bottom. Add wine (or heavy cream or additional stock, depending on what kind of sauce you want) and simmer 3 to 4 minutes, until reduced by about one quarter. Pour over the chicken breasts and serve.

Duck à l'Orange Treadway

SERVES 3 TO 4

*O*pened in 1957 and overlooking the Niagara River, the Treadway Inn of Niagara Falls, New York, featured a bar with airline posters from around the world and a dining room with an open kitchen that provided customers with a view of the chefs grilling steaks to order. House specialties included old-fashioned down-east lobster pie, newfangled baked shrimp stuffed with cheesy bread crumbs and—yes—pulverized potato chips, and, for sophisticates, duck à l'orange. Like quiche, duck à l'orange has paid a terrible price for its overpopularity at the height of the gourmet revolution, when it was a staple in every motel dining room with delusions of grandeur. Now considered vulgar and hopelessly out of fashion, it fell from grace not so much because of overexposure, as was the case with quiche, but because it was so often badly made: duck that was either flabby or charred, cloyed with sticky sweet jelly. But it doesn't have to be that way. Cooked to a turn (neither burnt black nor still pink) and sauced with plenty of Grand Marnier rather than orange soda pop (as in the original recipe we adapted from the *Treadway Inns Cookbook*, 1958), duck à l'orange deserves a second chance.

1 duck, 5 to 6 pounds
Salt and pepper
2 oranges
1 small onion, peeled
1 garlic clove, crushed
1 tablespoon butter
½ cup dry white wine
⅓ cup orange marmalade
2 teaspoons potato flour
1½ cups orange juice
½ cup Grand Marnier
1 tablespoon red currant jelly

Preheat oven to 375 degrees.

Season duck lightly with salt and pepper. Stuff it with 1 quartered orange, the onion, the garlic clove, and butter. Place it on its back on a roasting rack in a large shallow pan with the wine. Roast 2 hours and 15 minutes, basting every 20 minutes. As you baste, you may need to add more wine to the pan to keep at least 1/4 inch of liquid. After roasting 40 minutes, turn the duck on its breast, lifting with wooden spoons (do not pierce skin!). After 20 minutes more, turn the duck on its back again. After 2 hours, spread the duck's breast with marmalade. When done, remove to a warm platter and discard orange and onion stuffing.

As duck cooks, peel only the orange zest (no bitter pith) from the remaining orange and cut into small julienne strips.

Pour off all but 2 to 3 tablespoons of liquid in the roasting pan. Blend potato flour into pan juices. Pour in orange juice and Grand Marnier. Bring to a boil, stirring constantly. Add jelly and julienned orange strips. Simmer 3 to 4 minutes longer. Spoon a little of the sauce over each serving of duck and serve the rest in a gravy boat.

Pausing for lunch at one of the many quaint cafes along the boulevards of the world.

Baked Stuffed Shrimp, Surf 'n' Turf Style

SERVES 4 TO 6

*N*ext to the tails of spiny lobsters (a.k.a. "rock lobsters"), baked stuffed shrimp are the most common companion for filet mignon on plates of surf 'n' turf; and in some ways, they fill the bill even better than the big clumps of lobster meat found in grocers' freezers. Jumbo shrimp are eager to be butterflied and plied with all manner of edible enrichment, from (at their worst) soggy bread crumbs to this high-priced shrimp paste, as they used to serve at "The Restaurant in the Sky" at the Holiday Inn of Yonkers, New York. The gastronomic motto of the motel, as revealed in *Cooking the Holiday Inn Way (4th Edition)* in 1962, was "From 'Coffee and' to Coq au Vin."

3/4 pound raw medium shrimp
1/2 cup flour
1/2 cup bread crumbs
1 egg
1/4 cup minced shallots
1/4 cup white wine
1 garlic clove, minced
24 jumbo shrimp
2 tablespoons butter, melted

SAUCE

8 tablespoons (1 stick) butter
1/2 cup chopped shallots
1 tablespoon chopped parsley
1/2 cup dry white wine
1 garlic clove, chopped fine

Shell and devein the medium shrimp. Chop them very fine and combine with flour, bread crumbs, egg, minced shallots, 1/4 cup white wine, and minced garlic clove to make a paste.

Preheat oven to 350 degrees.

Clean and devein jumbo shrimp, then butterfly and stuff them with shrimp paste. Place them in a baking pan and drizzle with melted butter. Bake 25 minutes.

As shrimp bake, prepare sauce by melting the butter in a saucepan. When it begins to brown, add shallots and parsley, then wine and garlic. Bring to a simmer and drizzle over cooked shrimp.

Nothing was served unadorned at the Forum of the Twelve Caesars. What appeared to be an ordinarily sumptuous ¾-pound cylinder of filet mignon revealed its trove of treasure as soon as the customer's oversize knife glided through the crust and into the pillowy fibers of the meat: pâté de foie gras, packed inside the luscious flesh, warm and oozing among the juices.

Filet Mignon Caesar Augustus

SERVES 4

> 4 fillets of beef, 12 ounces each
> 4 ounces canned pâté de foie gras
> 2 tablespoons butter, melted
> Salt and pepper to taste
> Watercress as garnish

Press a 2-inch round cookie cutter into the top of each fillet, cutting about halfway through. Use a sharp pointed knife to excise the circle made by the cookie cutter, then use the knife to shave away a bit of the meat from the bottom of the plug. In the indentation in the steak place 1 ounce of pâté and cover it with the cut-out piece of meat. Brush each steak all around with melted butter and sprinkle with a generous grind of pepper.

Place the steaks under a broiler with the cut-out side down first, cooking just long enough to sear the bottom of the steaks, 1 to 2 minutes (you don't want the pâté leaking out). Turn the steaks and continue broiling until cooked to taste.

Season with salt to taste and serve garnished with watercress.

Beef Stroganoff Imperiale

SERVES 4 TO 6

Like coq au vin and boeuf bourguignonne, beef stroganoff was the gourmet's antidote to the stark dryness of many traditional American specialties (fried chicken, grilled steak, baked ham). Epicures, so this logic goes, want their food to be juicy and luscious, the meat cosseted in a rich gravy and accompanied by bouquets of vegetables and fulminations of spice. How much more sensuous it was to slurp a high-spirited stew than to saw at a sauceless, and hence puritanical, piece of meat! Nearly every significant "continental" dish provides the eater with plenty of gravy, melted cheese, and other moist adornments that are generally thought to separate epicurean from plebeian food. Of all the sloppy dishes favored by connoisseurs of continental cuisine, beef stroganoff was one of the most elegant, for the simple reason that sour cream makes everything seem deluxe. Another reason for beef stroganoff's popularity—at home as well in continental restaurants—is that it is so easy to make. The easiest recipes simply sauté slices of filet mignon, then mix sour cream with pan juices; this version, adapted from *The Playboy Gourmet*, creates a genial stew that is somewhat less elegant, but all the more cozy for a winter's eve.

¼ cup vegetable oil
2 pounds lean top sirloin, cut into 1-inch squares,
    ¼ inch thick
½ pound fresh mushrooms, washed and sliced
¼ cup minced onion
1 garlic clove, minced
½ teaspoon dried chervil
3 tablespoons flour
2 cups beef broth
2 tablespoons minced parsley
2 tablespoons tomato paste
1½ cups sour cream
Salt and pepper

Heat the oil in a stew pot and add the beef. Sauté over medium heat until browned. Add mushrooms, onion, garlic, and chervil and sauté until onion is limp. Sprinkle flour onto the beef, stirring well as you sprinkle it on. Stir in beef broth. Add parsley. Partially cover and simmer 2 hours, stirring occasionally. Stir in tomato paste. Remove from heat and add sour cream. Season to taste. Stroganoff may be chilled and reheated, but do not boil after adding sour cream. Serve over buttered noodles.

Beef Wellington to Impress All Who Dine

SERVES 6

arian Burros of *The New York Times* once wrote, "It took years of trying various recipes before I came to the conclusion that a rare fillet of beef and a flaky pastry are mutually exclusive." It might be true that Platonic beef Wellington—beef rosy pink, pastry flawlessly crusty—is an impossibility for all but master chefs and those armed with beet juice to make gray meat blush again; but that didn't stop gourmets from ordering it in restaurants and cooking and serving it at home, and actually enjoying it. Yes, the meat inside the crust can turn flaccid when it cooks its second time; and the cloak of dough almost always starts getting soft at the bottom even before you have a chance to slice it, and individual servings, with their torn crust and messy duxelles (or in the case of this recipe, faux-duxelles) are seldom picture-perfect. So, why be finicky? That's just the way beef Wellington is: a melt-in-the-mouth, lardaceous dish that is rich beyond reason and the height of sybaritism. For true sophisticates, its plushness was a curse, the curse of excess; but for novitiates to gourmet foodways, nothing was as symbolic an expression of food at its most deluxe. In 1965, *Gourmet* offered an extensive ode to all meats cooked inside pastry, rejoicing that "some of the most exquisite of man's creations have modestly hid beneath a crust." *Modest* is a word we would never apply to this recipe, based on *Gourmet*'s.

1 fillet of beef, 4 to 4½ pounds, well trimmed of fat
4 tablespoons butter, 2 of them melted
4 chicken livers, trimmed and chopped fine
½ pound mushrooms, cleaned and finely chopped
  (2 heaping cups)
¼ pound cooked ham, finely chopped (1 cup)
1 garlic clove, minced
1 tablespoon tomato purée
2 tablespoons sherry
3 truffles, finely chopped (optional, for rich people)
Puff pastry to wrap fillet (you can make your own or
  buy ready-made, frozen puff pastry)

Preheat oven to 500 degrees.

Roast the beef on a rack 10 minutes. Remove from oven and allow to cool. Reduce oven temperature to 375 degrees.

In the butter, sauté the chicken livers about 1 minute. Add mushrooms, ham, garlic, tomato purée, sherry, and optional truffles and cook over high heat, stirring almost constantly, until all the liquid evaporates, about 10 minutes.

On a lightly floured board, roll out 1 sheet of puff pastry large enough to encase the fillet. The pastry should be thin but not transparent, and there mustn't be any holes in it. Lay the beef in the center of the pastry and pile the mushroom mixture on and around it. Carefully wrap the fillet in the pastry, turning in the ends and pressing all the seams together firmly. Use one or two spatulas to gently ease the fillet onto a baking sheet, seam side down, taking care not to tear the wrapping. If desired, use additional puff pastry and cut decorative shapes (leaves, fleur-de-lis, crescents) and form them into swags on the dough. Brush the dough with melted butter. Bake 20 minutes, then raise the oven temperature to 450 and bake 7 to 10 minutes more, or until the pastry is nicely browned.

Use a sharp serrated knife to cut slices about 1 inch thick, trying to keep the crust intact.

Steak Diane

SERVES 4

For converts to the gourmet way of eating, who formerly thought of steak and potatoes as just about the greatest meal on earth, most continental restaurants offered a few handy ways to ease into a regime of fancy food without abandoning familiar cuts of red meat. There was surf 'n' turf, where at least you got a queen-size piece of beef; and chateaubriand for two with sauce béarnaise and vegetables bouquetière; there was steak *au poivre*, which had a French name and an abundance of pepper pressed into its crust, but was nonetheless meat and plenty of it; and there was steak Diane, a hammered slab of beef that was flamed in Cognac. Once considered a restaurant captain's tour de force requiring a big chafing dish and some pyrotechnical skill, steak Diane became a workable show-off dish for home cooks with an electric frying pan (providing everybody likes their steak rare: well-done Diane is a mistake). Because the beef ought to be cooked in a skillet that is extremely hot, the Cognac flames eagerly and abundantly. This recipe is based on steak Diane as served at Proof of the Pudding, a New York restaurant at the epicenter of the swinging singles scene (Sixty-fourth Street and First Avenue) that promised to "seduce you for dinner." It serves four, but you need a very large skillet to cook all four steaks at one time; anyway, this dish is best enjoyed by a cozy twosome. For two, simply cut the recipe in half—except for the Cognac, which should be ½ cup in either case, for the flames' sake.

> 4 boneless strip steaks, 5 to 6 ounces each
> 4 tablespoons prepared Dijon mustard
> 4 tablespoons clarified butter
> ¼ cup chopped shallots
> ¼ cup chopped parsley
> ½ cup warmed Cognac

Trim the steaks of fat and pound them to about ½ inch thick. Brush them with mustard on both sides. Heat the butter in a skillet over high heat. Sauté the steaks 20 to 30 seconds, flip, and add shallots and parsley. Sauté another 30 seconds or so, or longer if you insist on steaks cooked more than rare. Add Cognac and ignite. When flame dies, remove the steaks to a serving plate. Simmer sauce a few seconds and spoon over steaks.

$\mathcal{V}$incent Price got this recipe from Henri Soulé of the Pavillon. It is another of the great chef's dishes that is the soul of simplicity. But Price warned: "You *must* use Idaho potatoes, *break* them in half when they are baked [no slicing with a knife], use good butter and lots of it, sauté extremely slowly—in short, follow the directions to the letter. No improvising." The following recipe is for one serving. Multiply as needed, but it is best to make individual potato cakes. Bigger ones are hard to flip when sautéed in the skillet.

Pomme de Terre Macaire

SERVES 1

1 large Idaho potato
2 to 4 tablespoons butter
Salt and pepper

Preheat oven to 375 degrees.

Bake the potato 1 hour, or until soft inside. Remove from the oven and, when cool enough to handle, break it in half and scoop out the pulp with a fork. Into the pulp mash 1 tablespoon of the butter and salt and pepper to taste. Mash until smooth.

In a heavy skillet (nonstick preferred) over low heat, melt 1 tablespoon of butter. Place potato pulp in the skillet and spread it out with the back of a spoon into a cake about 1 inch thick. Sauté very, very slowly, adding butter if needed, until potato cake is golden brown on both sides.

Sauerkraut with Champagne

SERVES 10

*I*n keeping with the restaurant's seasonal theme and menu, the original *Four Seasons Cookbook* (1971) divided its recipes into seasons. In the autumn, when "aromatic fruits and vegetables of fall are metamorphosed," apples, game, nuts, and cabbages were featured, including this typically unlikely—but typically sensational—combination of high and low ingredients. The recipe makes a lot and can be cut in half; but leftover sauerkraut will keep well for several days in the refrigerator.

> 2 pounds fresh sauerkraut
> ½ pound of salt pork
> 1 large onion, chopped
> 1 cup champagne
> 1 tablespoon sugar
> 1 teaspoon white pepper

Wash the sauerkraut in cold water and squeeze it dry in a towel.

Place the salt pork in a saucepan and heat it long enough to render 2 tablespoons of fat. Remove the salt pork and reserve. To the melted fat, add onion and stir long enough for it to soften but not brown, about 5 minutes. Spread onion evenly over the bottom of the pan and place the solid piece of salt pork on top. Add sauerkraut, champagne, and enough water to cover the kraut by ½ inch. Add sugar and pepper. Stir gently. Cover and cook over low heat 1 hour. Remove salt pork before serving.

During World War II ice cream became the symbolic all-American dessert, especially prized by boys in uniform whenever they could get it. Until the creation of premium gourmet ice creams in the 1970s and 1980s, it remained an ingenuous kind of food—except when it was made into snowballs. Snowballs—a kind of lowbrow baked Alaska—magically transformed ice cream into something extraordinary; and while they were never embraced by true epicures (who were busy eating cheese and fruit at dessert, for heaven's sake!), snowballs appeared on the menu of many a continental restaurant. This recipe was a favorite at Treadway Inns since the 1950s, when they began adding continental items to the traditional dessert menu of such Yankee standards as Indian pudding and blueberry grunt. If you cannot find peppermint-stick ice cream, it is possible to improvise by crushing Starlight mints and folding them into softened vanilla, or you can simply roll the ice cream balls in the crushed mints along with the coconut.

Peppermint-Stick Snowballs with Fudge Sauce

SERVES 4

> 1 pint firm peppermint-stick ice cream
> 1½ cups shredded coconut
> 2 ounces unsweetened chocolate
> ¾ cup sugar
> ½ teaspoon salt
> ½ cup milk
> ½ cup white corn syrup
> 2 tablespoons butter
> 2 teaspoons vanilla extract

Use an ice cream scoop to fashion spheres of the ice cream. Place them in the freezer 30 minutes so they are firm, then roll them in coconut and return them to the freezer as you make fudge sauce.

Combine chocolate, sugar, salt, and milk in a heavy-bottomed saucepan over low heat. Cook and stir almost constantly as the chocolate melts. Add corn syrup. Cook 15 minutes over low heat, stirring frequently until medium-thick and silk smooth. Remove from the heat and stir in butter, then vanilla. Serve slightly warm over each snowball, or pour some into each dish and put a snowball on top.

Four Seasons Cappuccino Soufflé

SERVES 6

James Beard once gleefully recalled that when he helped Restaurant Associates open The Four Seasons in New York in 1959 and they found themselves with a soufflé oven but no experienced chef to make the soufflés, they recruited an unskilled boy from the bake shop, who was soon making several hundred a day. "It worked because he wasn't afraid," Beard explained. "The only thing that will make a soufflé fall is if it knows you are afraid of it. There is no mystery to cooking." Of all the soufflés for which The Four Seasons has been famous over the years, the best-known ones are those with a coffee flavor, in this case cappuccino—"the most glorious version we know of a coffee to end a meal," according to Tom Margittai and Paul Kovi, authors of *The Four Seasons* cookbook, from which this recipe is adapted.

4½ tablespoons butter
4½ tablespoons flour
1 tablespoon plus 2 teaspoons instant espresso coffee
1½ cups scalded milk
6 egg yolks
⅓ cup plus ¼ cup coffee liqueur
1 teaspoon ground cinnamon
8 egg whites, at room temperature
Pinch of salt
⅓ cup plus ¼ cup granulated sugar
1 cup milk
¼ cup confectioners' sugar

Preheat oven to 400 degrees.

Butter and sugar an 8-cup soufflé dish and fit it with a well-buttered collar of doubled-over heavy-duty aluminum foil that extends about 2 inches above the top of the dish. Secure the overlapping ends of foil with a straight pin and tie it to the dish with string.

Melt the butter in a saucepan over medium-low heat. Stir in flour and cook, stirring constantly, 2 minutes. Do not let the mixture brown.

Add 1 tablespoon of the instant coffee to the scalded milk and stir to dissolve. Stir the milk into the butter and flour mixture and whisk until smooth and thickened.

Remove pan from the heat and quickly beat in 6 of the egg yolks, 1 at a time, beating well after each addition.

Stir in ⅓ cup coffee liqueur and ½ teaspoon ground cinnamon.

In a separate bowl, beat the egg whites with a pinch of salt until frothy. Gradually add ⅓ cup granulated sugar and beat until stiff peaks form.

Fold about one quarter of the beaten egg whites into the base mixture to lighten it. Fold in the remaining egg whites. Spoon into prepared dish. Bake about 40 minutes. The soufflé should still be slightly underdone in its center.

As the soufflé bakes, prepare the sauce by heating 1 cup milk with 2 teaspoons of instant coffee and ¼ cup sugar in a small saucepan over medium heat, stirring until blended. Beat the 2 remaining egg yolks. Remove pan from the heat and stir a little of the hot mixture into the egg yolks to warm them, then stir the warmed yolks back into the milk. Cook over low heat, stirring constantly until mixture thickens. Do not boil. Remove from heat and stir in ¼ cup coffee liqueur.

When the soufflé is done, sprinkle confectioners' sugar and remaining cinnamon over the top through a sieve. Serve immediately with cappuccino sauce.

Ecole Cordon Bleu Chestnut Cream Tart

SERVES 8 TO 10

*T*elevision viewers all across America knew Dione Lucas's Cordon Bleu restaurant at 117 East Sixtieth Street in New York, because its kitchen was her broadcast studio, as well as the place she taught students of her Cordon Bleu Cooking School. The only meal served to the public was lunch—an ever-changing repertoire of the classic recipes she taught students. In the autumn, lucky customers were likely to have a chance to savor Ms. Lucas's renowned tarte aux marrons—a dizzyingly luscious and playfully designed combination of crunchy, featherweight meringue and nutty buttercream.

3 eggs
½ cup superfine sugar
½ teaspoon cream of tartar
Pinch of salt
1¼ cups granulated sugar
¾ cup water
¾ pound (3 sticks) unsalted butter, at room temperature
1 pound unsweetened chestnut purée
3 tablespoons light rum
1 baked pie shell (10 inches)
1 cup heavy cream
3 tablespoons sifted confectioners' sugar
2 inches scraped fresh vanilla bean
1 tablespoon cocoa

Separate the eggs and reserve the yolks.

Beat the whites slowly until soft peaks form.

Sift together the superfine sugar and ¼ teaspoon of the cream of tartar. Add to the egg whites, beating constantly. Beat in salt. Beat until whites are stiff and shiny.

Preheat oven to 275 degrees.

Place whites in a pastry bag with a small plain tube. Place a dab of meringue at each corner of a jelly-roll pan. Cover the pan with wax paper and paste it down at the corners with the meringue. Pipe meringue mixture on top in 16 to 18 small domes with size and shape of halved eggs. Sprinkle their tops with granulated sugar, using about 2 tablespoons altogether.

Bake 30 minutes, until meringues are dry to the touch and just barely colored. Remove from the oven and allow to cool. Remove them with a spatula and store in an airtight tin until ready to make the tart.

In a heavy pan, mix 1 cup of the granulated sugar, water, and remaining ¼ teaspoon cream of tartar. Stir over low heat until sugar dissolves. Cook over medium-high heat until mixture forms a light thread (230 degrees).

Turn mixer on high and begin to beat yolks. Slowly pour sugar mixture over yolks as they are being beaten. Continue beating until mixture is thick and cold, about 5 minutes. Still beating, add butter by tablespoons, then beat in chestnut purée and rum. Place chestnut purée into the pie shell, using a spoon to keep it smooth.

Beat cream with confectioners' sugar and fresh vanilla bean until stiff peaks form. Spread this whipped cream across the top of the chestnut tart. Refrigerate. Dust the meringues with cocoa so they resemble toadstools. Just before serving, place meringues into whipped cream on top of tart. Cut with a serrated knife.

COOK YOUR WAY
TO ROMANCE

Being a gourmet in midcentury America was a way to enrich one's spirit, nourish and nurture one's body, and experience the diversity of human culture on earth. It was also a good way to get a date into bed. Fine food—cooking and eating it, but especially serving it—had sex appeal. As America's gastronomic savvy swelled, culinary sophistication became an ever more attractive trait, conferring great powers of seduction on the gourmet that were explored with glee by arbiters of sexual behavior from *Playboy* and *Cosmopolitan* to Gael Greene ("The Insatiable Critic") and a singular Chef Lou Rand Hogan, whose "complete compendium of campy cuisine and menus for men or what have you" was titled *The Gay Cookbook* and included instructions for compounding aphrodisiacs and a chapter called "What To Do With a Tough Piece of Meat."

No one ever covered the subject of gastronomic seduction as delectably as M.F.K. Fisher, particularly in 1949 in the "B is for Bachelors" part of her *An Alphabet for Gourmets*; but Fisher's writing was not in the form of a seducer's manual or even a cookbook. She simply made it clear that hunger, which inspired eating and cooking, was a desire just like lust. The bachelor's approach to gastronomy, she wrote, is sexual: "They use what tricks they have to make their little banquets, whether intimate or merely convivial, lead as subtly as possible to the hoped-for bedding down." Reading about "the most successful bachelor dinner I was ever plied with," you feel her passion stir and savor the thin strips of veal dipped in an artful mixture of grated parmigiano and bread crumbs, all of which is convincingly sensual; however she never really explains *how to do it*. In contrast, Mimi Sheraton's twenty-three-chapter *Seducer's*

Cookbook of 1962 began with this brazen statement of purpose: "What we are concerned with here is the delectable and subtle art of luring, tempting, enticing, leading someone into going to bed with you in the most delightful way possible"; and Billie Young's *The Naked Chef* (subtitled "An Aphrodisiac Cookbook") said flat-out and uppercase, "SEX BEGINS IN THE KITCHEN. Nourish him on exquisite food and watch him respond with voluptuous delight. . . . Yes! Even remove your clothes . . . serve him his dinner with the velvet euphoria of your nakedness to highlight his sensuality."

Every month *Playboy* featured an article about food or drink that meticulously explained what to serve and how to serve it and also provided enough food lore so that any host could impress guests with his culinary erudition. *The Playboy Gourmet*, a compilation of these articles, mostly from the sixties, described its purpose "to draw women as well as men together warmly, to crack the same bottle, to share the same sumptuous trencher." Studying this massive tome, we are reminded that *Playboy* was a whopping success in the late fifties and sixties, not merely because it ran pictures of naked women and intellectual articles (both of which could be found elsewhere), but because it supplemented the cheesecake and mental gasconade with step-by-step instructions to readers who wanted to live a sophisticated life. "It was fun then to enjoy the fruits of leisure including fine food," wrote Thomas Mario, the magazine's resident gourmet, about the early days of *Playboy*. "It was infinitely more fun, as *Playboy* demonstrated month after month, if you baked your own oysters Rockefeller, grilled your own thick shell steaks, and set your own *crêpes* ablaze." Just as men studied *Playboy* to learn how to dress smartly, how to have witty conversations like the ones Hef and his guests enjoyed at *Playboy* mansion parties, and where to go for a swinging vacation, they could also turn to *Playboy* and learn how to cook not mere meals, but "sumptuous repasts" guaranteed to lubricate the social intercourse for a convivial soirée or romantic dinner à deux.

It was still a fairly novel idea that macho men ought to be the ones making dinner. Before the food revolution that began in the 1950s, guys who called themselves gourmets and fussed over what they cooked and ate were likely to arouse suspicions that they were light in the loafers. Traditionally, a man could be a professional *chef* in a restaurant, or a sportsman who knew how to slap the trout he caught into a frying pan with butter, or a Sunday cook who could make pancakes or scrambled eggs, or (especially beginning in the fifties) a patio barbecuist who knew how to roast a mean weenie on the backyard grill: Those were pretty much the limits of a male's expected culinary skills. As for what they ate, the pre-gourmet cliché about guys was that they liked little other than beefsteak and potatoes and apple pie à la mode. Tastes any more varied or sophisticated than that were likely to be considered dangerous signs of dandyism. Back in 1945, *American Cookery* reviewed a book called *200 Dishes for Men to Cook* by Arthur H. Deute with these condescending words: "This is no over-all book. Nine vegetables appear, and only nine (bearing out a popular superstition about the masculine taste), but they are cooked with generous gobs of bacon fat and a lot of imagination, two almost unbeatable ingredients. It's a jolly book, uncomplicated, attractive, and totally innocent of any concern with rationing, dietetics, or anything but a desire to eat well." Twenty-five years later, *The Playboy Gourmet* observed that "Like a beautiful unattached woman, the independent vegetable course serves party purposes magnificently," and went on to eulogize such traditionally derided (by men) vegetables as Brussels sprouts, broccoli, and artichokes. The acclamation included an assurance that artichokes were what made Antony and Cleopatra so hot for each other, and that according to Horace there was once a nymph named Cynara who was so beautiful that an envious god transformed her into an artichoke (hence the globe artichoke's botanical name *Cynara scolymus*). By the sixties, it was actually OK for a red-blooded, masculine American guy to admit that he liked vegetables. To know something about cooking vegetables was a conclusive sign that he was modern and enlightened.

Prior to the gourmet revolution, the idea of a man using food to attract a woman was generally considered a tactic of Lotharios from the Continent, and basically pretty silly (as in television's *"The Continental"*). In

"As your organ of taste begins to be aroused, you must experiment, touch, savor, so that, by trial and error, as you arouse your lover's appetite, you slowly, with a light and gentle hand, bring the feast to its fruition."

—*A Cookbook for Lovers,* 1970

1950, when Niccolò de Quattrociocchi, proprietor of New York's El Borracho restaurant, wrote *Love and Dishes*, he explained that his refined culinary skills were a great assist in his lifetime "pursuit of lovely ladies," and suggested that readers who were also in pursuit of the opposite sex avail themselves of cookery's amorous powers. His restaurant helped diners get in the proper mood by featuring one dining room with walls covered completely by liprouge kisses from a thousand famous beautiful women, each smear captioned with an epigram about love such as "A kiss is worth nothing until it is divided by two." Another El Borracho room was called *La Salle des Amoureux* and had only tables for two. In these dens of passion customers ate expertly prepared continental cuisine, which was frequently rich and exotic: caviar blini; baby pork with bronzed cracklings and wild rice; mousse au chocolat El Borracho. Nikky "Q," as his adoring patrons called him, was dubbed "an incorrigible prankster" by *Gourmet* in a 1947 review: "A handsome and elegant young man, a Palerman nobleman full of laughter and wit . . . who is responsible for all the harmless mischief and unstuffy atmosphere." He got away with his rapturous shenanigans because he cast himself in the role of a Latin lover and played it for laughs, but it is hard to imagine that many American males of 1950

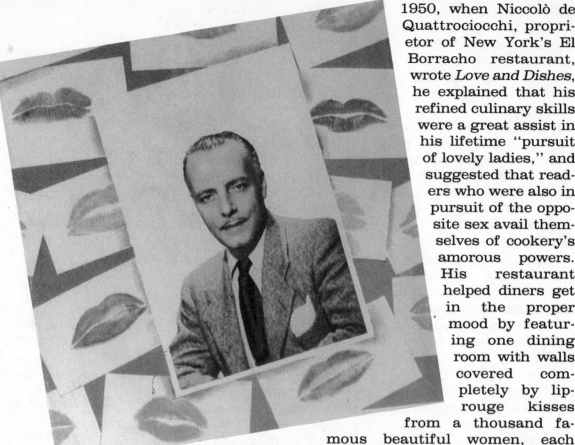

**Niccolò de Quattrociocchi
of El Borracho**

would have been comfortable making such a fuss about kissing, rouged lips, and "la cuisine d'amour."

Fifteen years later, with the gourmet revolution *and* the sexual revolution in full swing, international savoir faire of the sort displayed at El Borracho was no longer a laughable burlesque. Intimate knowledge of fine food had become not only a mark of sophistication, but an indication that a man's (or a woman's), refined sensibilities might extend beyond the dinner table into bed. "There *is* a relationship between food and sex," wrote *Cosmopolitan* editor Helen Gurley Brown. "One appetite can feed the other in a never-ending cycle of sensation. In both, we *need* sustenance, but *crave* enjoyment, too." Anyone who knew how to put a gourmet twist into a meal by cooking something romantic, such as flaming sherried Rock Cornish game hens or sucking on an artichoke leaf with suggestive savoir faire or serving plump strawberries (with stems) sopped in kirsch, was obviously a person who appreciated life's sensuous pleasures, which, by the late 1960s, were *always* thought to include adventurous sex.

Cosmopolitan advised, "Any with-it girl ought to know how to work sensual magic in more than one room of the house." *Playboy*'s treatise on salads encouraged men to elevate their greens consciousness and instead of seeing salads the way many American guys used to see them, as frilly fare for ladies, consider how macho they could be: Sicilian marinated octopus, French ox-mouth salad, Norwegian herring, spuds, apples, veal, and beets. "Now and then one of the newer crop of salad men may hesitate when he looks at some of the foreign salads for the first time," *Playboy* admitted, suggesting it took a real he-man to prepare (or ingest) such strong stuff; but the magazine went on to assure readers that proficiency as a saladier was downright Rabelaisian.

"The serious sensualist must find his own gastronomic style," Gael Greene proclaimed in an article titled "Kneesies at Nedick's and Other Gastronomic Foreplay." Greene, *New York* magazine's restaurant reviewer billed as "the insatiable critic," eagerly blurred the lines among sensual pleasures, writing about food in lascivious terms customarily reserved for descriptions of sex (and later, in her novels, writing about the flavors and aromas of sex as if she were describing hot lunch). For Greene, the very experience of eating in a restaurant became foreplay in her unceasingly libertine life. When she reviewed Chez Vito, she invited readers to "watch how he handles his '59 Richebourg and imagine how, a few hours from now, he will savor the *finesse* of you. Lust is kindled, passions postponed . . . sexual deals are consummated in a ritual *haute* foreplay forever linked to food." The food itself, when it was good, inspired her to multiple gastronomic orgasms. Writing about a meal at the Restaurant de la Pyramide in Vienne, she moaned "I vaguely recall a stirring confrontation with the cheese tray—a creamy St. Marcellin and something chalky and cinder-wrapped, classic manna of a goat. Then an offering of ice cream . . . is it possible we accepted? Were not our senses already seduced by the gâteau marjolaine, an essay in chocolate, four or five layers of absolutely everything you would want to do with that aphrodisiacal bean." And when the food was disappointing, Greene pouted like an unsatisfied lover: "The carry-out hot dog is shriveled, its bun unbuttered and unwarmed . . . the ice cream roster has been pruned to a puny 11 flavors. No buttercrunch!" (about Howard Johnson's).

Gael Greene's frankly erotic culinary sensibilities, which continue unabated in *New York* a quarter-century later, are a good indication of how food appreciation saturated pop culture in the sixties. Joining the ranks of the gourmet life in the Age of Pop did not necessarily require serious study of French monastic cheeses or of subcontinental chutneys; indeed, as a chic lifestyle among the trend-conscious, it seemed to require no hard-learned expertise of any kind, only a willingness to open oneself up to the sensuality of the dining experience. To a large degree in the popular mind, being a gourmet had come to mean little more than someone who relished food and ate plenty of it, i.e. a hedonist. Greene, who was in fact a knowledgeable epicure, wrote about herself not as a cultivated snob but as an ordinary person with ordinary taste ("My respect for the glories of French cuisine is unsurpassed, but I am a fool for junk food.") who was special only because of her unappeasable appetites. As she wrote about it, good eating, like good sex, was at least as much a matter of attitude as of technique. (And for this sacrilege, her writing was roundly condemned by those gourmet martinets, John and Karen Hess, as "East Side porno-chic.")

Greene is a pleasure lover whose equation of food and sex was customarily offered in the form of a review or a gauzy journalistic dalliance at some citadel of epicurean delight. Others who wove food and sex together were considerably more practical, and provided readers with specific advice about using good food to get a man into bed. In the pages of Helen Gurley Brown's *Cosmopolitan* magazine, single girls were told how important it was to know one's way around the kitchen, not for the old-fashioned reason that men are looking for women who will be efficient housekeepers, but because any man will be putty in a girl's hands if she feeds him lobster fra diavolo and peaches in red wine. More specifically, girls who thought of themselves as sophisticated ("they don't wear any underwear at all and own *two* ostrich boas") were advised that "Cooking and eating foreign food is the way to great sensuous pleasure with great sensuous men. Let other girls broil him a steak and slice a few tomatoes. You're out to rapture him with golden chicken paprikash gurgling in its pot and maybe even *capture* him by the time he's through the lemon chiffon crème."

Few people delineated the powers of gourmet cookery to attract the opposite sex with as much rigor as Jinx Kragen and Judy Perry in their book *Saucepans and the*

A Fawcett Crest Book
R1118
60¢
Surefire recipes for the quickest way to a man's heart
Saucepans and the Single Girl
By JINX KRAGEN & JUDY PERRY

Single Girl (1965). The authors were former coeds who discovered after graduation that while "TV dinners or hearty bowls of soup were enough to fill our inner needs, entertaining caused us many a migraine. We had visions of divine BBD&O men and intimate little dinners complete with candlelight and wine, but it wasn't long before we realized that it would take more than a fallen soufflé or a sticky fondue to give us the bravado one needs to entertain with ease and rakish glamour." The clever authors figured out not only how to mix a very dry martini and what to keep on the emergency shelf in an apartment, but exactly which foods please every sort of single man. "For each category of men there is a perfect menu," they observed. For the "Man in the Brooks Brothers Suit" they suggest a sophisticated dinner of fondue, spinach and bacon salad, and strawberries with kirsch. For a "Man's Man (who, they observe, is "something of a vanishing breed") the proper meal is steak with "masculine mushroom sauce," gnocchi à la Romana (or baked potato for the purist), salad, and fudge cake. "Remember, nothing fancy for the man's man!" To single girls faced with the daunting task of feeding a bona fide gourmet, *Saucepans and the Single Girl* suggests a truly classic sumptuous repast: hearts of palm salad, lobster thermidor ("any gourmet worth his chocolate-covered ladybugs dotes on seafood laced with sherry and a subtle cream sauce"), curried rice, and fruit and cheese for dessert, followed, natch, by brandy served in snifters ("from the dime store").

The authors of *Saucepans and the Single Girl*, which was subtitled "The cookbook with all the ingredients for that lighthearted leap from filing cabinet to flambé!" tackle even the most challenging gourmet dishes with can-do panache. If Julia Child cracked open the door for serious, aspiring gourmets, Jinx and Judy flung it wide enough for even the most dunderheaded culinary hopeful to join the fun. To impress someone with "homemade" bread, their recommendation is to "scrounge around the frozen-food department of your local supermarket until you find a loaf of unbaked frozen bread. Take it home and read the directions. Then follow them." To make an "aristocratic pâté that even your haughtiest acquaintances will cherish," they suggest mashing together three cans of liver pâté, cream cheese, onion, walnuts, and lemon juice and frosting it with more cream cheese festooned with pimiento strips and studded with sliced, pitted black olives. To assuage any skepticism that such culinary cunning really works, Ms. Kragen and Ms. Perry assure their readers that "It's easy enough to delude a male Saturday night dinner guest into believing he has discovered a real jewel of a gourmet." (The hard part is pulling the wool over the eyes of a surprise guest, for whom they suggest pauper's pizzas on English muffins or hamburger wiki wiki [with bananas].)

To seasoned connoisseurs of fine cuisine, such strategies were hardly gourmet cooking; but by the time *Saucepans and the Single Girl* offered its magic recipes as ammunition in the game of love, the term *gourmet* was part of popular culture and no longer meant only haute cuisine. It simply meant anything fancy; in this case, something allegedly seductive. The same principle applies to many of the recipes published in *Playboy* and later collected in *The Playboy Gourmet*. Every month, the magazine's inspirited essays about food and entertaining by Thomas Mario made little attempt to offer serious scholarship in gastronomy, but did provide readers with delightful tidbits of knowledge, as well as clever conversation topics about the food in question, and—most provocatively—an *attitude* to assume while preparing food and eating it. The attitude was knowledgeable but not pedantic, urbane without the intimidating edge of snobbery. In a June 1967 article about "Spit Roasting," Mario perfectly captured the spirit of the *Playboy* style of gourmet cookery: "The master of the turning spit knows that after he's built his fire and impaled his meat, his chief job will be to do nothing. He can leave his captain's chair and his Pimm's Cup to brush the spitted meat with its own fat or with a basting sauce. But even these minor duties aren't always necessary." There you have the master of modern cuisine: relaxing in his captain's chair, sipping a Pimm's cup, doing nothing while his hot meat is impaled and smoldering.

In another of the magazine's monthly culinary pep talks, in this case about shellfish, Thomas Mario made even a humble crustacean seem like a groovy kind of

> "The glorious thing about feeding and watering females is that you don't have to be the least bit exotic about the whole affair. Remember, they're tired of being coy and sophisticated about eating—all they want is food and plenty of it."
>
> —*Saucepans and the Single Girl*

In a world where food was foreplay, few tableside rites were considered more seductive than setting the victuals on fire.

cat: "The lobster is the playboy of the deep; he is a night person, an epicure, a traveler. During the daylight hours, he remains relatively stable on the ocean bed, but after sundown he becomes noticeably restless, moving about with vigor and dash despite his armor-plated bulk." Mario waxed poetic (in *Playboy*'s alliterative idiom) when he informed his readers which foods were the most luxurious: "Veal has been synonymous with sumptuous supping ever since the Prodigal Son sat down to that feast of the fatted calf." As for dessert he advised (in an article titled "Saturnalian Sweets") that "Until recent years, the man-of-the-world paid scant attention to desserts. He was content to round off his meal with a wedge of ripe Camembert cheese while his gentle companion munched her *meringue glacée* with marrons." Mario reassured readers that it had become acceptable for men-of-the-world to express a fondness for sweet desserts, too, and offered recipes for such lady- (and man-) killers as pineapple flambé with coconut cream, coupe with bananas flambé and crêpes suzette with brandy-benedictine liqueur. Anyone who studied these essays in food appreciation and learned how to eat (and possibly even cook) such foods as lobster, veal, and bananas flambé could easily impress a tableful of dinner guests or a single fair companion that he (or she) was a truly swinging gourmet.

In a world where food was foreplay, few tableside rites were considered more seductive than setting the victuals on fire. Given a modernist cachet by Joe Baum at the Newarker and other Restaurant Associates establishments, flaming presentations had become a popular sign of hedonistic gastronomy. To watch a waiter do it in a dimly lit restaurant could be very romantic; to bask in the glow of flaming food during dinner-for-two in the privacy of a bachelor or bachelorette pad was the epitome of enchantment. Acclaiming the "primordial, universal lure of the open flame," John J. Poister's *The Pyromaniac's Cook Book* (1968) explained that flambéed things have special appeal because they are primitive, but they also remind us that we are civilized; we have mastered fire; it is our servant. To command the flames with a sure flourish (accompanied by mood lighting and pulsating savage music) had the same kind of animal sex appeal as a lion tamer who exercises power over a jungle beast. Since the late forties, many men had attained mastery over backyard barbecue flames and thereby expressed their primitive masculinity; but by the sixties patio grills seemed so domesticated; there was nothing very wild and dangerous about grilling beef patties and franks. On the other hand, a midnight supper of *homard à l'absinthe flambé* or a dinner date that climaxed with glorified *café brûlot framboise* could take an eater's breath away; for a man (or woman) to present such flaming splendors to an evening's companion was to practically guarantee that sex would follow. See if you can find the hidden sexual innuendo in this testimonial to the pleasures of flambé cookery from a December 1962 *Playboy*: "It's hard to say which of the two, eating or firewatching, is more fun. Certainly, the aureoles around such heavenly bodies as northern lobster, ring-necked pheasant, and soufflé omelets rate all the attention they arouse."

Aphrodisiacal as it may have been, flambéing foods was fairly tricky work. There were easier and more convenient ways to enjoy the magic properties of shimmying flames at mealtime, including the hibachi grill (perfectly sized for dinner à deux), the monkeywood puu-puu platter with Sterno can, and the most cozy open-flame appurtenance of all, the fondue pot. The discovery of fondue is one of the great unsung events of America's postwar food revolution: Because of it, aspiring gourmets with little or no cooking ability had a way to serve a meal that was foreign, flamed, and gobs of fun. Even when seduction was not an issue, the fondue pot was a wonderful social stimulant because it was entertainment as well as dinner. No matter how hackneyed it became, it was always "different" and always lent a whiff of jet-set glamour to a party because of its association with the chic ski lodges of Switzerland (where, according to most fondue cookbooks, the "international set" discovered it in the 1950s). A fondue pot was especially appropriate for the gourmet host or hostess because it encouraged people to talk about food and play with it as well as eat it. The very act of swabbing bread or fruit through the communal crock of melted cheese or chocolate was an unorthodox gastronomic experience that made everyone feel like a bit of a connoisseur. And, too, there was the merriment that resulted from the inevitable dribbling. There is perhaps no clearer symbol of the role that good food played in The Good Life of the swinging sixties than the fondue pot: positioned altar-like at the center of the table (perhaps in the living room or den rather than the formal dining room), with acolytes gathered around dipping into the great hot crucible for their exotic nourishment, and having a gay time sharing the culinary experience.

The fondue pot was informal and therefore friendly and suited for festive groups of six; yet its bewitching foreign personality was also appropriate for the most intimate of meals shared by two inamorati. "Lovers will sit by a fire for hours, watching quietly and unaware of time as the dancing flames cast their spell," suggested *A Cookbook for Lovers* (1970) in its introduction to a recipe for beef fondue, which it proposed as a source of "romantic togetherness from the first simmer to the last drop of wine." With a fondue pot, it was natural for lovers to put speared food in each other's mouths, as well as to do much lip-licking and to perform suggestive gestures while scooping out some of the hot stuff from the pot.

For an intimate dinner intended as a prelude to sex, fondue was the ideal food. Once it was prepared, the seducer could devote all of his or her attention to the object of desire. "Place your fondue pot near the fireplace and plug it in so that it rests on the floor," advised Billie Young in *The Naked Chef*. Ms. Young recounts the time she made fondue for her "lecherous lover" who ate it by the fire, then became so aroused that he pushed the pot aside and made love to her then and there. "I think it's something you put in the food," he mused in his post-coital reverie. Then he thought about it, and comprehension dawned on him: "It *is* the food!"

Even when a fondue meal was served for more than two, it could function as the catalyst for sexy games. Anita Prichard, a stewardess who wrote *Fondue Magic: Fun, Flame, and Saucery Around the World* (1969), explained that fondue dinners were especially erotic because the "rules" of fondue cookery (she didn't mention who wrote these rules) dictate that if you drop your speared food, you must kiss or be kissed by the person on your right.

Nearly every course of a meal could be served enrobed in flames or presented on top of a blazing Sterno can. (Once, *Playboy* suggested an entirely incandescent dinner, from onion soup flambé to flaming soufflé and ceremonial ignition of an after-dinner panatela.) But it seemed especially appropriate to cauterize food as the grand climax of a feast. "Fire lovers seem to be in complete agreement on at least one thing," observed *The Pyromaniac's Cookbook*. "When the final curtain is rung down on the dinner table, it is far more festive, and frequently more flavorful, if it is a curtain of flames." Blazing desserts, which had been part of the repertoire of flashy restaurants at least since cherries jubilee were first set ablaze at London's Carlton Hotel, and an alluring aspect of contemporary French restaurant cuisine in America (*crêpes suzette* and *bombes flambés*) since the Pavillon, became an ever more popular way for gourmet hosts at home to show that they could end a meal with a rousing flourish. *Playboy* put it this way: "Nothing warms the cockles of an epicurean's heart as much as the festively flavorsome pyrotechnics of setting good food ablaze." To serve dessert on fire was intimate as well as exciting—a special compliment to a guest (or guests) that told them they inspired fireworks.

Flaming coffees, especially if imbibed away from the dinner table in a teak-paneled study, were the most intimate incandescent thing of all, and a nearly surefire initiator of postprandial sex. Not only did they provide the proper combustible theatrics; they also could be concocted to contain a good dose of alcohol (burned away in most flaming food recipes) in order to chemically overwhelm a date's moral scruples. Like a crackling hearth, the diaphanous blue flames of high-proof liqueur were touted by many a seductive mixologist as a guaranteed method of making a guest's heart pound faster. *A Cookbook for Lovers* reminded its readers that "King Louis XV of France—and who knew more about seduction than Louis?—amused his paramours by brewing their coffee over a tiny spirit lamp."

Using liquor to get sex is at least as old a tactic as the Benjaminites of Israel, whose men raided the annual wine festival in Shiloh to snatch dancing girls among the vineyards; but the tactic of getting someone drunk to ravish them (now known as date rape) was pursued with unprecedented frankness by legions of randy American gourmets of the 1960s for whom the pleasures of the table and the bed were complementary: "You've just refilled his glass with that exquisite Montrachet, and together you lie in bed," begins *Cosmo Cookery*, edited by Helen Gurley Brown and published in 1971. Mrs. Brown went on to delineate a plan for "gourmet meals from the first drink to the last kiss," including advice about a subject she called "Sense-Reeling Drinks" to ensure a night of fun and sexual bliss. *Playboy's Host and Bar Book* lauded exotic aperitifs as a wondrous stimulant for the onanistic pleasure of fantasizing: "Observe the Frenchman in his natural habitat, as each afternoon he sits at his favorite café table and partakes of his Byrrh, Amer Picon or vermouth cassis with attentive enjoyment. . . . He observes its color, savors its scent and samples it with a relish one usually associates with newfound pleasures. His senses then undergo the most salutary of metamorphoses: Taste buds tingle in anticipation of the evening repast; the local scenery becomes more vivid; and the passing *mesdemoiselles*, though they may be the same *jeunes filles* who promenade daily past his table, are surveyed with fresh appreciation." As for after-dinner drinks, *Playboy* advised, "A chick who doesn't have the faintest idea of what ingredients go into pastis or prunelle will nevertheless receive the same luxurious wavelengths from either of these drinks."

The liquors most doted on by male rakes were gin and vodka—not so much because they could get a date drunk swiftly and sneakily (although these qualities made them especially valuable in the arsenal of seduction), but because they had qualities considered manly at the time: They were strong and not the least bit sweet. Before the gourmet revolution, most real men drank slugs of whiskey. But as tides of connoisseurship made a whiskey drunk seem so home-grown American, whiskey assumed a lunkheaded and low-class aura. On the other hand, gin and vodka—formerly the toast of ladies, Lotharios in lounging jackets, and tortured novelists—became symbols of a manly taste in potables. "I never have more than one drink before dinner," James Bond explains in *Casino Royale* as he instructs the bartender how to mix a vodka martini. "But I do like that one to be large and very strong and very cold and very well made." Through the fifties and sixties, martinis got drier and drier, going from three-to-one (gin to vermouth), and winding up at sixty-to-one, or stronger. Their legendary power to get people gassed and cause them to lose their inhibitions made the martini some seducers'—including James Bond's—favorite drink, as well as the subject of innumerable party jokes and even a book in 1965 by Johnny Carson called *Happiness is a Dry Martini*. The art of making the martini super-dry (hence, ultra-potent) inspired its own substantial branch of mixological folklore: For utmost dryness, use an atomizer or eyedropper to implant the minimum amount of vermouth into the gin; or simply store the bottle of gin in the shadow of the bottle of vermouth. Whether made of gin or vodka, for drinking oneself or serving to a fair companion, martinis were considered by many to be the ultimate path to sexual triumph.

An obsession with properly mixed cocktails—martinis in particular—became the mark of many a male who considered himself a gourmet of all of life's pleasures, not only fine cuisine. A martini fixation—on the strength of the drink, and on all the stirring, chilling and mixological folderol that went into it—was an excellent way to prove one's virility and connoisseurship simultaneously. "The martini drinker of today isn't just a conspicuous fusspot," *Playboy*'s Thomas Mario assured readers. "The years have refined his martini sense. His taste buds are imbued with the same kind of informative sensitivity an Italian enjoys when he drinks one of

"Happiness is . . . finding two olives in your martini when you're hungry."

—Johnny Carson in *Happiness is a Dry Martini*

the wines he's known since he was old enough to hold a glass in his hands."

Many epicures who had honed their palates on European eating habits turned up their noses at the very idea of someone being a connoisseur of martinis and other hard stuff. To the classically enlightened snob, drinking any kind of hard liquor before dinner was hopelessly crude. Among the sternest gourmets, the only proper libation was wine, with the possible exception of preprandial aperitifs or after-dinner digestifs. To drink a pitcher of martinis before a meal was sheer blasphemy against the niceties of a cultivated palate. Mimi Sheraton explained to readers of her *Seducer's Cookbook* what was wrong with the way Americans drank. Beer, she said, "can hurl one into a torpid flatulence that will defeat your prime purpose; bed is the object, not sleep." And she especially damned such typical American cocktails as the martini and Gibson as having "probably done more to set both sex and gastronomy back than anything since the Reformation." She pointed out that some French restaurants simply *refuse* to serve martinis before dinner because they believe that a person's tastebuds are so damaged by such cocktails that good food is wasted on them; and she extrapolated that the same is true of sex: Hard liquor was unacceptable because it rendered drinkers too insensitive for the "finer intricacies of sex play." Wine, on the other hand, she puffed, was replete with "amorous properties and romantic implications." She concluded her treatise on sex and booze with a comparison: "Like a fine wine, a woman should be handled carefully, warmed slowly, and taken leisurely." There is no equivalent simile given for men (bologna or a risen soufflé come to mind); but the equation of gastronomy and sensuality among horny gourmets of Mimi Sheraton's day was not gender-specific. For women as well as for men, it was common practice to compare connoisseurship of sex to connoisseurship of wine and food. All were aspects of the libertine life that increasing numbers of restless American pleasure lovers were hungry to know.

Recipes

Aphrodisiacal Artichokes

Vichyssoise Salle des Amoureux

Zorba the Greek Salad

**Creamy White Chicken Breasts in
    Champagne Véronique**

Homard à l'Absinthe Flambé

**Flaming Sherried Rock Cornish
    Game Hens**

Seducer's Potatoes Dauphinoise

Naked Chef's Carrots

Helen Gurley Brown's Ghastly Eggs

Kiss and Twirl Fondue

Madison Avenue Chocolate Fondue

Pots de Crème au Chocolate

Cherries Jubilee à Quatre

Café Brûlot Framboise

Pyromaniac's Café Diable

007's Potent Martini

Aphrodisiacal Artichokes

SERVES 4

The sex appeal of artichokes is irrefutable: The tight layering of their pliant, tapered leaves and the integument of pulp that is retrieved by scraping with a firm but gentle bite make tugging at them and eating them a sensual experience. According to food lore, they actually have aphrodisiacal powers; and *The Naked Chef* reports that street vendors in Paris once chanted:

Artichokes! Artichokes!
Heat the body and the spirit;
Heat the genitals!

Never one to miss an opportunity to insinuate sex into food, *The Naked Chef*'s author, Billie Young, offered these suggestions for cooking any vegetable, especially artichokes: "Always have the water boiling lustily. . . . My own favorite way of keeping my vegetables virile is to cook them inside a French salad basket . . . set in a huge pot of boiling water. When the vegetables are ready, I simply lift the basket out. That way they stay sleek and lusty." Good advice, even if you aren't going to have sex between courses or immediately after eating.

4 artichokes
2 lemons
½ teaspoon dry mustard
5 tablespoons olive oil
3 tablespoons tarragon vinegar
1 garlic clove, minced
Salt and pepper
1 teaspoon finely chopped green olives

Strip the tough outer leaves from the artichokes. Cut 1 lemon in quarters and use these quarters to rub the artichokes all over, which will help them retain their color. Cut off the end of each artichoke within 1 inch of the base and tug the leaves open from the inside. Place them head down in a few inches of boiling salted water to which the juice of 1 lemon has been added. Cover and simmer until tender, 15 to 20 minutes. When the leaves pull off without great effort, the artichoke is done. Drain well.

Make sauce by vigorously mixing mustard, olive oil, vinegar, garlic, and salt and pepper to taste, adding green olives when mixed. Serve the sauce in tiny individual bowls, suitable for dunking, alongside the artichokes.

Vichyssoise
Salle des
Amoureux

SERVES 4 TO 6

*N*iccolò de Quattrociocchi, proprietor of El Borracho and the man who designed it as a lovers' hideaway, had much to offer in the way of advice to gentlemen and ladies wishing to seduce their dates over dinner. Among his tips were:

1. Leave your pipe and cigars at home. Cigarettes make you look debonair.

2. If you are a girl, you will look ravishing and very alluring as you comb your hair in a restaurant, but who wants alluring hair flying into his soup? Use the powder room.

3. Don't neck in a restaurant. There is a time, place, and a quiet room for things of that sort.

4. Chew with your mouth closed.

5. Don't rinse your mouth with coffee.

Señor Quattrociocchi revealed that when prizefighter Jack Dempsey dined at El Borracho, he began his meal of steak and French fried potatoes with a bowl of vichyssoise. This potato and leek soup has been a gourmet favorite since its invention by chef Louis Diat of New York's Ritz-Carlton Hotel sometime after 1910. It had fallen out of favor during World War II because its name suggested the puppet government of Vichy (near which Diat had been raised), and some French chefs in New York had begun offering it as *crème Gauloise*; but after the war, its popularity soared, as vichyssoise, a swanky soup with an elegant French name and delicate flavor, but with a good, honest potato heft. These qualities made it easy to like, not only among polished-palated epicures, but among meat-and-potatoes men who wanted to put on the dog and show their dates they were genteel by ordering it at civilized places like El Borracho.

4 leeks, sliced (white part only)
1 medium onion, diced
2 tablespoons butter
4 medium thin-skinned potatoes, peeled and sliced thin
3 cups chicken broth
Salt
1 cup milk
2 cups heavy cream
4 tablespoons chopped chives

In a heavy saucepan, lightly brown the leeks and onion in butter. Add potatoes, broth, and salt if broth is not salty. Bring to a boil. Simmer 30 minutes, or until vegetables are tender. Pass soup through a sieve, strainer, or food mill, crushing potatoes.

Return to the heat. Stir in the milk and cream. Season to taste. Bring to a boil and immediately remove from heat. Cool, then for maximum smoothness, run the soup through a very fine strainer. (The second straining is not necessary if you don't mind a few food flecks in your soup.) Serve chilled, topped with chives.

Zorba the Greek Salad

SERVES 4

*O*f all the robust salads discovered by connoisseurs of international cuisine, none was more hale than Greek salad, which like nearly all things that came from Greece in the 1950s and 1960s, was considered not only hearty but downright lusty. Brawny-palated types who wanted to be gourmets especially liked Greek salads because they contained so many strong-flavored things, often including anchovies or sardines, marinated artichoke hearts, Kalamata olives, and brackish feta cheese. As a contrast to the much-repined timidity of so much ordinary American food, chilled green salads in particular, such impertinent ingredients had sure sex appeal. To eat them was to declare oneself game, eager to embrace life with gusto, and probably not a prude. This recipe, from *The Playboy Gourmet*, even throws in *mashed* potatoes, for gosh sake, as part of the dressing. It is a mighty meal.

> 2 ounces shelled pine nuts
> 3 garlic cloves
> ½ cup olive oil
> 2 tablespoons lemon juice
> 1 small thin-skinned potato, boiled and mashed (no milk)
> 1 quart salad greens, washed, dried, and torn into
>   bite-size pieces
> 8 anchovies, drained of oil
> 8 Kalamata olives
> 1 jar (8 ounces) tiny stuffed eggplants, drained
> 1 jar (4 ounces) artichoke hearts, drained
> 1 green pepper, seeded and cut into long thin slices
> 2 firm, ripe tomatoes, cut into eighths
> ½ cucumber, cut into thin slices
> 1 cup crumbled feta cheese
> Salt and pepper
> 1 can (8 ounces) sliced beets

In an electric blender, combine the pine nuts and garlic. Slowly add oil and lemon juice while blending at low speed. Add the potato and blend until smooth. Chill.

In a large bowl, combine all other ingredients except beets. Add the dressing and toss well, seasoning to taste.

Place the salad on 4 serving plates, using the beets as a garnish.

To entertain one's lover on Valentine's day, Ernest J. Carteris, author of *A Cookbook For Lovers* (1970), suggested raw oysters by candlelight, French champagne, and pale chicken breasts in a creamy champagne sauce, followed by a heart-shaped coeur à la crème (page 41). The chicken in champagne was given added distinction by the addition of grapes (hence the véronique appelation); but it is important in this scheme of things that the grapes not be fresh. They have too much body, and their skin needs to be crushed by teeth, and they may even have seeds—all of which can rend the gauzy softness of the meal. Canned grapes are *de rigueur*: tender and bland as a sigh, sugary sweet, and without any of the coarseness of raw fruit. We have had some trouble finding canned grapes (they *are* still available); and one time actually raided cans of fruit cocktail to get them for this recipe.

Creamy White Chicken Breasts in Champagne Véronique

SERVES 2

2 small breasts of chicken, boned but not skinned
¼ cup flour
½ teaspoon salt
¼ teaspoon black pepper
3 tablespoons butter
1 tablespoon vegetable oil
¼ cup chicken broth
½ cup heavy cream
White pepper
¼ cup champagne
4 ounces cooked, buttered noodles
Chopped parsley
1 cup canned white grapes, drained

Wash the chicken breasts and pat them dry. Mix flour, salt, and black pepper together on a piece of wax paper and use this mixture to coat the breasts.

Heat the butter and oil in an 8-inch skillet over medium heat. Place chicken, skin side down, in pan. Brown for 3 to 4 minutes; turn and brown the other side 3 to 4

continued

minutes. When the breasts are springy to the touch, they are done. Remove them to a hot platter and keep them warm in a very low oven while making the sauce.

Add chicken broth to drippings in the pan. Cook over medium heat, scraping up shreds of chicken, until broth is thickened and syrupy, 1 to 2 minutes. Turn heat to low and drizzle in heavy cream, cooking and stirring until sauce has thickened slightly, 1 minute. Do not boil. Season with salt and white pepper to taste. Stir in champagne. Continue heating over low heat 1 minute more.

Serve chicken breasts over cooked, buttered noodles. Top with sauce. Sprinkle with chopped parsley and grapes.

Homard à l'Absinthe Flambé

SERVES 4

To the dismay of hedonists in search of sexual stimulants, absinthe had been banned in America since 1912 because the wormwood from which it was made was found to corrode brains and absinthe itself was habit-forming. Nonetheless, its reputation as the drink of love continued in potions and recipes that used Pernod or Herbsaint (both of which had a bitter licorice taste similar to absinthe, but only the normal narcotic effect of alcohol). *The Pyromaniac's Cookbook* suggested a large variety of brandies and gins for setting lobsters on fire, including Pernod as an absinthe substitute to make lobster the old-fashioned French way. Lobster, of course, was a seducer's big gun: Even out of the shell, as in this recipe, its juicy succulence made eating it à deux a sensuous experience.

1 liter dry white wine
6 fresh tarragon sprigs
2 lobsters, 2 pounds each
6 tablespoons butter
2 tablespoons flour
2 tablespoons chopped fresh chervil, or ½ teaspoon dried
1 teaspoon chopped fresh dill, or ¼ teaspoon dried
Salt and pepper
¼ cup Pernod

In a large skillet or saucepan, bring the wine to a simmer with 4 sprigs of the tarragon. Add lobsters and simmer 20 minutes. Remove lobsters and reserve wine.

Preheat oven to 200 degrees.

When they are cool enough to handle, split the lobsters lengthwise, removing the sac from their head and the intestinal vein. Remove and reserve the coral and tomalley. Cut meat from the tails and claws into bite-size pieces and place in a large heatproof casserole with 3 tablespoons of the butter. Place in the oven.

As lobster heats, place remaining 3 tablespoons of butter in a saucepan with the coral and tomalley and mix in flour to make a smooth paste. Heat gently and stir in 1¼ to 1½ cups of the wine in which the lobsters were boiled—enough so the mixture is light and creamy. Chop remaining tarragon fine and add it to the sauce with chervil, dill, a pinch of salt, and about ½ teaspoon of ground black pepper. Blend well and heat, but do not boil.

Remove lobster meat from the oven. Heat Pernod. Pour over the lobster and set it on fire. When the flames extinguish, cover the lobster pieces with the sauce and serve.

Flaming Sherried Rock Cornish Game Hens

SERVES 2

*H*elen Gurley Brown's *Single Girl's Cookbook* had a recipe and a menu for every occasion, including different things to eat at each of five different stages of a love affair, and suggestions for what to do when a boy you like brings you a fish he has caught. "Toujours gai, toujours l'amour—and aren't you glad you've become such a fabulous cook?" Mrs. Brown enthused when writing about that special Valentine's Day meal for that special boy. She discouraged readers from making their paramours Jell-O salad that spelled out their initials, a large baked roll with mouth, eyes, and nose made of pimientos, or anything topped with pink-tinted whipped cream. Such extravagances, she advised, "tend to give most men the creeps and the 'what am I doing here with this *dame*?' feeling." On the other hand, single girls were advised that Rock Cornish game hens were always in good taste—far more impressive than mundane chicken, but not as daunting to prepare as duck or goose. An all-white-meat crossbreed that weighs scarcely more than two pounds dressed, Rock Cornish game hens were a twentieth-century American invention, and they were beloved by many American gourmets for a flavor considered more robust than ordinary fowl, but not nearly as gamy as waterfowl, and without risk of eating bird shot.

This single girl's recipe purposely ignores the juices left over in the roasting pan, which would make a nice sauce for a dowdy married couple, but are far too messy looking for the presentation Mrs. Brown suggests: served on white dishes on a pretty pink cloth with long white candles, red and white flowers, and plenty of rosé wine.

2 Rock Cornish game hens, defrosted
4 tablespoons butter
Salt and pepper
¼ cup sherry
¼ cup brandy

Remove giblets from the defrosted birds and store for later use. Wash and dry the birds.

Preheat oven to 350 degrees.

Melt the butter in a heavy skillet with a heatproof handle. Sprinkle the hens with salt and pepper, then brown them delicately all over in the butter, turning frequently. This should take about 20 minutes. When the hens are browned, add sherry to the pan and transfer it to the oven. Roast 45 to 60 minutes, until the hens are tender, basting often.

Transfer the hens to a heated (and heatproof) serving dish. Warm the brandy in a small saucepan and ignite it. Pour over the hens and serve flaming.

Seducer's Potatoes Dauphinoise

SERVES 2

To accompany elegant entrées such as Rock Cornish game hens or lobster, or even a tender filet mignon, a seducer (male or female) was best advised to serve an aristocratic starch: wild rice, risotto, rice pilaf, etc. What was a girl to do when the boy she loved was a meat and potatoes man? That was simple. Make him potatoes dauphinoise, which are hearty enough for a man-size appetite, but have a tender, soaked-in-milk consistency that reminds the man being seduced that they were cooked by gentle hands. "Rich, yes," wrote Helen Gurley Brown, "but just this once, could you forget how fat you're getting?"

4 medium-size thin-skinned potatoes
½ teaspoon salt
½ teaspoon freshly ground pepper
¾ cup scalded cream
1 garlic clove, cut in half
3 tablespoons butter
½ cup shredded Gruyère cheese
Milk

Peel the potatoes and slice them in rounds ⅛ inch thick. Place them in a bowl. Sprinkle on salt and pepper and pour in cream. Toss lightly, taking care not to break potatoes.

Preheat oven to 400 degrees.

Rub an 8-inch baking dish about 2 inches deep with the cut sides of the garlic clove. Use 1 tablespoon of the butter to generously butter the dish. With a slotted spoon, transfer half the potatoes to the prepared dish. Dot with 1 tablespoon butter. Sprinkle with half the cheese. Add the remaining potatoes. Dot them with the remaining butter and sprinkle on the remaining cheese. Pour the seasoned cream over the potatoes and, if necessary, add enough milk to barely cover them. Bake 40 to 45 minutes, or until the potatoes have absorbed the milk and are tender.

The *Naked Chef*'s author, Billie Young, surmised that it was carrots' resemblance to penises that made them known in Hellenic times as a "love philter used to increase potency and desire." In ancient Greece, Ms. Young advises readers, their tumid flesh was admired equally by both sexes because "men were able to switch from one gender to the other with equal facility." If she is correct about carrots' symbolic meaning, her recipe, although quite delicious and easily made, seems rather strange: *The Naked Chef* says to use only very thin ones, and to begin by hacking them into bite-size disks.

Naked Chef's Carrots

SERVES 4

1 pound carrots, scrubbed clean and sliced into
  ¼-inch disks
3 tablespoons butter
2 teaspoons brown sugar
¼ cup brandy

Boil carrots until barely tender, about 10 minutes. Drain. Stir in butter and brown sugar, mixing to coat the carrots. Place in a flameproof serving dish. Heat the brandy, pour over the carrots, and ignite. Sauté 15 to 20 seconds, tossing to extinguish flames.

Helen Gurley Brown's Ghastly Eggs

SERVES 2

*T*housands of recipes were disseminated to help girls and guys make someone fall in love with them. Only Helen Gurley Brown had the foresight to provide readers of her *Single Girl's Cookbook* with recipes designed to drive away a man when the love affair goes sour. For dinner, she suggested liver, kidneys, or sweetbreads because "the average American male—and you know by now he *is* average—turns poison green at the mention of 'innards,'" accompanied by broccoli or turnips and followed by baked grapefruit. If that didn't do the trick, and somehow he managed to spend another night and the poor girl awoke sick to her stomach at the sight of him, Mrs. Brown had just the recipe, which she called her coup de grace: ghastly eggs. "No man confronted with a purple egg in the morning—particularly if he's had anything to drink the night before—is apt to return to your house for more of *anything*." The wine sauce is indeed purple, which isn't really too ghastly; but the egg whites turn a hue known to artists as caput mortuum, like something out of a horror movie about living corpses. The taste is quite nice if you like wine sauce with your eggs in the morning, but still, we would never want to serve these unsightly oddities to anyone but houseguests who overstay their welcome.

3 tablespoons butter
½ cup minced onion
2 cups Burgundy wine
1 teaspoon salt
¼ teaspoon pepper
1 whole clove
1 bay leaf
2 tablespoons flour
4 eggs
4 slices of bread, suitable for toasting

In a pan big enough to poach 4 eggs, melt 2 tablespoons of the butter. Sauté onion until pale gold. Add wine, salt, pepper, clove, and bay leaf. Bring to a boil, reduce heat, and let the mixture simmer slowly for 15 minutes.

Mix the remaining tablespoon of butter with flour to make a paste. Set aside.

One by one, break the eggs onto a saucer and slip them into the slowly simmering liquid. Cover the pan. As the eggs poach, make the toast.

The eggs will take about 8 minutes to cook. Remove them gently with a spoon, draining off the poaching liquid, then lay them on toast on plates. Slide the plates into a low oven to keep them warm. Pour the poaching liquid through a sieve. Return the flour and butter mixture to the heat and slowly add about 1 cup of the strained poaching liquid, stirring as the sauce thickens. Continue cooking about 2 minutes. Pour the sauce over the eggs and serve.

"P.S.: A few drops of Kitchen Bouquet will take the horrid purple look away from the sauce if you aren't trying to revolt anybody and just want something unusual and delicious for breakfast."—Helen Gurley Brown

P.P.S: Mrs. Brown's suggestion does make the sauce look harmless; but there is no way to disguise the color of the eggs themselves.—J. & M. S.

PLEASE NOTE: In modern times, eggs cooked like this might scare off even a blind houseguest who is worried about salmonella. Alas, salmonella anxiety has made *all* poached eggs ghastly; so unless you are certain that your eggs are salmonella-free, don't blame us if you want to die after trying this recipe.

Kiss and Twirl Fondue

SERVES 4 AS A
MAIN COURSE,
8 TO 10 AS AN APPETIZER

*A*nita Prichard filled her book *Fondue Magic: Fun, Flame, and Saucery Around the World* with many fondue-eating rules of undisclosed origin, all of them designed to make the experience a more sophisticated version of spin-the-bottle. Discussing basic cheese fondue, a specialty of Zurich, she revealed that it was traditional to scoop out the cheese by spearing a bread cube on the end of one's fondue fork, then twirling it, first in a cup of kirsch, then in the fondue itself. "This charming custom, now eagerly accepted everywhere, carries with it its own special consequences: If a lady, in the course of dunking, loses her bread in the fondue, she pays the kind of forfeit that's bound to catch on internationally—a kiss to the nearest man. If it's a man whose bread cube gets away, he provides the next bottle of wine."

1 garlic clove, cut in half
2 cups dry white wine (Neuchâtel, Moselle, or Rhine)
1 tablespoon lemon juice
1 pound aged Swiss cheese, grated
3 tablespoons flour
3 tablespoons kirsch, plus 1 cup for dipping
¼ teaspoon grated nutmeg
Dash of paprika
1 large loaf of French or Italian bread, cut into bite-size cubes and lightly toasted

Rub the fondue pot with the cut sides of garlic. Discard the garlic. Pour the wine in the pot and add lemon juice. Set over moderate heat but do not boil.

Toss cheese with flour. Lower fondue pot heat and add cheese, a third at a time, stirring constantly with a wooden fork or spoon until cheese is melted. Raise heat and bring to a bubble for a few seconds; add 3 tablespoons of the kirsch, the nutmeg, and paprika.

Reduce heat so fondue stays hot to serve.

Pour 1 cup kirsch into a wide bowl next to the fondue pot.

Guests should spear a cube of bread, quickly twirl it in the kirsch, then in the fondue to scoop out cheese, giving the cheese a good stir with each scoop. The crust that forms at the bottom of the fondue pot is a delicacy and should be divided at the end of the meal among the guests.

ew people doubt that chocolate has some kind of magic power, if not actually aphrodisiacal, then awfully close. Considering how people pant for it and fall into deliriums while eating it, it was inevitable that chocolate would find its way into the agitated ecstasies of the fondue pot. It happened not in Switzerland, but in America, on Madison Avenue in New York, in the test kitchens of the Switzerland Association, which was looking for a way to promote the use of Toblerone Swiss chocolate bars in cooking. They devised chocolate fondue— suitable for dessert at the end of a meal, or as an excuse for a chocolate party. The taste of this dish depends entirely on the chocolate you use. Ordinary sweet baking chocolate or semisweet chips taste fine; but use high-quality semisweet chocolate bars, and this fondue sings. (By the way, it also makes a wonderful chocolate sauce for ice cream: Use it slightly warm, like hot fudge.)

10 ounces semisweet chocolate of choice
1½ cups heavy cream
2 ounces Cognac, kirsch, or Cointreau (¼ cup)
Ladyfingers or pound cake, cut into bite-size pieces
Fruit of choice: fresh strawberries, fresh peach slices,
    orange sections, stemmed maraschino cherries,
    bananas, pitted dates, chunks of canned pineapple

Melt the chocolate in the cream over medium-low heat, stirring frequently. When blended, add liquor and continue stirring until smooth. Keep warm at low heat in a fondue pot or a pot that can be placed over a Sterno or gas heat, somewhere easily accessible for guests. (Be sure heat is low: chocolate scorches easily.) Provide long fondue forks and invite guests to spear fruits and cake and dunk them in the warm chocolate.

Pots de Crème au Chocolate

SERVES 2

*B*efore restaurants discovered how lucrative brunch could be and turned it into an opportunity for families to fill up cheap at serve-yourself food bars, the Sunday late-morning meal had romantic and intimate implications. It was the repast after the night before, an opportunity for lovers who had tripped the light fantastic to rekindle their energies and renew their passion by eating sumptuous food at a leisurely pace. In his *A Cookbook for Lovers* (1970), Ernest Carteris suggested that during "an unexpected breakfast-after, love can walk in at any moment, ravenously hungry, not willing to wait longer than it takes to boil an egg." His brunch recipes were, therefore, suitably expeditious; and he suggested that anyone who suspected that a Saturday night date might last through Sunday prepare the pots de crème au chocolate before the date begins. Pots de crème were a delightful gourmet affectation: rich and lush, but without the grandiose connotations of mousse. Mr. Carteris advised serving them as dessert, with coffee, after a quick and simple meal of eggs and English muffins.

1¼ cups heavy cream
½ teaspoon vanilla extract
2 ounces sweet chocolate, chopped
2 egg yolks
2 teaspoons granulated sugar
2 teaspoons confectioners' sugar, sifted
Dash of vanilla extract

Preheat oven to 325 degrees. Place a pan with 1 inch of hot water in the oven.

Combine 1 cup of the cream and the vanilla extract with the chocolate in a small heavy saucepan over low heat and cook until the chocolate is melted and completely blended with the cream.

Beat the egg yolks until thick and lemon-colored. Beat in granulated sugar. Add a little hot cream to the egg yolks to warm them, then add the rest, stirring vigorously. Pour into 2 custard cups. Set the cups in the baking pan in the oven. Cover them with aluminum foil and bake 20 to 25 minutes, or until a knife inserted in the center of each pot comes out clean. Cool, then chill in the refrigerator 4 to 8 hours, covered with plastic wrap. Serve with chantilly cream made by whipping remaining ¼ cup of cream with the sifted confectioners' sugar and a dash of vanilla extract.

"You'll love this place . . . the prices are exorbitant!"

Cherries Jubilee à Quatre

SERVES 4

*I*n his ode to ice cream, *Playboy*'s gourmet, Thomas Mario, pitied the Emperor Nero who, instead of ice cream, had to make do with snow, brought in buckets from the Alps and flavored with fruit syrup. Modern epicures, he rejoiced, have a whole world of ice cream flavors and frozen desserts at their command. "For the knowledgeable bachelor chef," Mario wrote, "there could be no more fitting finale to a cool terrace tiffin than . . . a chilled treat." So much the better if it was topped with flaming sweet cherries. The combination of vanilla ice cream, dark cherries, and an inebriant has been a favored fancy dessert since early in the century when maraschino cherries came packed in liqueur. For *Playboy*'s flaming version, Mario advised the neophyte to practice privately before trying to set the dessert on fire among company; he also insisted on the importance of using fine buffet ware. "You can flame desserts in an old frying pan if you wish, of course, but the applause meter will register much higher if you perform the same fire ritual in a gleaming chafing dish or a properly proportioned pan of copper."

1 can (17 ounces) pitted black cherries in heavy syrup
1 tablespoon cornstarch
2 tablespoons sugar
2 teaspoons butter
2 ounces light rum (¼ cup)
2 ounces curaçao (¼ cup)
1 pint vanilla ice cream

Drain the cherries well. Put ¼ cup of their syrup (save the balance) into a small bowl and mix with cornstarch and sugar until the cornstarch dissolves. In a small saucepan over a low flame, bring the remaining cherry juice to a boil. Stirring constantly, gradually stir in the cornstarch mixture. Simmer 2 minutes. Add butter and 1 ounce of the rum. Remove from the heat and set aside. This is the sauce.

When ready to serve dessert, heat cherries with curaçao and remaining rum in a chafing dish over a direct flame until hot but not boiling. Scoop very cold ice cream into serving dishes and top with hot cherry sauce. Set cherries on fire and let flames flicker a few seconds. Spoon over ice cream and sauce.

The most famous flaming coffee is café brûlot, a grand New Orleans end-of-meal flourish made by pouring strong chickory-root coffee into a cauldron of spiced, flaming brandy (*brûlot* means both "incendiary" and "seasoned"). Absolutely authentic recipes require specially shaped heatproof brûlot bowls, although any chafing dish or saucepan will suffice. Traditionally, Cognac is the fuel that is burned. This recipe using framboise was suggested by *The Pyromaniac's Cookbook*. Nearly any flammable liqueur works; other good brûlot recipes call for Grand Marnier, B & B, Kahlúa, crème de cacao, or Drambuie.

Café Brûlot Framboise

SERVES 4

 2 tablespoons honey
 2 cinnamon sticks
 6 whole cloves
 Zest of ½ lemon
 Zest of ½ orange
 ¼ cup framboise liqueur
 2 cups piping hot strong black coffee

Place all ingredients except framboise and coffee in a chafing dish or brûlot bowl. Heat framboise and pour it into the bowl, igniting it immediately. Let it blaze a few seconds, then pour in the coffee to extinguish the flames. (Don't let all the framboise burn up.) Pour into demitasse cups and serve immediately.

Pyromaniac's Café Diable

SERVES 4

An after-dinner powerhouse suggested by *The Pyro-maniac's Cookbook*, which called it (in language stunningly reminiscent of *Playboy*'s impassioned prose) one of "the more famous blazable brews that have well-established pyric popularity." The book of all-flaming foods also gave its readers a warning that bears repeating here: "Anything, but anything can be flamed. And as some too casual chefs have learned, this can include fingers, eyelashes, hair, tablecloths, rugs, and draperies." Special caution was aimed at "Compulsive martini drinkers who have reached a high state of euphoria, and anyone else who thinks it might be clever to see how much flammable spirit they can get into their chafing dish. Don't waste your booze in overly large tabletop conflagrations. You may spoil both the dinner *and* the dining room."

> 2 cinnamon sticks
> 8 whole cloves
> 5 whole coffee beans
> 1 ounce Cointreau
> 1 ounce curaçao
> 2 ounces Cognac
> 2 cups piping hot strong black coffee

Place all ingredients except Cognac and coffee in a chafing dish or brûlot bowl. Warm over low heat and mix well. Warm the Cognac, ignite, and pour into the bowl. Blaze a few seconds, then pour in coffee to extinguish the flames. Pour into demitasse cups and serve immediately.

"*I*'m going to patent it when I can think of a good name," James Bond said of his favorite preprandial cocktail when he instructed the barman in *Casino Royale* how to make it. It is a martini, of sorts—at least that is what 007 called it when he first stepped up to the bar—but it contains both gin *and* vodka, as well as Lillet, and there is no vermouth. Note, please, that Bond said he had only one of these extra-large libations before dinner.

3 jiggers gin
1 jigger Russian vodka
½ jigger Lillet
1 large thin slice of lemon peel

In a cocktail shaker with plenty of ice, combine gin, vodka, and Lillet. Shake very well until ice cold. Strain into a deep champagne goblet and top with lemon peel.

5

6

GOURMANIA

The changes that took place on American tables and in attitudes toward food in the two-and-a-half decades after World War II were a revolution: An ambivalent revolution, to be sure, for this was not only a time of upward-spiraling culinary yearning; it was also the glory day of convenience cookery and corporate-encouraged culinary sloth.

In one way, the desire to cook using time-honored techniques imparted by the likes of Julia Child and to partake of the world's classic cuisines was a reaction against the boom in ready-to-eat products and bake-'n'-serve cookery. Real epicures reviled any recipe that didn't start with natural ingredients from the farm, fishmonger, or butcher shop. In an era that prized convenience foods, they marched to the beat of a different drummer, and condemned what they saw as the inevitable loss of quality implied by shortcut cooking.

But at the same time, increasing numbers of less fussy consumers yearned to have a taste of the gourmet pleasures that had become a symbol of The Good Life; and if they could get these pleasures conveniently, from the grocer's freezer case or out of a can, so much the better. Like foreign travel, fancy food got popular; and as it became readily accessible—off-the-shelf, no kitchen skills required—the word *gourmet* lost its glow. Most genuine connoisseurs of fine food learned to disdain the very word, as they still do today, as a sign of bogus delicacies and callow-palated parvenues. When we asked James Beard about being a gourmet in the early eighties, he told us, "*Gourmet* has become a hideous term"; and he went on to complain that most people who called themselves gourmets were nothing but food fetishists who would rather talk about a four-star meal than cook or eat a tasty plate of food.

Genuinely sophisticated epicures had championed all good food, even peasant fare that wasn't necessarily fancy, and they had learned to savor excellence at every level of sociogastronomic refinement. But for increasing numbers of people who became enamored of gastronomy in the sixties and seventies, *gourmet* always signified a meal that was fancier than normal, even if it wasn't any better. For these nouveaux epicures, cooking and eating pretentious food was culturally approved evidence that their life was not mediocre and their lifestyle was in the groove. By 1970, gourmania was unbounded. No longer confined to authentic foreign dishes or choice regional Americana, "gourmet fare" became a meaningless term like "designer fashion": formerly an exclusive mark of distinction, now a garden-variety label for indulging one's palate or advertising one's own good taste.

Knowing how to cook interesting food became such a valuable status booster that a healthy little publishing industry arose producing amusing books that informed kitchen klutzes how to fake it. *The Madison Avenue Cookbook* (1962) promised to "tell you how to appear to know a good deal about cooking when actually you know little or nothing." Included among its recipes are chilled Portuguese sardines cut in half and put on squares of crustless black bread, accompanied by a dab of Bombay chutney: "completely captures the spirit and calls for no cooking at all." Even Peg Bracken's hilariously obstinate *The I Hate to Cook Cookbook* (1960) contained a supply of eight highfalutin menus to impress demanding guests, including chicken with a can of artichokes and French beef stew, with the suggestion that almost any mediocre meal could be saved if it concluded with a bang: "that lovely orange-cream sherbet at the fancy-food store . . . or a rare, fine, immortal glass of Irish coffee." Irish coffee is especially excellent for the inept cook, Ms. Bracken suggested, because it is coffee, dessert, and liqueur all in one, thus eliminating the fuss over dessert plates, forks, coffeepots, sugar bowls, etc.

Cheating aside, no single gesture by a host or hostess announced culinary sophistication quite so handily as the serving of impressive appetizers. For many newcomers to the pleasures of gastronomy, appetizers were, along with wine, the telltale mark of the gourmet. They were important because even if they were unimaginative, they made any meal into an occasion; they distinguished a sumptuous repast from a TV dinner that could be fitted into a single plate. To nouveau sophisticates intent on experiencing the fullness of epicurean pleasure, appetizers were a way of separating themselves from rubes and vulgarians who fed themselves but did not *dine*. Only mundane farm families and construction workers in strap T-shirts plunked themselves down at tables to ingest drab, one-plate, meat-and-potatoes meals. On the other hand, gourmets gathered on the porch or patio or in the conversation pit before dinner and savored imaginative cocktails and hors d'oeuvre.

Successful hors d'oeuvre set a tone for a meal that even an ordinary entrée might not blot out. *The Instant Epicure Cookbook (for Terribly Tired Gourmets)*, published in 1963, put it bluntly: "A clever hostess, with little effort and expense, can produce appetizers and hors d'oeuvre that will so completely fill her guests that dinner can be a meager main course with fruit and coffee to follow." *The Instant Epicure* also warned that nothing was quite as gauche as tearing open a bag of potato chips or opening a can of salted peanuts: "Guests feel neglected and approach dinner with understandable doubts and depression." *The Graham Kerr Cookbook* stated the point even more forcefully: "Hostesses who provide nuts, potato chips, and olives before dinner announce to the world their total indifference."

The quest for appetizers that were different had been a fundamental aspect of the gourmet revolution since James Beard started it all with *Hors d'Oeuvre and Canapés* in 1940. Despite his aversion to dips and dunks, they remained in the culinary armory of American hosts—gourmet as well as conventional—because they were the do-it-yourself way of serving. Among most of us Americans, all but the snootiest guests enjoy "dipping our own" because it seems a more democratic and social way of eating (as opposed to being proffered a ready-made canapé, which always has an upper-crust connotation). "What with the growth of informality in entertaining, dips and spreads have come into their own," observed Lila Perl in her 1961 book, *What Cooks in Suburbia;* and she went on to suggest a number of such specialities with the power to lift a humdrum occasion onto a cloud of culinary elegance: sour cream and caviar dip, smoked salmon spread, brandied blue cheese dip ("very exotic"). A surefire way for a host to use a dip to establish gourmet reknown was to serve it *hot.* Hot dips made of seafood were especially soigné because they smacked of such blue-ribbon preparations as Newburg and thermidor, yet required little more effort than opening a can of crab, clams, or shrimp (or even tuna), a package of cream cheese, and a bottle of inexpensive sherry. Ceil Dyer, author of *Best Recipes From the Backs of Boxes, Bottles, Cans, and Jars,* called hot crabmeat appetizer, featuring Philadelphia brand cream cheese and a can of crabmeat "a short cut to becoming the hostess with the mostess."

Despite such facile (and frequently counterfeit) elegance in the dip-and-dunk department, gourmets who were serious about showing off served top-of-the-line hors d'oeuvre of the type James Beard had pioneered: individual mouthfuls of food each with a unique pasticcio of flavor. Canapés, cheese puffs, tiny turnovers, or bite-size astonishments of infinite variety were the incontestable way to establish a reputation as a gourmet cook.

Of all the ambitious appetizers, there were two that became enshrined as gourmet paradigms: quiche and rumaki. Quiche made its first notable appearance in America at the Cheese Cellar of the New York World's Fair in 1939; and it was soon popularized at swank cocktail parties in New York, particularly those catered by James Beard's Hors d'Oeuvre, Inc. "I am convinced I am the one who introduced quiche to America," Beard reminisced in the 1980s; but in 1946 it was still so strange that Mrs. Louis B. Newell of Wayzata, Minnesota, wrote to *Gourmet* requesting a recipe for "a cheese dish with a creamy or custardy consistency that sounds like *'Quietsch à la Reine'.*" She asked, "Does that mean anything to you?" *Gourmet* responded, "It certainly does—it means that very tasty appetizer tart," and provided Mrs. Newell with the recipe for quiche Lorraine.

Within a decade, quiche would begin its ascendance into general popularity and rumaki would make its appearance (from sources unknown). Passé and nearly forgotten now, rumaki—a strange assembly of chicken livers, water chestnuts, and bacon—had nearly as stunning an impact as quiche on the hors d'oeuvre repertory of aspiring gourmets and especially caterers with an upscale image. It was still novel enough in 1965 so that *Gourmet*'s "You Asked For It" column ran the recipe in response to a reader's request; but within ten years it, too, would become an overly popularized parody of gourmet foodways. Lush, exotic, and sumptuously pinguid, rumaki required a fair amount of work to assemble, and until they became a common ingredient of weddings, bar mitzvahs, and the suburban patio parties of culinary strivers, they were an emblem of a home where connoisseurship reigned. They became so popular that by the late 1970s the Underwood ham company had developed a jiffy recipe for them, which saved time and money by substituting liverwurst spread for chicken livers.

Other than ritzy appetizers, one sure way to make eating a novel experience was to join a gourmet group and create *theme meals*. PTA-published cookbooks with "international" chapters suggested potluck party night: Each invited guest brings a dish from a different country, the result being a grand United-Nations feast, a sort of edible Tower of Babel. The more common way to sample international cuisines was to do them one at a time, at a party keyed to the food and culture of a single country. Such a soirée was a great opportunity for gourmets to share their epicurean tastes with like-minded connoisseurs, or to strut their savoir vivre among impressionable guests by flaunting what they had learned abroad on vacation or during their sabbatical. In 1970 *The New York Times Cocktail Party Guide* suggested entertaining with "international flavor," which meant not only serving foreign food, but steering conversation to amusing topics suggested by events in foreign countries: "Whip up some traditional Greek appetizers [*The Times* suggested tyropitakia and hummus] and get ready to tell your guests what *The Times* reported about hippies hiding out in the caves of Crete." To accompany quiche and chilled wine, hosts were supposed to talk about the day Parisians were encouraged to paint graffiti on the walls of an art museum. ("You may have even clipped the story from *The Times*.") Another *Times* party scheme instructed aspiring gourmets to focus on Russia, with a special appeal to world travelers: Serve piroshki "and discuss the merits of a boat trip down the Volga compared with a Siberian bus tour." All these far-flung menus were fine if you knew your company was as sophisticated as you, but Barbara Taylor Bradford's *Entertaining to Please Him* (1969) warned, "It's wise not to serve only extremely exotic fare in case some of your guests have fairly conventional tastes." Her recommendations of sophisticated but not-too-scary meals included paella, cassoulet, Indian beef curry, or a "French Seashore Supper" of fish stew, bread, and salad followed by peppermint whirl ice cream . . . unless the boss was coming to dinner, in which case she emphatically urged her reader to "stay with well-cooked American dishes. . . . A roast of some kind is preferable to anything else."

In the hands of a conscientious host, virtually any international gourmet menu could be the inspiration for a theme party. With appropriate music on the stereo (Herb Alpert and the Tijuana Brass for guacamole and chicken mole; Verdi for eggplant caponata and lasagne), an embroidered hostess gown recently purchased during a trip to Lisbon or Cancun, and a handful of conversational gambits from *The New York Times* clipping file, anyone's attempt to cook and serve foreign food could easily be complemented by a soupçon of proper atmosphere. At the high end of the culinary status hierarchy, dinner guests might eat a genuinely French *poulet poêlé à l'estragon* with potato crêpes straight out of a Julia Child book and drink a spritely Bordeaux-Médoc, accompanied by Edith Piaf tapes and perhaps even smatterings of conversation actually in French. On the other end of things, guests came to a party wearing sandals, shorts, and open shirts and ate pork chops Waikiki with rum and tonics while listening to Don Ho on the record player. Among less sophisticated gourmets, there was nothing quite so much fun as a patio luau.

As gourmet foodways trickled (or rather, flooded) down the ladder of status, certain specific ingredients or combinations of ingredients, as well as a large repertory of distinct dishes, all became instantly recognizable signs of the gourmet touch. Some of the more obvious examples include anything flambéed, cheese balls infused with wine and studded with nuts, smelly cheese such as Liederkranz or Camembert, shellfish in cream and sherry sauce, duck all ways but especially dripping with fruity sauce, soup with melted cheese in it, cold soup (gazpacho, vichyssoise), quiche and fondue, any dish that could rightfully (or wrongfully) be called curried, glacéed, souffléed, moussed, mulled, melba'd, deviled, scalloped, stuffed or à la française, as well as anything containing lumpfish caviar, capers, croutons, canned French fried onion rings, slivered almonds, hearts of artichoke, shriveled black olives (preferably with pits), marrons, mint, or Major Grey's chutney.

To our present-day culinary sensibilities, the concepts of instant epicureanism and gourmet food from a can are anathema; but from the beginning of the gourmet revo-

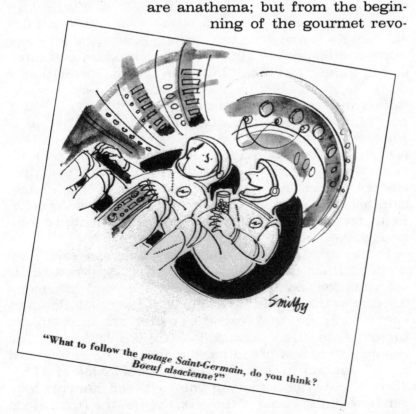

"What to follow the potage Saint-Germain, do you think? Boeuf alsacienne?"

lution to the time ostentatious foodways became readily available to one and all in the early 1970s, there was no automatic discrepancy in many American cooks' minds between haute cuisine and jiffy meals. In fact, at the outset of the renaissance of international cooking in America after World War II, cans and jars were the only place to get many foreign, rare, and fascinating foodstuffs. Consider the "gourmet shelf" that could be found (and still is found) in many supermarkets: Here were cans and jars of such deluxe exotica as pâté de foie gras, snails (with shells), boned ringneck pheasant, smoked oysters, Danish sausage sticks, crabmeat and tiny shrimp, garlic paste (for no-fuss garlic bread), sauces béarnaise and hollandaise, brandied cherries, crystallized violets, and Chinese kumquats; also, perhaps, international soups including mock turtle, consommé madrilène, and seafood bisque. By the time most comfortable households acquired freezers, instant epicureanism became even easier, in the form of such buy-'em-and-bake-'em gourmet entrées as lobster tails, chicken Kiev, and assorted cordons bleus. And for those hosts and hostesses who actually wanted to cook interesting things, but didn't have the time or inclination to do it the night they were entertaining, there were innumerable recipes disseminated for "do-ahead" dinners. In 1964 Helen Quat's *The Wonderful World of Freezer Cooking* promised "you can entertain in the finest gourmet tradition and yet have most of the cooking done weeks before the party." Included in her ritzy freezer collection were such dishes as crêpes divine, coulibiac of salmon and lobster, crabmeat quiche, Roquefort cheese biscuits, and crème de menthe chocolate bombe.

To understand how American cooks so easily reconciled their deep freeze and can opener with their yearning for sophisticated food, it is crucial to remember that at the beginning of the gourmet revolution, foreign food in cans and from the freezer was *modern* and, therefore, to many forward-looking people, good. "The can opener is fast becoming a magic wand," exclaimed Poppy Cannon in *The Can Opener Cookbook* of 1951. "Our new way of achieving gourmet food can only happen here—in the land of the mix, the jar, the frozen-food package, and the ubiquitous can opener."

Not everyone was so ecstatic about the new way of shortcut deluxe cooking. From the beginning, *Gourmet* magazine made a point of separating itself from the processed-food enthusiasts; its original manifesto in 1941 assailed progress, expressing instead nostalgia for "the mellow moods and manners of a bygone day," and offering its readers mostly recipes that produced fancy dishes the old-fashioned way, without mixes, jars, and frozen packages. Nonetheless, as World War II came to a close, legions of overwrought gastronomic journalists were singing the praises of a future in which nearly all the food we eat would be dehydrated, dessicated, irradiated, or otherwise embalmed; and kitchen drudgery of any kind would be a thing of the past.

In the spirit of this prediction, a stunning shift of culinary values was engineered by big food-processing companies, cheered on by enthusiastic recipe writers eager to seem modern, and embraced with glee by housewives looking for ways to save time and yet live The Good Life: Home cooking from scratch was made to look obsolete and démodé. Advertisements for wonder convenience products implied that only old codgers in babushkas shlepped from greengrocer to baker to butcher to fishmonger. Modern cooks one-stop shopped in the supermarket and used jet-age convenience foods. Only farm wives and hillbillies kneaded bread and stirred pots on the stove for hours. Sophisticates, this logic asserted, used processed groceries and all the timesaving techniques they could muster. "Some of these delicious dishes take to shortcuts the way a duck takes to orange sauce," advised Esther Riva Solomon's *Instant Haute Cuisine* in 1963. Even venerable Clementine Paddleford, who had been a fixture at *Gourmet,* writing "Food Flashes" in the idealistic beginning years, got on the bandwagon and proclaimed in 1966 that "Cooking from 'scratch' is no longer the brag thing. Even Grandma and her league practice being instant gourmets." Ms. Paddleford's *Cook Young Cookbook* glorified a "revolt in the ways of cooking, as in the manner of clothing. Cooking is done the easy way, with convenience foods as the timesaving ingredients."

Except for a genuinely well-informed elite and a co-

"Our new way of achieving gourmet food can only happen here—in the land of the mix, the jar, the frozen-food package, and the ubiquitous can opener."

—Poppy Cannon in
The Can-Opener Cook Book

terie of purists, there were large numbers of modern Americans who had come to see themselves as having enlightened palates, and who relished processed foods as symbols of their savoir faire, using all the work-saving tricks in the book to separate themselves from frumpy old cooks who spent all day in the kitchen. *Simple Cooking for the Epicure* distinguished between dowdy housewife cooking, which it described as "usually quite simple and often extremely dull," and stylish epicurean cooking, which was never simple, yet always required less time and effort than the old, plodding ways and inevitably produced food that was "interesting and cosmopolitan."

A clever quickie-gourmet host didn't merely buy and serve canned or frozen things. He or she bought them, doctored them up, then served them. This gave the dish in question a genuinely personal touch; and—to the horror of fastidious idolators who spent hours preparing court bouillon exactly the way *Mastering the Art of French Cooking* instructed—made the host a gourmet cook: presto! To many housewives (and men learning how to cook, too) the glory of the gourmet revolution was not discovering a genuine and arduous recipe for *feuilleté du chef*, as described in the now overly quaint-seeming *Bouquet de France,* but rather learning how to make a wacky, nonconformist dish like Noodle Doodle & Cheese using five cans of wet food, one can of French fried onions, and a defrosted brick of chopped spinach, as instructed by Beverly Ann Ault in *Go Go Gourmet* (1973), which guaranteed that none of its recipes took longer than thirty minutes to prepare, and served as a testament to something more modern even than fine food: creativity.

To the devil-may-care gourmaniac, creativity is what counted, not authenticity. Classical gourmets gag at the concept, but there was an ingenuous exuberance about this utterly novel concept of epicureanism. Unlike old-fashioned fine cooking, which required knowledge, skill, and possibly apprenticeship with a master, the new gourmania was absolutely democratic, accessible to anyone with enough energy and the will to be creative. For these packaged-food enthusiasts, to cook an "authentic" haute cuisine recipe wasn't merely hard, daunting work; it was *uncreative,* it was doing only what had been done thousands of times before by other old-fashioned cooks who knew nothing about the wonders of modern appliances and jet-age food preparation technology. Where was the creative joy in that? On the other hand, there were few cooking experiences that seemed as radically creative—and as modern—as mixing and matching various processed foodstuffs as no person had ever done before. Like a frenzied scientist in a laboratory, America's gourmaniacs stocked their kitchens with packets of soup mix, cans of gravy, boxes of skillet dinner, jars of dried herbs, and frozen blocks of seafood and vegetables and went positively wild combining them and inventing new dishes with a brazenness unknown in any of the world's tradition-bound cuisines. Never mind that what they made didn't necessarily taste so good; what mattered was that through their crazy-quilt methods the world would come to see them as gourmets, no longer content to put mere roasts and potatoes on the family table.

Like so many hand crafts that gained immense popularity at the same time (macramé, creative denim, tie-dyeing), this style of cookery recycled commercially available products into something new and different. These restless culinary artisans took cans and boxes from the grocery shelf and added their personal touch with a fusillade of stuff from other cans and boxes to invent a dish that they could call their own: an original piece of American gourmet cooking. One of the most popular such ways to make ordinary food special was to infuse it with hails of dried herbs from jars, because the use of herbs was the mark of an epicure. Even uncooked dishes such as salad dressings and dips frequently contained sandy streaks of dried, uncooked basil, savory, or oregano, making them practically inedible . . . but nonetheless sophisticated.

Gourmaniac creativity did not have to be difficult or complicated. *Instant Haute Cuisine,* the guide to "French Cooking—American Style" included several recipes for the host who is pressed for time and yet knows that "sauce is the very essence of France, reduced in a pan," and therefore insists on always serving sauce to make the meal excellent. Here are three such alleged recipes, sure to make Escoffier spin in his grave:

E-Z Hollandaise Sauce To one small jar of Hollandaise, add a squeeze of lemon juice. Heat in the top of a double boiler and serve at once.

Lazy Daisy Brown Sauce Heat canned beef gravy until very hot but not boiling. Stir in an equal amount of red or white wine. Heat but do not boil. Serve.

Sauce Mornay in a Minute To a can of cheese soup, add 1 cup of light cream. Heat, stirring, but do not boil. Pour over broccoli, asparagus, etc.

In addition to featuring the customization of store-bought products, many jiffy dishes were elevated to gourmet status by their presentation or by an impressive name. "If I put a gob of chocolate pudding in a glass dish, it's chocolate pudding," observed Esther Riva Solomon in *Instant Haute Cuisine.* "If I put it in a French-looking tiny white porcelain pot, it becomes *petit pot de crème au chocolat.* Put a crystallized violet on top of vanilla ice cream—suddenly it's French." *Instant Haute Cuisine* suggested that any ordinary fare at dinner could bask in the gourmet glow if it was preceded by soup ("To the French a dinner without soup is unthinkable"); it also informs that no one can really tell the difference between a canned soup and one that is slow-simmered from scratch.

Because this style of crafty cookery was so relentlessly artistic, even many of its simplest recipes acquired gourmet charisma; e.g., California dip (sour cream and dried onion soup), green bean bake (frozen beans and mushroom soup), and the Famous Chocolate Wafer cake (cookies and whipped cream frozen into a log). Some of the cleverest gourmet doctoring-up ideas were inspired by a single store-bought product—Stouffer's frozen spinach soufflé, for which recipes abound in community cookbooks from the 1960s—always with a ceremonial title such as "Spinach d'Elegance," "Continental Spinach Bake," or "Easy Connoisseur Soufflé." Cooked as directed in its aluminum tin, spinach soufflé was a luxurious-tasting but prosaic-looking block of rich, green mush. Partially defrosted and decanted from the tin, it could be repacked into a ring mold either alone or with a can of sliced mushrooms, or with artfully arranged cross sections of hard-boiled egg, then baked until set. Once the puffy wheel of spinach soufflé was unmolded onto a serving tray, the chef poured a can of warmed Campbell's cheese soup or a jar of mushroom gravy into its center, then sprinkled the whole thing with bacon bits or Bacos, and voila! The artful dish was an eye-popper—jiggly and verdant, ever so much more attractive than an ordinary brown soufflé made from eggs, etc. that does nothing but puff up in a big, boring, flaccid cloud. For eager gourmaniacs, big food companies such as Stouffer's were prep-chefs, providing basic materials that allowed the home cook to cut loose and shine.

And so it came to pass that out of the ignominious depths of convenience cookery arose what was the strangest and most impertinent contribution of the gourmet revolution—an entirely new cuisine in America, known as brand-name cookery. The basic principle of brand-name cookery was (and is) to mix and match store-bought processed food products in novel and fantastic ways. Its imaginative masters have been home economists and recipe developers employed by food companies, energetic housewives, and writers for voracious weekly newspaper food pages—all of whom have worked feverishly to contribute to an avalanche of brand-name recipes that have come tumbling into American kitchens since the fifties.

Not all the repertory of brand-name cookery aspires to noble gourmet status, to be sure (there have always been plenty of uninspired burger-stretcher stews, tuna casseroles, and Rice Krispies cookies); but as the gourmet revolution crested in the late sixties and early sev-

No one can really tell the difference between a canned soup and one that is slow-simmered from scratch.

enties, nearly every food company hoped to capture the imagination of these unafraid and untutored new gourmets. Campbell's, which was known among brand-name cooks primarily for the condensed soup from which plebeian casseroles were made, invented meat loaf Wellington—chopped beef stuck together in an emulsion of golden mushroom soup and enrobed in Pillsbury refrigerated crescent dinner rolls. Kitchen Bouquet went upscale from pot roast to gourmet duck (basted with undiluted concentrated orange juice and Old Virginia currant jelly). Mrs. Paul's offered fish fillet cordon bleu, for which the frozen fillets of pollack, et al. were blanketed with boiled ham and Swiss cheese and cosseted in nearly full-strength condensed cream of celery soup. Here was the best of both worlds: easy prepared foods that allowed for the signature of creativity.

Brand-name gourmet cookery was no mercurial fad. As countless new fashions in epicureanism have been embraced and discarded by upscale gourmets since the mid-seventies, America's brand-name cooks have stayed true to their creative principles and continue to enlarge their recipe files by incorporating the latest products, regional flavors, and serving trends into their repertory; i.e. instant nachos and taco salad (eat the shell!); cold Szechuan noodles with chunky Skippy peanut butter; Sock-It-To-Me Cake; and elaborate Jell-O molds that emulate the work of world class presentation-food chefs by creating scenes inside the gelatin out of Gummi Bear implants. Unshackled by ancient gastronomic tradition and freed of ordinary cooking's drudgery, these enthusiastic cooks continue to wing their way through supermarket aisles collecting ingredients for their audacious art without ever having to worry about such antiquated rituals as whisking eggs, kneading dough, or stirring a roux. That they blithely consider what they make out of the boxes and cans they buy a kind of gourmet cuisine is resounding evidence that in America no man or woman is denied the opportunity to believe that he or she has savored excellence.

Recipes

Supreme Cocktail Cheese Ball

Clam Dip Classique

Cocktail Hour Brandied Blue Cheese Dip

**Quiche Lorraine, the Way It Was
    Meant to Be**

King for a Day Hot Crabmeat Appetizer

Wedding Reception Rumaki

Hibachi Tidbit Marinade

Noodle Doodle & Cheese

Royal Rock Lobster Tail Kabobs

Chicken Marengo

Roast Duck with Gala Soda Pop Glaze

Meat Loaf Wellington

Shell Steak in a Paper Bag

Green Bean Bake à la Campbell's

**Giant Nutty Cheesy Bacony Mushroom
    Caps d'Elegance**

Avocado, Yes Avocado, Ice Cream

Angostura Bitters Ice Cream

**Ultimate Famous Chocolate Wafer Roll:
    Nesselrode**

Supreme
Cocktail
Cheese Ball

SERVES 8 TO 10

*T*he invention of the cheese ball is an event lost in the mists of culinary history; but if its origins are obscure, its heyday was only yesterday. As the centerpiece of a cocktail party, as a welcome gift to bring that new neighbor, as a do-ahead snack for watching television with special friends, the regal, colorful orb was a totem of hospitality, a way of showing that you took pains to make something extra special and deluxe (as opposed to just slapping down a brick of unadulterated cheese or a jar of ready-made spread). The laws of cheese ball making require that the finished creation always be spherical; but beyond that, a ball maker is limited only by imagination. The primary question to consider is whether the various cheeses that go into it ought to be fully blended, thus creating an even taste and texture. The alternative is only partially compounding them, resulting in interesting veins and lodes of different flavors as the cheese ball is eaten (but also risking structural flaws and a ball that splits in pieces when a fissure is exposed). On the outside, it is traditional to use ground nuts; but the following recipe, based on one in Wish Bone's *Not For Salads Only* book, is for a ball encrusted with chopped pimiento-stuffed olives. The red and green scheme makes it especially appropriate for Christmas parties.

1 cup shredded Cheddar cheese
½ cup shredded blue cheese
4 ounces (half a large brick) of cream cheese
½ cup Thousand Island dressing
1 hard-boiled egg, chopped
2 tablespoons diced green pepper
2 teaspoons Worcestershire sauce
⅛ teaspoon hot pepper sauce
1 cup chopped pimiento-stuffed olives

Combine all ingredients except the olives. Mix thoroughly. Wrap the mixture in plastic wrap and refrigerate until it is firm, 2 hours or more. Form the mixture into a smooth ball and roll it in the chopped olives. Chill again, lightly covered, until ready to serve. Serve with crackers and provide a few cheese knives.

One of the unsung advances in American postwar gastronomy was the invention of the corrugated, heavy-duty potato chip, which made possible a whole world of dips too ponderous for ordinary, fragile chips. Perhaps the greatest and most fondly remembered of these mighty compounds was clam dip—a fundamental fusion of ocean zest (in the form of canned minced clams) and dairy luxury (cream cheese). Of this recipe, adapted from the "Hooray for Holidays and Parties" chapter of Helen Gurley Brown's *Single Girl's Cookbook,* Mrs. Brown wrote, "here is my favorite, favorite cocktail party dip. Sometimes I make up a batch just for *me.*" She suggested that in addition to crinkled potato chips for dipping, this hearty amalgam could be served with a spoon and dolloped onto little rounds of cocktail rye bread.

Clam Dip Classique

SERVES 6 TO 8

2 garlic cloves
2 teaspoons lemon juice
1 can (7½ ounces) minced clams
1 small onion, finely minced
3 packages (3 ounces) cream cheese, softened
2 to 4 tablespoons sour cream

Put the garlic cloves through a press and let the juices fall into a small mixing bowl. Add 1 teaspoon of the lemon juice. Drain the clams, reserving a few teaspoons of their juice, and add the clams to the garlic. Add the minced onion.

In a separate bowl, mash the cream cheese with a fork, adding just enough sour cream to make the mixture smooth and stirrable, but not so much it gets soupy. Add the cheese to the clams and mix, adding lemon juice and the reserved clam juice to taste. Store the dip in the refrigerator (up to several days), but serve it at room temperature.

Cocktail Hour Brandied Blue Cheese Dip

SERVES 6 TO 8

*L*ila Perl introduced her "Saturday Buffet Supper" chapter of *What Cooks in Suburbia* by saying, "The aim of this book is to present recipes that are 'different.'" Among the novelties she suggests are literally dozens of hors d'oeuvre, cocktail snacks, dunks, turnovers, and spreads, all of which were well suited to the new style of informal—and yet culinarily sophisticated—entertaining. Serve yourself was the smart way to do things, she advised, at chafing dishes, bowls of dip, and platters of canapés. Among the recipes considered most soigné at this type of finger-food party was any combination of cheese and wine or brandy. In fact, crocks of already brandied cheese were a popular item in gourmet shops and even supermarkets. It is our guess—speculation only—that somehow the combination trickled down and into the American cocktail hour from the time-honored British tradition of serving port and Stilton *after* a meal. Whatever its lineage, this dip

has a long-forgotten luxury flavor that launches us back to the 1950s and to Saturday night cocktail parties given by our parents. Oh, how glamorous those evenings seemed! The bed in the guest room was piled with ladies' minks and Persian lamb jackets redolent of perfume; grown-ups smoked cigarettes and drank sweet Manhattans with bright red maraschino cherries in them; and before bedtime, children were allowed out of their rooms to meet the company and act sophisticated by eating a celery rib stuffed with brandied blue cheese dip. That is how Mrs. Perl suggests serving this nostalgic amalgam: surrounded by ribs of celery and enough small knives so guests can "stuff their own."

    4 tablespoons butter, softened at room temperature
    4 ounces cream cheese, softened at room temperature
    4 ounces blue cheese, crumbled
    4 tablespoons mayonnaise
    2 teaspoons Worcestershire sauce
    1½ tablespoons brandy
    ½ cup chopped walnuts

Mash together or beat with an electric mixer the butter, cream cheese, and blue cheese. Add all remaining ingredients except nuts, beating until smooth and fluffy. Fold in walnuts. Dip may be covered and refrigerated, but it should be served only slightly cool (so it is spreadable), garnished, if desired, with additional chopped walnuts.

Quiche Lorraine, the Way It Was Meant to Be

SERVES 4 TO 6 AS
AN ENTRÉE, 8 TO 10 AS
AN HORS D'OEUVRE

*T*his is an adaptation of the recipe that *Gourmet* provided its reader from Minnesota who wrote in 1946 asking about the strange and wonderful cheese dish she had discovered in the course of her exploration of good food and foreign cooking. Over the next fifteen years quiche was popularized both in little pieces as an hors d'oeuvre and in big, pie-slice portions as a perfect centerpiece for Sunday brunch until it became one of the definitive symbols of gourmet cuisine. For at least a dozen more years it retained its connoisseur's aura; in fact, as late as 1978 we sat in a fairly important Detroit dining room and listened as the waitress carefully explained to her customer, a sophisticated-looking executive from the auto industry, that quiche Lorraine was "like bacon and eggs in a crust." By this time however, quiche had overstayed its welcome in many gourmets' repertoires. It was too easy to make in advance and had become a caterer's platitude. Despite its still being out of fashion, freshly made quiche Lorraine with multiple strata of thick bacon and melted veins of Swiss cheese throughout its quivering custard *is* a well-nigh perfect flavor combination.

Dough for a 1-crust 9-inch pie (a frozen pie crust is fine)
6 thick slices of bacon
5 ounces Swiss cheese, cut into 10-12 slices about the
    same size as the cooked bacon
4 eggs
1 tablespoon flour
Generous grating of nutmeg
½ teaspoon salt
Pinch of cayenne
2 cups heavy cream
1½ tablespoons butter, melted

Line a 9-inch pie plate with dough.

Preheat oven to 375 degrees.

Fry the bacon until it is cooked but not crisp. Drain on paper towels.

Layer the bacon and cheese in a crosshatch pattern on the pie dough.

Beat together the eggs, flour, nutmeg, salt, and cayenne. Gradually beat in the cream and, finally, the melted butter. Beat well and strain the mixture over the bacon and cheese in the pie crust. Bake 45 to 50 minutes, or until the custard is set and the top is nicely browned. Serve slightly warm.

King for a Day Hot Crabmeat Appetizer

MAKES 1½ CUPS

"*N*obody, but nobody can resist it!" raved Ceil Dyer when she wrote about the classic hot hors d'oeuvre popularized by Kraft to sell cream cheese. No question about it: To gobble from a big bowl of this hot, creamy, seafood-flavored pabulum, with all the Ritz crackers you can eat for dipping into it, makes any guest feel like royalty.

1 package (8 ounces) cream cheese
¼ cup mayonnaise
2 tablespoons finely chopped onion
2 tablespoons milk
1 teaspoon prepared horseradish
½ teaspoon Dijon mustard
¼ teaspoon salt
¼ teaspoon garlic salt
Dash of pepper
1 can (7 ounces) flaked crabmeat, drained
⅓ cup sliced almonds, toasted

Preheat oven to 375 degrees.

Combine all ingredients except the crabmeat and almonds. Mix well until blended or process in a food processor. Fold in the crabmeat and spoon the mixture into a small ovenproof baking dish. Sprinkle with almonds and bake 15 minutes.

Serve warm with crackers, chips, or crudités.

$\mathcal{T}$rader Vic revealed that rumaki originally came from Hawaii and were of Chinese origin, but with a Japanese name. In his words, they were "thoroughly integrated"—which is one reason that American gourmets of the 1960s, with their United Nations idealism about the cuisines of the world, loved them so. They are indeed beguiling—and a conspicuous refinement beyond common salted nuts, chips and dip, or even pigs in blankets. Rumaki are best cooked quickly over open coals. They can also be broiled or—Trader Vic's way—fried in deep fat.

Wedding Reception Rumaki

SERVES 6 TO 8

    1 tablespoon sugar
    1 bay leaf
    1 teaspoon ground cinnamon
    1 piece (1 inch) fresh ginger, peeled and diced
    2 tablespoons 5-spice powder
    1 cup chicken broth
    1 garlic clove, crushed
    1½ cups soy sauce
    1 pound chicken livers
    ½ pound thinly sliced bacon
    1 can (8 ounces) sliced water chestnuts
    1 bunch of scallions, sliced lengthwise into thin strips

Mix sugar, seasonings, broth, and garlic with soy sauce in a saucepan and bring to a boil. Reduce heat. Simmer uncovered 5 minutes. Add chicken livers and bring to a boil again. Reduce heat. Simmer 10 minutes. Remove chicken livers from sauce and let them cool.

When chicken livers are cool enough to handle, slice and wrap a third of a strip of bacon around 1 bite-size piece of chicken liver, 1 piece of water chestnut, and a few small strips of scallion. Secure each packet with a toothpick.

Cook over hot coals or broil 5 to 10 minutes, turning, until bacon is crisp. Serve immediately.

Hibachi
Tidbit
Marinade

ENOUGH FOR ABOUT
12 SKEWERS

"*Y*ou will find that the delicate lemon-lime flavor of 7-Up lends sparkle, subtle tang, and a light airiness to your favorite party dishes," instructed a 1961 brochure called "7-Up Goes to a Party." Cooking with soda pop had been a venerable tradition among American home cooks since southerners discovered the invigorated savor that a country ham developed when basted with Coca-Cola; but it wasn't until the 1950s that soda makers began exploring with zeal more unlikely possibilities. Dr. Pepper stepped forth with a recipe for home-baked bread made sweet and prune-flavored by an infusion of warmed pop; thousands of cooks discovered the wonder of baking Coca-Cola cake and using soda for their Jell-O molds; and 7-Up circulated brochures galore with recipes for the likes of tuna chow mein (in 7-Up and cornstarch gravy), 7-Up fondue, and peas provençal (simmered in 7-up). One of the brightest ideas was using 7-Up in a marinade on hibachi-cooked, skewered foods, thus giving them the sweet zest that nearly all luau-things were supposed to have.

1 garlic clove, minced
1 tablespoon curry powder
1 tablespoon soy sauce
½ tablespoon crushed peppercorns
1 teaspoon salt
⅛ teaspoon MSG (omit if it paralyzes you)
½ cup olive oil
1 bottle (7 ounces) 7-Up (or a scant cup)

Thoroughly mix all the seasonings with olive oil. Stir in 7-Up. Thread about 12 skewers with shrimp, meat cubes, green pepper pieces, cherry tomatoes, small onions, and mushrooms. Soak loaded skewers in the marinade about an hour before cooking, then cook on a hibachi grill or underneath an oven broiler, using the marinade to baste the skewers frequently as they cook.

*B*everly Ann Ault, the *Go Go Gourmet*, is described on her book jacket as a "Navy wife, mother of three, teacher, lecturer, Cub Scout leader, culinary award winner, choir director, horticulturalist, civic leader, world traveler, interior decorator, and children's literature consultant [who] has only thirty minutes to prepare dinner." Apparently Mrs. Ault was so busy that the only introductory remarks she had time to compose about her recipe for Noodle Doodle & Cheese dish were: "Super good!" What we wonder is: Which ingredient is the *doodle*? Another mystery: The original recipe calls for *cans* of macaroni and cheese, a supermarket ingredient with which we are unfamiliar. We prepare this nice meal-in-a-casserole using Kraft Dinner, which does prolong the preparation time by a few minutes; but if you've got a microwave to defrost the broccoli, you can still whip it up in under ten. The cottage cheese and broccoli help de-salinize the Kraft Dinner; and if you want to make this practically health food, you can leave out the canned French fried onions.

2 packages Kraft macaroni & cheese dinner
½ cup cottage cheese
1 package (10 ounces) frozen chopped broccoli
1 bunch of scallions, chopped
½ teaspoon dried oregano
1 can (3½ ounces) French fried onions

Prepare the macaroni and cheese dinners according to the directions on the box, but use ½ cup of cottage cheese (¼ cup for each dinner) instead of milk when mixing them. As the noodles cook, cook the frozen broccoli in a microwave oven (about 8 minutes at full power, stirring once halfway through).

Preheat oven to 350 degrees.

In a 3-quart casserole, stir together the prepared dinners with the broccoli, scallions, oregano, and half the French fried onions. Sprinkle the remaining onions on top and bake uncovered 15 to 20 minutes.

Royal Rock Lobster Tail Kabobs

SERVES 6 TO 8

*L*obsters are undeniably fancy—a gourmet staple going back to la belle époque, but it is hard to eat them elegantly. If you are a host who wants to conduct a dignified dinner at which you can show off your nice table linens and serve wine in refined crystal goblets, whole lobster is out of the question. There is simply no polite way to break the shells and extract the meat at the table. Soon, wineglasses will be clouded by buttery thumbprints, the tablecloth will be sotted with juice, and instead of carrying on soigné conversations, guests are likely to be grunting and slurping meat from the creature's joints and sucking on its tentacles. You can always take the meat out of the shell yourself and make lobster thermidor or Newburg, but in the 1960s as epicures broadened their horizons and ate lobster in the Greek isles and langouste in Paris, the classic cream-sauced seafood dishes began to seem old-fashioned and tearoomy. The modern—and spotless—way to serve lobster was to serve lobster *tails*.

America fell in love with lobster tails after World War II, and by the late 1960s we were gobbling 12 million pounds of them a year—as the seafood half of surf 'n' turf in restaurants, and by themselves on home barbecues across the land. Although not as delicately fleshed or as subtly flavored as a whole north Atlantic lobster, tails (which are the best part of the clawless spiny lobster found in waters farther south) provide a kind of basic sawing-with-knife and chewing satisfaction equivalent to beefsteak, as well as the kingly satisfaction of knowing that all your food can be extracted from its shell as one, giant pink tread. For cooking à deux, tails fit nicely on a hibachi grill; and in 1969, *Gusto International*, the "magazine for the modern epicure," proclaimed, "The langouste, the royal rock lobster that master French chefs have immortalized the world over, is one of the ideal foods for barbecuing." Unlike north Atlantic lobsters, which are best bought alive, tails are convenient and eliminate the distress of deciding how to kill them. They are sold frozen solid, and keep that way for months.

8 medium-size rock lobster tails
2 navel oranges, unpeeled and quartered
8 cling peach halves
8 tablespoons (1 stick) butter, melted
⅓ cup dry sherry
2 tablespoons lemon juice
1 can (6 ounces) frozen concentrated pineapple-orange
   juice, thawed

Thaw the lobster tails and fire up the coals in an outdoor grill or hibachi. Use scissors to cut the underside membrane of the tails, then carefully remove the meat in one piece. Thread the meat lengthwise on a skewer with an orange quarter and a peach half. Combine all remaining ingredients. Brush the kabobs with this mixture and put them on a rack 6 inches above white-hot coals. Turn the kabobs and brush them with sauce as they cook. Grill them until the lobster meat is opaque and slightly browned. Serve drizzled with remaining sauce.

Chicken Marengo

SERVES 4

*F*or enthusiastic newcomers to deluxe cookery, one of the most satisfying ways to ply their skills was chicken Marengo, a gaudy entrée with a pedigree going back to Napoleon, who allegedly ate it after every battle. Originally, it was created by his chef out of chicken, tomatoes, mushrooms, and onions, all of which were found around Marengo, where the Emperor had enjoyed a great victory. From that time on, practitioners of haute cuisine were forever gilding it with ever more opulent ingredients. This recipe from *Instant Haute Cuisine (French Cooking, American Style)* (1961) shows just how easy and nearly instantaneous fancy food could be. It uses canned mushroom gravy instead of mushrooms and tomato paste instead of tomatoes, and forsakes olives altogether, but adds already cooked chunky lobster tail, croutons, and to top the whole thing off, fried eggs. The finished dish is a sight guaranteed to bring tears of joy to gourmaniacal eyes.

> 1 frying chicken, about 3 pounds, cut up
> Salt and pepper
> 4 tablespoons butter
> 1 tablespoon tomato paste
> ¾ cup canned mushroom gravy
> ½ cup white wine
> 4 eggs
> 4 small rock lobster tails, cooked in their shells
> ½ cup garlic-flavored croutons
> Chopped parsley

Wash chicken parts and pat them dry. Season with salt and pepper. Heat the butter in a large frying pan. Brown the chicken parts on both sides over medium heat. Reduce heat. Add tomato paste, gravy, and wine, adding more wine if sauce is pasty. Cover and cook slowly until chicken is tender, about 25 minutes. Uncover for the last 10 minutes.

When the chicken is nearly done, fry the eggs and trim them with a round cookie cutter so they are perfect circles. Set aside.

When the chicken is done, add the lobster tails and heat through. Add croutons. Immediately turn out onto a warmed serving platter. Sprinkle with parsley. Top with fried eggs.

*E*sther Riva Solomon, author of *Instant Haute Cuisine*, described duck's importance to the connoisseur of fine food this way: "When you say *Paris* . . . I say *duck*. Duck with black cherries, pressed duck, duck with olives. I remember walking the streets, map in hand, searching for the restaurants famous for duck." One recipe we'll wager Mrs. Solomon did not find in the boites and bistros of Paris was roast duck with gala soda pop glaze, which we discovered in a 1963 brochure called "Quick Recipe Favorites," published to promote the use of 7-Up in cooking. Soda pop and poultry were a natural combination in the hands of jiffy gourmets who had seen for themselves in continental restaurants that the modish thing to do with a duck was to bathe it with something sweet and sticky. Using 7-Up, Dr. Pepper, or ginger ale saved a cook the trouble of preparing an elaborate sauce à l'orange. In fact, the lemon-lime tang of 7-Up is an inspired foil for the gamy flavor of a crisp-skinned duck. The original recipe calls for ½ cup of brown sugar and a tablespoon of cornstarch, both of which we have halved. Soda pop makes this glaze just sweet enough, and too much cornstarch is the ruination of any sauce.

Roast Duck with Gala Soda Pop Glaze

SERVES 4 TO 6

  1 duck, 4 to 5 pounds, ready to cook
  4 cups prepared seasoned bread crumb stuffing
  ¼ cup brown sugar
  1½ teaspoons cornstarch
  1 teaspoon caraway seeds
  ¼ teaspoon salt
  1 bottle (7 ounces) 7-up (scant cup)
  1 cup halved seedless white grapes

Preheat oven to 325 degrees.

Fill the duck with bread crumb stuffing. Close it with poultry pins; lace the pins with string to keep the stuffing inside. Secure the neck skin over the back with another poultry pin. Place the duck, back side down, on a rack in a shallow, open baking pan and bake 2½ to 3 hours, until tender. After 2 hours, spoon on glaze.

To make the glaze, mix brown sugar, cornstarch, caraway seeds, and salt in a saucepan. Add 7-Up. Cook over low heat, stirring, until slightly thickened. Brush sauce on duck. When ready to serve, add grapes and simmer 3 minutes. Use this as a sauce for the duck.

Meat Loaf
Wellington

SERVES 6 TO 8

*M*eat loaf is rightfully considered by most people to be a plebeian dish; that is its charm. But gourmaniacs of the 1950s and 1960s found ways to make even this blue-collar food seem opulent, thus satisfying a meat-hungry family while providing them the aesthetic education gained by eating their loaf of meat in the manner of a British Lord—en croute. The simplest way to do this was to encase the cooked loaf in a soft blanket of seasoned mashed potatoes, then sprinkle the spuds with grated Cheddar cheese and bake it until the cheese got crusty: a lumpish-looking gloss on shepherd's pie. The truly swank (and actually quite tasty) way to dress up meat loaf was to use refrigerated crescent rolls to make a fancy crust, as follows.

1 can (10½ ounces) Campbell's condensed golden
   mushroom soup
2 pounds ground beef
½ cup fine dry bread crumbs
1 egg, slightly beaten
⅓ cup finely chopped onion
1 minced garlic clove
1 teaspoon Worcestershire sauce
¼ cup ketchup
1 can (8 ounces) refrigerated crescent dinner rolls
⅓ cup sour cream

Preheat oven to 375 degrees.

Mix ½ cup of the soup with beef, bread crumbs, egg, onion, garlic, Worcestershire sauce, and ketchup. Form the meat into a firm 8 × 4-inch loaf and place the loaf on a shallow baking pan. Bake 65 minutes.

Spoon fat out of the meat loaf pan. Separate rolls and overlap them on a floured pastry board, pressing to form them into one large blanket of dough big enough to completely cover the loaf. Place the blanket over the loaf and mold it to fit, trimming excess dough. (Use excess dough to make fleur-de-lis patterns or happy faces to stick on the crust, if desired.) Return to the oven and bake 15 to 20 minutes longer, or until the crust is light golden brown.

In a saucepan, blend the remaining soup and sour cream and warm it over very low heat, thinning with up to ¼ cup of water to create a smooth gravy. Ladle over individual slices of meat loaf en croute.

Shell Steak in a Paper Bag

SERVES 1

*A*lan Koehler's *Madison Avenue Cookbook* ("For People Who Can't Cook and Don't Want Other People to Know It") advised readers that one of the most uncouth things a person could do was to cook or eat meat well done. Curiously, the doneness of meat has become one of our culture's litmus tests of sophistication. Proverbial wisdom asserts that true epicures like it only rare, barely cooked, or even raw. One *bec fin* who considered rare steak a pillar of sophistication was Maurice C. Dreicer, whose achievements in the 1950s included cutting a 78 r.p.m. record billed as the world's only aural bartender's guide (complete with sound effects), the creation of The Order of the Great Dining Establishments of the World (a list of his favorite restaurants), and serving as president, simultaneously, of Cigar Smokers United and The Ale League of the World. Whenever Mr. Dreicer ordered steak in a restaurant, he presented the waiter with a tasteful little card on which had been engraved

his precise instructions for the preparation of beef as he preferred it: extra blood rare, meaning seared for a minute or less per side. Upon chefs who complied, he bestowed the Dreicer Silver Butter Knife Award.

Of the following clever recipe for seasoned steak cooked in a bag, the *Madison Avenue Cookbook* advises, "Inquire of your guests whether they prefer their steak rare, medium, or well done, but serve it only rare." In fact, it is virtually impossible to cook steak in a paper bag any way other than rare; locked inside the brown paper with garlic and spice, the meat miraculously imbibes the savory flavors with which it has been packed and assumes the quality of being cooked; yet it shows little of the darkening or crustiness associated with well-done or even medium-done grilled or broiled steaks. The recipe is for one serving. Multiply as you wish, using an individual bag for each steak.

> **1 shell steak, about ¾ pound and 1 inch thick**
> **1 tablespoon olive oil**
> **1 small garlic clove, minced**
> **½ teaspoon bouquet garni**
> **½ teaspoon cracked black pepper**
> **½ teaspoon kosher salt**
> **2 tablespoons unflavored dry bread crumbs**

Preheat oven to 400 degrees.

Rub the steak with oil. Combine the garlic, seasonings, and bread crumbs and rub them into the steak, pressing to make them cling as well as possible. Put the steak in a brown paper bag on a roasting pan, fold the bag closed, and cook 25 minutes.

Carefully remove the bag with the steak still inside to a serving platter and carry it to the table. Peel the bag away and serve.

Green Bean Bake à la Campbell's

SERVES 4 TO 6

*T*here aren't many vegetable dishes plainer or sadder looking than unadorned string beans, especially if they come from a can or a frozen box. In the 1960s Campbell's figured out a way to lift beans from the doldrums by suspending them in cream of mushroom soup. Borrowing a trick from advanced tuna-casserole chefs, the company laced its invention, known as Green Bean Bake, with a can of French fried onions, giving it such a high-class aura that many people came to know it, spuriously, as French green beans.

> 1 can (10¾ ounces) Campbell's condensed cream
>   of mushroom soup
> ½ cup milk
> 1 teaspoon soy sauce
> Dash of black pepper
> 2 packages (9 ounces each) frozen green beans,
>   defrosted, cooked, and drained
> 1 can (2.8 ounces) French fried onions (Durkee brand)

Preheat oven to 350 degrees.

In a 1½-quart casserole, mix soup, milk, soy sauce, and pepper until smooth. Add the beans and half the onions. Bake uncovered 25 minutes. Stir. Top with remaining onions. Bake 5 to 10 minutes more, until onions are golden brown.

Among the many excellent uses ambitious cooks found for Stouffer's spinach soufflé, other than its intended purpose as an elegant side dish, this awe-inspiring but easily made concoction was one of the most popular. For giant mushroom caps, you will need a knife and fork; use smaller mushrooms and half-strips of bacon and you have swank finger food that makes yummy little hot hors d'oeuvre.

Giant Nutty Cheesy Bacony Mushroom Caps d'Elegance

SERVES 4 TO 6

1 box Stouffer's spinach soufflé, cooked as directed
1 cup grated Cheddar cheese
½ cup chopped walnuts
18 extra-large mushroom caps (1½ to 2 inches in diameter), washed and scrubbed clean
18 strips of bacon

Heat oven to 375 degrees.

Combine cooked spinach soufflé with grated Cheddar and walnuts. Dollop into the mushroom caps and wrap each cap with a strip of bacon. Place the caps on a baking sheet and bake 25 minutes, then broil about 5 minutes, or until bacon is crisp.

Avocado, Yes Avocado, Ice Cream

2 PINTS; SERVES 6 TO 8

*A*vocados had been cultivated for centuries by natives and newcomers to the New World, but in the 1950s and 1960s they were suddenly embraced with a new kind of enthusiasm. Those nurtured from pits into trees that grew indoors in the kitchen, bathroom, or dining room became the kookiest, merriest, most offbeat fun fruit since tropical bananas were glorified in the 1920s. Somehow, they seemed exotic (they were not); and although it wasn't only gourmets who relished them (skinny single perky girls often grew avocado trees to signify their zaniness), eating them was a sign of a relatively sophisticated palate and a person who knew how to enjoy life. "The avocado is instantly the first and exclusive subject of conversation whenever a group gathers in my living room," wrote Hazel Perper, the self-coronated "Avocado Lady" in her 1965 book, *The Avocado Pit Grower's Indoor How-to Book*. Ms. Perper's rival for avocado domination was Helen Rosenbaum, whose *Don't Swallow the Avocado Pit—and What to Do with the Rest of It* not only told how to care for avocado plants, but included chapters about "Avocadoitis," "Sex and the Single Avocado," and "Avocado People" (thumbnail biographies of men and women who have been conspicuously successful growing avocado plants). "Avocados are not just another pretty face on the fruit counter, Ms. Rosenbaum instructed readers, then went on to offer "gourmet" recipes for the likes of avocado egg-nests for breakfast, avocado pizza, even avocado cocktails made with vodka, milk, Galliano, and avocado pulp.

The common thing to do with avocados was to use them in salads, or as edible bowls for salads of shrimp or crabmeat; but *Hawaiian Cuisine*, published in 1963 by the Hawaii State Society to commemorate the Aloha State's incorporation into the Union, included a wacky, deliciously unctuous recipe that connoisseurs of exotic food were supposed to serve after a meal of South Seas seafood or kabobs cooked outdoors. It is a truly unusual and likable flavor combination, and the pale hue is a bewitching reminder of the avocado green color scheme of so many modern 1960s kitchens.

2 egg yolks
1 cup sugar
2 cups heavy cream
Dash of salt
½ teaspoon vanilla extract
½ teaspoon almond extract
2 cups well-mashed avocado pulp (about 2
    good-size avocados)

Beat the egg yolks and ½ cup sugar until thoroughly mixed, then beat in the cream. Cook in the top of a double boiler over simmering water, stirring frequently, until thickened enough to coat the back of a spoon, about 5 minutes. Add salt, vanilla extract, and almond extract. Chill.

Add the remaining ½ cup sugar to the avocado pulp. Add the chilled custard mixture and freeze until the mixture is about half-frozen. Remove it from freezer, scoop it into a chilled bowl, and beat it with a balloon whisk until it is smooth but not melted, about 30 seconds. Return it to the freezer and freeze until firm.

Angostura Bitters Ice Cream

2 PINTS; SERVES 6 TO 8

*O*ne of the methods by which some epicures learned to separate themselves from the rest of the eating world was to disdain things that were too sweet: Jell-O, bread recipes that called for sugar, fruits in syrup, even any wine that wasn't bone dry. The corollary to this proposition is that bitter, pungent things are always interesting. This logic made it easy for the Angostura company to sell its aromatic bitters in a 1968 brochure: "a secret ingredient by famous chefs and practicing gourmets for almost a century and a half." One of the genuinely intriguing recipes invented by the Angostura company was for ice cream: an inspired counterpoint of bitters and sweetened, iced cream. The recipe, as follows, was the basic freezer method, which makes a fairly dense ice cream. If you have an ice cream maker, use a recipe for vanilla, reduce or eliminate the vanilla bean or vanilla extract, and add a tablespoon of Angostura bitters for each pint. The results, without vanilla flavoring, are clever and delicious—ice cream with an eye-opening twist. The extremely lazy way to do it is to take a pint of good vanilla ice cream, semi-defrost it, mix in the Angostura, and re-freeze it.

> **3 eggs**
> **½ cup sugar**
> **2 cups milk**
> **2 cups heavy cream**
> **2 tablespoons Angostura bitters**

Whisk eggs, adding sugar gradually.

Heat the milk and cream to the boiling point. Whisk ¼ cup of warmed milk and cream mixture into eggs, then gradually add the warmed egg back into milk and cream mixture, whisking constantly until mixture thickens enough to coat the back of a spoon, about 5 minutes. Do not allow it to boil. If there are any lumps, strain the mixture. Cool to room temperature. Stir in Angostura bitters.

Pour into two shallow freezer trays (as for ice cubes) and freeze until the mixture is about half-frozen. Remove it from the freezer, scoop it into a chilled bowl, and beat it with a balloon whisk until it is smooth but not melted, about 30 seconds. Return it to the freezer and freeze until firm.

The recipe for Famous Chocolate Wafer roll is an un-dying classic, still on the box of Nabisco Famous Chocolate Wafers. Made exactly as instructed, and cut on the diagonal, it is spiffy and tasteful; but gourmaniacs have always liked to dude it up, mostly by tinting the whipped cream with food coloring or flavoring it. Probably the most luscious thing to do with the black and white log (known to some as zebra cake) is to pack the whipped cream with the mixture of candied fruits, nuts, and crumbled macaroons frequently called nesselrode—a lavish mélange found only in affluent dining rooms, customarily in the form of frozen pudding or gelatinized pie.

> **2 cups cream**
> **⅓ cup confectioners' sugar**
> **½ teaspoon vanilla extract**
> **⅓ cup chopped raisins**
> **⅓ cup candied citrus peels, finely chopped; plus ⅓ cup coarsely chopped**
> **2 tablespoons ground almonds**
> **⅔ cup crumbled macaroons**
> **20 Nabisco Famous Chocolate Wafers (about half a package)**

Whip the cream with the sugar and vanilla, and chill a little more than 1 cup. To the whipped cream that remains, fold in the raisins, finely chopped citrus, almonds, and macaroons. Generously spread the wafers with this mixture, stacking them up in fives, as neatly as possible, on wax paper on a plate. Chill the wafer stacks for 15 minutes. Lay the stacks on their sides, end to end, on a serving plate, forming a single long roll. If desired, whip a drop of food coloring into the reserved whipped cream, then spread it around the outside of the roll, forming a smooth tube. Sprinkle the tube with the coarsely chopped candied citrus peels. Cover it lightly and freeze at least 4 hours. Use a serrated knife to cut the tube *diagonally*, then allow each serving to warm slightly at room temperature before serving.

By the early 1970s, another culinary insurrection was stewing.

The savory crusade that had begun with high hopes and idealism after World War II encouraged many Americans to elevate their taste beyond square meals and popularized food as a social pleasure; but like all revolutions that succeed, gourmet dogma turned stale. The principle of glorifying gastronomic excellence had hardened into its own set of clichés that seemed to value pretense above gusto. For those who had been stirred by the populist ethics of the 1960s, the word *gourmet* had returned to its earlier connotations of elitism: Too many snobs indulged in haute cuisine to display their wealth and status; too many professedly gourmet restaurants specialized in arrogance rather than good meals.

It was no longer necessarily a badge of distinction for a home cook to call the food he or she served *gourmet*. For those serious gastronomes who had mastered the art of French cooking, and perhaps of other countries' cooking, too, the word had lost its charisma as it was liberally applied by advertisers to envelopes of powdered instant sauce béarnaise and frozen dinners of bogus haute cuisine that made it possible for any culinary parvenu to palm himself off as a gourmet host by defrosting heat-n-serve factory-processed boxes of fancy foodstuffs.

Gourmet food was beginning to seemed old-fashioned rather than modern. Its traditional prodigalities, heavy on the cream and butter, ran contrary to many Americans' growing infatuation with fitness and nutrition. And if *real* haute cuisine was bad for you because it was too rich, the chemically impregnated prosthetic gourmet fare sold in supermarkets and dished out by spinning continental restaurants was an even greater crime against a cultivated palate and a healthy self. The revolution of the 1970s was a backlash against overrich, overprocessed, overpackaged meals—gourmet and faux gourmet as well. The new breed of American epicures exalted culinary probity above all things and glorified a style of eating that seemed closer to nature and natural life. Their enemy was big business, which they saw as having drained all the flavor (as well as nutritional value)

Alice Waters in the kitchen of Chez Panisse: A new era begins.

from food by refining it, sterilizing and homogenizing it, overcooking it and thereby separating it from the wholesomeness of a garden in the good earth. Just as gourmets a quarter century earlier had felt the exhilaration of being at the front lines of a battle against the Puritan austerity of American taste, the new epicures believed they were leading an uprising against an establishment that conspired to turn food into flavorless aliment more suitable for bionic robots than for human beings.

No phenomenon expressed the new attitude toward food more convincingly than the widening eminence of Chez Panisse through the 1970s. Certainly the most charismatic restaurant of its era, and possibly the most pretentiously unpretentious one in history, Chez Panisse, which opened in Berkeley in 1971, offered none of the pageantry of traditional deluxe dining. It was country casual; its customers wore jeans and turquoise jewelry rather than bouclé silk and diamonds. Yet its pursuit of excellence was as relentless as that which characterized the Pavillon two and three decades earlier. Chef and owner Alice Waters formulated a Franco-Italo-California cuisine out of spicy watercress and suckling pigs from Amador County, Zinfandel from the Napa Valley, local garlic and goat cheese, Pacific oysters, sun-dried tomatoes, backyard herbs and produce, and what she described as "perfect little lettuces carefully hand-picked from the hillside garden and served within a few hours." The goal, she said, was self-sufficiency and freedom from the food establishment that for her and many like her had come to symbolize the mediocrity of American eating habits. Her standards of personal commitment verged on culinary fetishism: Customers ate the meal she decided to make that evening, whether they liked it or not. "When people come to the restaurant, I want to insist that they eat in a certain way," she wrote. Her mania for that "certain way" of eating became a litany among passionate eaters in the 1970s, who romanticized almost any food that was like hers: charcoal-roasted or locally grown, glistening with olive oil, oozing warm goat cheese, festooned with surprising salad greens, or—most important of all—*fresh*.

Fresh became the highest encomium for food, not just because its antonym is *stale*, but because it implied that the food had not been tampered with or adulterated. The closer anything was to its living, natural state, the more America's nouvelle epicures liked it. Heavy sauce, frequently used by second-rate gourmet chefs to mask crummy food, became anathema; and one of the nostrums of fashionable eating was that nearly everything ought to be undercooked, therefore more purely itself. Vegetables and pasta were always served painfully *al dente*; bloody rare duck breast and pink-fleshed chicken were considered proper; salmon was sautéed on one side only, uncooked slabs of tuna fish were pounded into oceanic carpaccio, and even beans were frequently cooked so briefly that they broke when bitten.

In the quest to avoid food with a corporate taint (and the diminution of flavor and quality that taint implied), almost anything produced by a cottage industry was treasured by post-gourmet epicures, who fell into rapture over organically grown, hand-picked baby vegetables and artisanal cheeses produced on boutique farms by medieval history PhDs getting back in touch with nature.

Worn-out bourgeois restaurants dishing up pasty quiche, onion soup topped with rubbery cheese, canned pâté, and cloying duck à l'orange were passé, along with their great, beribboned, leatherette-bound menus listing canonical French dishes by their name in flowery script (i.e. *Le Coq au Vin en Casserole du Chevalier du Tastevin*). In their place came chic bistros with young chefs who took up the gauntlet of gastronomic excellence but shunned the hoary rituals now associated with gourmet dining rooms. And in the place of the worldly *bec fins* who considered classic haute cuisine the holy grail came a new generation of epicures, the foodies. Foodies had their own peculiar set of standards and rituals: just as *le*, *la*, and *les* had once been *de rigueur* on any menu purporting to offer first-class food, obsessive accounts of each ingredient's origins became the way stylish chefs let customers know they were eating authentic things rather than cryonautically preserved mystery meat hiding under a rich sauce. Instead of "steak with mushroom gravy," a modern American bistro menu might entice a diner with "entrecôte cut from a two-year-old, corn-fed, Montana steer of Frisian-Holstein lineage, dry-aged five weeks, broiled over mesquite and grape vine clippings, served with a natural Gilroy-garlic gravy of *Morchella semilibera* mushrooms harvested by the Syfert family in the woods outside Boyne City, Michigan."

The ascendance of the Chez Panisse style among trend-conscious home cooks as well as among celebrity chefs in chic restaurants marks the end of the story of the American gourmet. To describe her cuisine and its spiritual meaning, Alice Waters' introduction to the *Chez Panisse Menu Cookbook* in 1982 used such enchanting expressions as "earthiness," "nourish and nurture," "freshest and finest," "aesthetics of food," and "idealism and experimentation." Not once in the description of the way she cooked did she use the word "gourmet."

Adams, Charlotte. *The Four Seasons Cookbook.* New York: Ridge Press, 1971.

Armitage, Merle, et al. *"Fit For A King."* New York: Duell, Sloan & Pearce, 1939.

Au, M. Sing. *The Chinese Cook Book.* Reading, Penn.: Culinary Arts Press, 1936.

Ault, Beverly Ann. *Go Go Gourmet.* Washington: Acropolis Books, 1973.

Barber, Edith. *Silver Jubilee Super Market Cook Book.* New York: Super Market Publishing Co., 1955.

Batterberry, Michael and Ariane. *On the Town in New York.* New York: Charles Scribner's, 1973.

Beard, James. *American Cookery.* Boston: Little, Brown, 1972.

———*Cook It Outdoors.* New York: M. Barrows, 1941.

———*Delights and Prejudices.* New York: Atheneum, 1964.

———*The Fireside Cookbook.* New York: Simon & Schuster, 1949.

———*Hors d'Oeuvres and Canapés.* New York: M. Barrows, 1940.

———*The New James Beard.* New York: Alfred A. Knopf, 1981.

Beard, James, and Alexander Watt. *Paris Cuisine.* Boston: Little, Brown, 1952.

Bergeron, Victor J. *Frankly Speaking.* Garden City, N.Y.: Doubleday, 1973.

———*Trader Vic's Helluva Man's Cookbook.* Garden City, N.Y.: Doubleday, 1976.

Bracken, Peg. *The I Hate to Cook Cookbook.* New York: Harcourt Brace, 1960.

Bradford, Barbara Taylor. *Entertaining to Please Him.* New York: Simon & Schuster, 1969.

Brillat-Savarin, Jean Anthelme. *The Physiology of Taste,* translated by M.F.K. Fisher. New York: Alfred A. Knopf, 1971.

Brown, Helen Gurley. *Cosmo Cookery.* New York: That Cosmopolitan Girl Library, 1971.

———*Single Girl's Cookbook.* New York: Bernard Geis Associates, 1969.

Burgess, Gelett. *Look Eleven Years Younger.* New York: Simon & Schuster, 1937.

Campbell, Jean Hamilton, and Gloria Kameran. *Simple Cooking for the Epicure.* New York: Viking Press, 1949.

Cannon, Poppy. *The Can Opener Cookbook.* New York: Thomas Y. Crowell, 1951.

Carson, Johnny. *Happiness is a Dry Martini.* Garden City, N.Y.: Doubleday, 1965.

Carteris, Ernest. *A Cookbook for Lovers.* New York: Hearthside Press, 1970.

Chamberlain, Samuel with recipes by Narcisse Chamberlain. *Bouquet de France.* New York: Gourmet, 1952.

Chamberlain, Samuel. *Clémentine in the Kitchen.* New York: Gourmet, 1943.

Child, Julia. *The French Chef Cookbook.* New York: Alfred A. Knopf, 1968.

Child, Julia; Louisette Bertholle; and Simone Beck. *Mastering the Art of French Cooking.* New York: Alfred A. Knopf, 1961.

Claiborne, Craig. *The New York Times Cook Book.* New York: Harper & Row, 1961.

——*New York Times Guide to Dining Out in New York.* New York: New York Times Co., 1964–1968.

de Quattrociocchi, Niccolò. *Love and Dishes.* New York: Bobbs-Merrill, 1950.

Dyer, Ceil. *Best Recipes From the Backs of Boxes, Bottles, Cans, and Jars.* New York: McGraw-Hill, 1979.

Dyer, Ceil and Rosalind Cole. *All Around the Town.* New York: Bobbs-Merrill, 1972.

Fisher, M.F.K. *An Alphabet for Gourmets.* New York: Viking Press, 1949.

——*Serve It Forth.* New York: Harper, 1937.

Fodor, Eugene, et al. *France in 1951.* New York: David McKay, 1951.

Fussell, Betty. *Masters of American Cookery.* New York: Times Books, 1983.

Garvin, Fernande. *The Art of French Cooking.* New York: Bantam Books, 1958.

The Gourmet Cookbook. New York: Gourmet, 1950.

Gourmet's Guide to Good Eating. New York: Gourmet, 1946–1958.

Greene, Gael. *Bite.* New York: W.W. Norton, 1971.

Hawaiian Cuisine. Tokyo: Charles E. Tuttle, 1963.

Hess, John L. and Karen. *The Taste of America.* New York: Grossman Publishers, 1977.

Hines, Duncan. *Adventures in Good Eating.* Bowling Green, Ky.: Adventures in Good Eating, Inc., 1937–1957.

Hogan, Lou Rand. *The Gay Cookbook.* New York, Sherbourne Press, 1965.

Hutchinson, Thomas. *Here is Television, Your Window to the World.* New York: Hastings House, 1946.

Kerr, Graham. *The Graham Kerr Cookbook.* Garden City, N.Y.: Doubleday, 1969.

Klein, Jerome E. *Alitalia Views to Dine By.* New York: View Books, 1961.

Koehler, Alan. *The Madison Avenue Cookbook.* New York: Holt, Rinehart & Winston, 1962.

Kragen, Jinx, and Judy Perry. *Saucepans and the Single Girl.* Garden City, N.Y.: Doubleday, 1965.

Langseth-Christensen, Lillian. *The Instant Epicure Cookbook (for Terribly Tired Gourmets).* New York: Coward-McCann, 1963.

Lucas, Dione with Darlene Geis. *Gourmet Cooking School Cookbook.* New York: Bernard Geis Associates, 1964.

Lucas, Dione. *The Cordon Bleu Cookbook.* Boston: Little, Brown, 1947.

MacKall, Lawton. *Knife and Fork in New York.* Garden City, N.Y.: Doubleday, 1949.

Malone, Ruth M. *Cooking the Holiday Inn Way (4th Edition).* Little Rock, Ark.: Pioneer Press, 1965.

Margittai, Tom, and Paul Kovi with recipes by Joseph (Seppi) Renggli. *The Four Seasons.* New York: Simon & Schuster, 1980.

Mario, Thomas. *The Playboy Gourmet.* Chicago: Playboy Press, 1972.

McCarthy, Josephine. *Josie McCarthy's Favorite Recipes.* Englewood Cliffs, N.J.: Prentice-Hall, 1958.

The New York Times Cocktail Party Guide. New York: New York Times, 1970.

Oliver, Raymond. *A Man's Cookbook.* Garden City, N.Y.: Doubleday, 1961.

Paddleford, Clementine. *Cook Young Cookbook.* New York: Pocket Books, 1966.

Patrick, Ted, and Silas Spitzer. *Great Restaurants of America.* New York: J.B. Lippincott, 1960.

Perl, Lila. *What Cooks in Suburbia.* New York: E.P. Dutton, 1961.

Perper, Hazel. *The Avocado Pit Grower's Indoor How-to Book.* New York: Walker & Company, 1965.

Platt, June. *Serve it and Sing.* New York: Alfred A. Knopf, 1945.

Poister, John J. *The Pyromaniac's Cookbook.* Garden City, N.Y.: Doubleday, 1968.

Price, Mary and Vincent. *A Treasury of Great Recipes.* New York: Ampersand Press, 1965.

Price, Vincent. *I Like What I Know.* Garden City, N.Y.: Doubleday, 1959.

Prichard, Anita. *Fondue Magic: Fun, Flame, and Saucery Around the World.* New York: Hearthside Press, 1969.

Quat, Helen. *The Wonderful World of Freezer Cooking.* New York: Hearthside Press, 1964.

Rieman, Margo. *Twelve Company Dinners.* New York: Simon & Schuster, 1957.

Robbins, Ann Roe. *Treadway Inns Cookbook.* Boston: Little, Brown, 1958.

Roberson, John and Marie. *Complete Small Appliance Cookbook.* New York: A.A. Wyn, 1953.

Rombauer, Irma S. *Joy of Cooking.* New York: Bobbs-Merrill, 1931–.

Root, Waverley, and Richard de Rochemont. *Eating in America.* New York: Ecco Press, 1981.

Sheraton, Mimi. *The Seducer's Cookbook.* New York: Random House, 1963.

Solomon, Esther Riva. *Instant Haute Cuisine.* New York: M. Evans, 1962.

Wason, Betty. *A Salute To Cheese.* New York: Hawthorn Books, 1966.

Waters, Alice. *Chez Panisse Menu Cookbook.* New York: Random House, 1982.

Wechsberg, Joseph. *Dining at the Pavillon.* Boston: Little, Brown, 1962.

Williams-Heller, Ann. *Mr. & Mrs. Roto-Broil Cookbook.* Long Island City, N.Y.: Jay Broiler Co., 1953.

Wood, Morrison. *With a Jug of Wine.* New York: Farrar, Straus & Giroux, 1949.

Young, Billie. *The Naked Chef.* Port Washington, N.Y.: Ashley Books, 1971.

Your Favorite Guests

"So much of the pleasure of good dining depends on the friends we break bread with that we felt this book would not be complete without some guest pages," wrote Vincent and Mary Price at the end of *A Treasury of Great Recipes*. We second the idea. When your dinner party draws to its conclusion, ask guests to sign their names here and jot down some comments about what they ate and drank and what the evening's conversation was about. Then after they leave, add your own comments so you can remember whether or not you want to invite them back.

Date	Your Favorite Guests	Menu Notes

Date	Your Favorite Guests	Menu Notes

Date	Your Favorite Guests	Menu Notes